GeoServer Cookbook

Boost your map server's performance using the power and flexibility of GeoServer

Stefano Iacovella

open source*
community experience distilled

BIRMINGHAM - MUMBAI

GeoServer Cookbook

First published: November 2014

Production reference: 1201114

Published by Packt Publishing Ltd.
Livery Place
35 Livery Street
Birmingham B3 2PB, UK.

ISBN 978-1-78328-961-5

www.packtpub.com

Credits

Author

Stefano Iacovella

Reviewers

Dan Blundell

Daniela Cristiana Docan

Antonio Santiago

Commissioning Editor

Usha Iyer

Acquisition Editor

Subho Gupta

Content Development Editor

Vaibhav Pawar

Technical Editor

Pooja Nair

Copy Editors

Roshni Banerjee

Adithi Shetty

Project Coordinator

Kranti Berde

Proofreaders

Simran Bhogal

Ameesha Green

Paul Hindle

Indexers

Mariammal Chettiyar

Tejal Soni

Production Coordinators

Kyle Albuquerque

Arvindkumar Gupta

Cover Work

Arvindkumar Gupta

About the Author

Stefano Iacovella is a long-time GIS developer and consultant living in Rome, Italy. He also works as a GIS instructor.

He has a PhD in Geology. Being a very curious person, he developed a deep knowledge of IT technologies, mainly focusing on GIS software and related standards.

Starting his career as an ESRI employee, he was exposed to and became confident in proprietary GIS software, mainly the ESRI suite of products.

In the last 14 years, he has been involved with open source software, integrating it with proprietary software. He loves the open source approach, and really trusts in collaboration and sharing knowledge. He strongly believes in the open source idea and constantly manages to spread it, not only in the GIS sector but also in others.

He has been using GeoServer since the release of Version 1.5, configuring, deploying, and hacking it in several projects. Some of the other GFOSS projects he mainly uses and likes are GDAL/OGR, PostGIS, QGIS, and OpenLayers.

Prior to this cookbook, Stefano worked on *GeoServer Beginner's Guide*, which covers the basics of GeoServer.

When not playing with maps and geometric shapes, he loves reading about science (mainly physics and math), riding his bike, and having fun with his wife and two daughters, Alice and Luisa. You can contact him at `stefano.iacovella@gmail.com` or follow him on Twitter at `@iacovellas`.

Acknowledgments

I would like to thank all those people who helped me make this book a real thing.

A special mention for GeoServer's developers; they are the wonderful engine without which this software, and hence, this book too, would not exist.

I would like to thank all the people at Packt Publishing who worked on this book. They helped me a lot and were very patient and encouraging when I had difficulties meeting deadlines.

A special thanks to my technical reviewers; they constantly checked for my errors and omissions. This book has become better thanks to all their hard work.

Last but not least, I want to express my gratitude to Alessandra, Alice, and Luisa for their support and patience when I was working on this book.

About the Reviewers

Dan Blundell is a designer and developer with over 10 years of experience. He has worked in both the public and private sector, from the government to creative agencies. With clients ranging from district authorities and local businesses to international brands, Dan not only has a breadth of experience, but also a reputation for delivery. Today, he is working towards making the government more open, creative, and collaborative.

Daniela Cristiana Docan is a survey engineer. She works as a lecturer for the Faculty of Geodesy, Technical University of Civil Engineering Bucharest, Romania.

Formerly, she worked for ESRI Romania and ANCPI (National Agency for Cadastre and Land Registration).

While working for ESRI Romania, Daniela trained teams from different private or state companies as an authorized instructor in ArcGIS by Environmental Systems Research Institute, Inc., USA.

In 2009, she created the logical and physical data model of the National Topographic Dataset for ANCPI on a large scale (TOPRO5). She was also a member of different workgroups that elaborated on technical specifications and country reports for INSPIRE (Infrastructure for Spatial Information in the European Community) in 2010.

Antonio Santiago is a Computer Science graduate with more than 10 years of experience in designing and implementing systems.

Since the beginning of his professional life, his experience has always been related to the world of meteorology, working for different companies dealing with meteorology as an employee or a freelance programmer. He has experience in developing systems to collect, store, transform, analyze, and visualize data. He is interested in and actively pursues any GIS-related technology, with preference for data visualization.

As a restless person, which is what one mainly experiences while working in the Java ecosystem, he has also been actively involved with many web-related technologies, always looking to improve the client side of web applications.

As a firm believer of software engineering practices, he is an enthusiast of Agile methodologies involving customers as the main key for a project's success.

Antonio is also the author of *OpenLayers Cookbook, Packt Publishing*.

www.PacktPub.com

Support files, eBooks, discount offers, and more

You might want to visit www.PacktPub.com for support files and downloads related to your book.

Did you know that Packt offers eBook versions of every book published, with PDF and ePub files available? You can upgrade to the eBook version at www.PacktPub.com and as a print book customer, you are entitled to a discount on the eBook copy. Get in touch with us at service@packtpub.com for more details.

At www.PacktPub.com, you can also read a collection of free technical articles, sign up for a range of free newsletters and receive exclusive discounts and offers on Packt books and eBooks.

https://www2.packtpub.com/books/subscription/packtlib

Do you need instant solutions to your IT questions? PacktLib is Packt's online digital book library. Here, you can access, read and search across Packt's entire library of books.

Why Subscribe?

- ▶ Fully searchable across every book published by Packt
- ▶ Copy and paste, print and bookmark content
- ▶ On demand and accessible via web browser

Free Access for Packt account holders

If you have an account with Packt at www.PacktPub.com, you can use this to access PacktLib today and view nine entirely free books. Simply use your login credentials for immediate access.

Table of Contents

Preface

Until a decade ago, spatial data and the art of map building were considered tricky and complex—almost reserved for highly skilled and specialized professionals.

The advent of web mapping has changed the way geography is perceived by people. This has been largely powered by a few types of open source software that made it possible for everyone to collect, manage, and publish spatial data on the Internet.

GeoServer is one of these precious gems. Along with open JavaScript frameworks such as OpenLayers and Leaflet, it gives everyone the tools they need to create a powerful map server and lightweight applications that run in modern browsers. This allows users to show data visualizations, create online data editors, and do much more.

GeoServer is a complete and powerful type of server software that can publish data to a web mapping application. In recent releases, support for geoprocessing operations has been added, which lets you use GeoServer as a data processor.

Since the beginning, GeoServer has support to standards from Open Geospatial Consortium (OGC), which is kept compatible with its recent most relevant releases (for more information on OGC, have a look at `http://www.opengeospatial.org`).

This book will guide you through the details of configuring data for publication, creating geoprocessing tasks, and optimizing your server for optimal performance.

What this book covers

Chapter 1, *Working with Vectors*, discusses vector data publication with WFS. It covers how to use the data with a JavaScript client. It also explores how to use parametric SQL views and how to enhance performance with feature generalization.

Chapter 2, *Working with Rasters*, explores the different raster data types you can publish with GeoServer. It also covers the mosaic data creation and adding support for more formats that integrates GDAL libraries in your server.

Chapter 3, *Advanced Styling*, deals with the art of representing data on a map. Using the CSS module, you will explore how to create symbols for vector data and how to build a renderer for raster data.

Chapter 4, *Geoprocessing*, teaches you how to create data processing tasks on GeoServer. By following the recipes, you'll understand how you can use GeoServer to create complex server-side functions and use them in your client.

Chapter 5, *Advanced Configurations*, deals with some advanced configuration tasks. You'll explore database connection optimization, configuring the cache to improve performance, and Spatial Reference System (SRS) optimization.

Chapter 6, *Automating GeoServer Configurations*, explores the GeoServer REST interface. Using the operation published in that interface, you will discover how to create automatic tasks to update your site's configuration.

Chapter 7, *Advanced Visualizations*, focuses on some visualization techniques. You will explore how to add time support in WMS, create animated maps, and export data to Google Earth.

Chapter 8, *Monitoring and Tuning*, teaches you the use of the control flow and how to monitor extensions for GeoServer. With the tools provided, you can control how the requests are filtered and queued to your server. You will learn how to save information about users' requests and analyze them to build reports.

Appendix, OGC for ESRI Professionals, discusses a brief comparison between GeoServer and ArcGIS for Server, a map server created by ESRI. The importance of adopting OGC standards when building a geographical information system is stressed. You will learn how OGC standards lets you create a system where different pieces of software cooperate with each other.

What you need for this book

You will need a working instance of the following types of software:

- Tomcat
- GeoServer
- PostGIS

The recipes work both with Linux and Windows operating systems, so you may select the one you prefer.

All the software used in this book is freely available, mostly as open source projects. Hardware requirements for development purposes are not very high. A relatively modern laptop or desktop will be enough to run the examples. Source code and data used in this book are freely available on the Packt Publishing site.

Who this book is for

If you are a developer or an analyst familiar with GIS, WMS, WFS, and spatial data, and you wish to get the most out of GeoServer, then this book is for you.

You can use it as a desktop quick reference guide to solve the common issues you find in your day-to-day job.

Sections

In this book, you will find several headings that appear frequently (Getting ready, How to do it..., How it works..., There's more..., and See also).

To give you clear instructions on how to complete a recipe, we use these sections:

Getting ready

This section tells you what to expect in the recipe, and describes how to set up any type of software or any preliminary settings required for the recipe.

How to do it...

This section contains the steps required to follow the recipe.

How it works...

This section usually consists of a detailed explanation of what happened in the previous section.

There's more...

This section consists of additional information about the recipe in order to make the reader more knowledgeable about the recipe.

See also

This section provides helpful links to other useful information for the recipe.

Conventions

In this book, you will find a number of text styles that distinguish between different kinds of information. Here are some examples of these styles and an explanation of their meaning.

Code words in text, database table names, folder names, filenames, file extensions, pathnames, dummy URLs, user input, and Twitter handles are shown as follows: "Save the file in a folder published on your server, such as TOMCAT_HOME/webapps/ROOT, and point your browser to it."

A block of code is set as follows:

```
<layer>
  <defaultStyle>
    <name>simple_roads</name>
  </defaultStyle>
  <enabled>true</enabled>
</layer>
```

When we wish to draw your attention to a particular part of a code block, the relevant lines or items are set in bold:

```
<layer>
  <defaultStyle>
    <name>simple_roads</name>
  </defaultStyle>
  <enabled>true</enabled>
</layer>
```

Any command-line input or output is written as follows:

```
$ curl -u admin:geoserver -XDELETE -H 'Accept: text/xml'
  http://localhost:8080/geoserver/rest/workspaces/MyOrganization
```

New terms and **important words** are shown in bold. Words that you see on the screen, for example, in menus or dialog boxes, appear in the text like this: "Move to the bottom of the screen and select the **Guess Geometry type and srid** checkbox and click on **Refresh**."

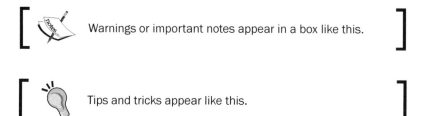

Warnings or important notes appear in a box like this.

Tips and tricks appear like this.

Reader feedback

Feedback from our readers is always welcome. Let us know what you think about this book—what you liked or disliked. Reader feedback is important for us as it helps us develop titles that you will really get the most out of.

To send us general feedback, simply e-mail `feedback@packtpub.com`, and mention the book's title in the subject of your message.

If there is a topic that you have expertise in and you are interested in either writing or contributing to a book, see our author guide at `www.packtpub.com/authors`.

Customer support

Now that you are the proud owner of a Packt book, we have a number of things to help you to get the most from your purchase.

Downloading the example code

You can download the example code files from your account at `http://www.packtpub.com` for all the Packt Publishing books you have purchased. If you purchased this book elsewhere, you can visit `http://www.packtpub.com/support` and register to have the files e-mailed directly to you.

Downloading the color images of this book

We also provide you with a PDF file that has color images of the screenshots/diagrams used in this book. The color images will help you better understand the changes in the output. You can download this file from `https://www.packtpub.com/sites/default/files/downloads/9615OS_coloredimages.pdf`.

Errata

Although we have taken every care to ensure the accuracy of our content, mistakes do happen. If you find a mistake in one of our books—maybe a mistake in the text or the code—we would be grateful if you could report this to us. By doing so, you can save other readers from frustration and help us improve subsequent versions of this book. If you find any errata, please report them by visiting `http://www.packtpub.com/submit-errata`, selecting your book, clicking on the **Errata Submission Form** link, and entering the details of your errata. Once your errata is verified, your submission will be accepted and the errata will be uploaded to our website or added to any list of existing errata under the **Errata** section of that title.

To view the previously submitted errata, go to `https://www.packtpub.com/books/content/support` and enter the name of the book in the search field. The required information will appear under the **Errata** section.

Piracy

Piracy of copyrighted material on the Internet is an ongoing problem across all media. At Packt, we take the protection of our copyright and licenses very seriously. If you come across any illegal copies of our works in any form on the Internet, please provide us with the location address or website name immediately so that we can pursue a remedy.

Please contact us at copyright@packtpub.com with a link to the suspected pirated material.

We appreciate your help in protecting our authors and our ability to bring you valuable content.

Questions

If you have a problem with any aspect of this book, you can contact us at questions@packtpub.com, and we will do our best to address the problem.

1
Working with Vectors

In this chapter, we will cover the following recipes:

- Using different WFS versions in OpenLayers
- Using WFS nonspatial filters
- Using WFS spatial filters
- Using WFS vendor parameters
- Filtering data with CQL
- Filtering data with CQL spatial operators
- Creating a SQL view
- Creating a parametric view
- Improving performance with pregeneralized features

Introduction

Vector data is probably the main source of spatial information that is used inside GeoServer to build maps. You may use the data both to render maps on the server side, that is, using the **Web Map Service** (**WMS**) standard, or have the client get the shapes and manipulate or render them in a map, that is, using the **Web Feature Service** (**WFS**) standard.

In this chapter, we will use both these standards, and we will focus on how to filter data and optimize configuration for better performance. We assume that you're already comfortable with the standard WMS and WFS requests and you know how to configure a data store and a layer with the GeoServer web interface.

The recipes in this chapter use a few datasets. Configuring and publishing them is quite easy, so we are not covering these steps in detail. We will use publicly available data from NASA Earth Observatory (`http://neo.sci.gsfc.nasa.gov`) and Natural Earth (`http://www.naturalearthdata.com`). Configuration and publication of datasets is straightforward, and hence not covered in detail.

You should download the Blue Marble dataset from NASA Earth Observatory. In the home page, you can find it by navigating to the **LAND** section. Use the GeoTiff format with 0.1 degrees resolution to match the exercises provided in this book. You should publish this dataset as `NaturalEarth:blueMarble` for use with exercises that require a map that looks like the one in this book.

You also need a couple of datasets from Natural Earth: the datasets for countries and populated places in the 1:10,000,000 scale. Go to `http://www.naturalearthdata.com/downloads/10m-cultural-vectors/` and download the datasets for countries and populated places in the shapefile format. Publish the countries' data as `NaturalEarth:countries`.

We will be using the populated places dataset to create a SQL view. To be able to create it, you should load the data in a spatial RDBMS. Our choice is PostGIS, as it is a very good option; it is powerful, easy to deploy, and free.

We won't cover how to install and configure a PostGIS installation. In fact, PostGIS is not an RDBMS, but a spatial plugin for PostgreSQL. So, you should first install the latter and then add the former. If this sounds new and somehow complicated for you, there are a lot of nice guides on the Internet that you can use for a quick start.

The procedure to install on Linux can be found at:

`http://trac.osgeo.org/postgis/wiki/UsersWikiInstall`

For Windows, a good choice is downloading the binary packaged by Enterprise DB:

`http://www.enterprisedb.com/products-services-training/pgdownload#windows`

Using different WFS versions in OpenLayers

You are probably comfortable with WMS and including WMS layers in a web application. When you need more control over your data, it's time to switch to WFS.

Unlike WMS, a WFS request brings you the actual raw data in the form of features. By working with the features directly, you are no more dealing with a static rendering of features, that is, a map; you can take fine control of the shapes by setting drawing rules on the client side.

WFS comes in several different flavors or, more precisely, in different protocol versions. GeoServer supports 1.0.0, 1.1.0, and 2.0.0. Each version differs in the formats supported and the query capabilities supported. For example, WFS 2.0.0 supports the use of temporal queries and joins.

 If you are curious about the details of WFS and GML, check out the reference documents for WFS and GML in the OGC repository at `http://www.opengeospatial.org/standards/is`. Here, look for the following files:

- OpenGIS® Geography Markup Language Encoding Standard (GML)
- OpenGIS® Web Feature Service (WFS) Implementation Specification

The following screenshot shows the map you're aiming for:

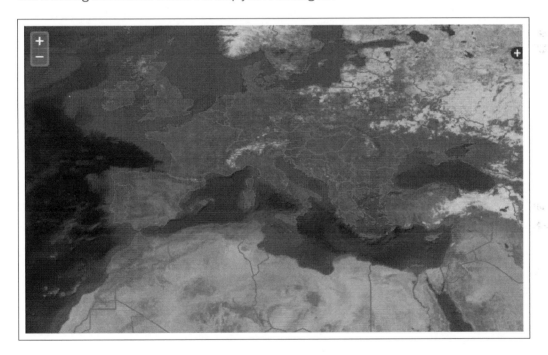

 We will build the code step by step. For your reference, check out the code bundle provided with the book and have a look at the `ch01_wfsVersion.html` and `ch01_wfsVersion101.html` files.

How to do it...

1. Create an HTML file and insert the following code snippet:

```
<html>
  <head>
    <title>Dealing with WFS version</title>
    <meta http-equiv="Content-Type" content="text/html;
      charset=UTF-8">
  <body onload="init()">
    <div id="myMap"></div>
  </body>
</html>
```

Downloading the example code

You can download the example code files for all Packt books you have purchased from your account at http://www.packtpub.com. If you purchased this book elsewhere, you can visit http://www.packtpub.com/support and register to have the files e-mailed directly to you.

2. Create a style for the map, defining the size and aspect:

```
<style type="text/css">
  #myMap {
    clear: both;
    position: relative;
    width: 750px;
    height: 450px;
    border: 1px solid black;
  }
</style>
```

3. Insert a reference to the OpenLayers library:

```
<script type="text/javascript"
  src="http://openlayers.org/api/2.13.1/OpenLayers.js"
  ></script>
```

4. Now start coding in JavaScript and add new map objects:

```
<script type="text/javascript">
  function init() {
    map = new OpenLayers.Map({
      div: "myMap",
      //We don't want any layers as base map
      allOverlays: true,
```

5. Add the Blue Marble layer, which is a standard WMS layer:

```
layers: [
    new OpenLayers.Layer.WMS("Blue Marble",
        "http://localhost/geoserver/wms",
        {layers: "NaturalEarth:blueMarble", format:
            "image/png", transparent: false}
    ),
```

6. Now, add a vector layer using the WFS protocol:

```
new OpenLayers.Layer.Vector("countries", {
    strategies: [new OpenLayers.Strategy.BBOX()],
    protocol: new OpenLayers.Protocol.WFS({
        url: "http://localhost/geoserver/wfs",
        featureType: "countries",
        featureNS:
            "http://www.naturalearthdata.com/",
        // Mind the geometry column name
        geometryName: "geom"
    }),
```

7. Insert a style to render the vector features:

```
styleMap: new OpenLayers.StyleMap({
    strokeWidth: 3,
    strokeColor: "#FF0000",
    strokeWidth: 1,
    fillColor: "#ee9900",
    fillOpacity: 0.3
    }),
    })
],
```

8. Zoom in to the map and center it on Europe:

```
center: [12.48, 42.60],
zoom: 4
});
map.addControl(new
    OpenLayers.Control.LayerSwitcher());
}
</script>
</head>
```

9. Save the file in a folder published on your server, such as TOMCAT_HOME/webapps/ ROOT, and point your browser to it. You should get a map that looks like the one shown in the introduction to this recipe.

10. Now, switch the request to another version. We will use v1.1.0 and the JSON format:

```
new OpenLayers.Layer.Vector("countries", {
    strategies: [new OpenLayers.Strategy.BBOX()],
    protocol: new
      OpenLayers.Protocol.WFS.v1_1_0({
      url: "http://localhost:8080/geoserver/wfs",
      featureType: "countries",
      featureNS:
        "http://www.naturalearthdata.com/",
      geometryName: "geom",
      outputFormat: "JSON",
    }),
```

11. Reload your document inside the browser and check that your map looks the same.

How it works...

We are using a JavaScript application to perform a WFS query on GeoServer. This is a common use case in the era of web mapping, besides using the OpenLayers framework to assist you in building a complicated request.

The HTML and CSS part of the script is quite easy. As you must have noticed, the core of this little program is the `init()` function, which is called at page loading.

We first create a `map` object and set the `allOverlays` variable to `true`. The default value of `false` makes it mandatory for a layer to be `basemap`; in this recipe, we don't want to have `basemap`, which is a layer that is always turned on in the map:

```
allOverlays: true,
```

Then, we start to add data on the map. First, we use the raster data from the NASA Blue Marble dataset. We use the `OpenLayers.Layer.WMS` class; you just need to set a name and URL for the WMS service. The `format` and `transparent` parameters are optional, but they let you control the file produced by GeoServer. The code is as follows:

```
layers: [
  new OpenLayers.Layer.WMS("Blue Marble",
    "http://localhost/geoserver/wms",
    {layers: "NaturalEarth:blueMarble", format:
      "image/png", transparent: false}
  ),
```

 While we are using a raster dataset in this request, you can, of course, use vector data in the WMS request

Then we create a new layer using the `OpenLayers.Layer.Vector` class, and this layer can use a different source data format:

```
new OpenLayers.Layer.Vector("countries", {
```

We add a strategy, `BBOX`, to let `OpenLayers` query the server for data intersecting the current map extent:

```
strategies: [new OpenLayers.Strategy.BBOX()],
```

With the `protocol` parameter, we set the data format. Of course, we use WFS, and this class defaults to the 1.0.0 version of the standard:

```
protocol: new OpenLayers.Protocol.WFS({
```

We need to set some mandatory parameters when invoking the constructor for the WFS class. The `geometryName` parameter is optional, but it defaults to `the_geom` value. So, you need to set it to the actual name of the geometry column in your data. The code is as follows:

```
url: "http://localhost/geoserver/wfs",
featureType: "countries",
featureNS: "http://www.naturalearthdata.com/",
geometryName: "geom"
```

WFS returns raw data, not an image map like WMS. So, you need to draw each feature yourself; you have to set some rules for feature drawing. Inside the `StyleMap` class, you set the color, line width, and other rendering parameters that will be used to represent features in the map, as shown in the following code:

```
styleMap: new OpenLayers.StyleMap({
    strokeWidth: 3,
    strokeColor: "#FF0000",
    strokeWidth: 1,
    fillColor: "#ee9900",
    fillOpacity: 0.3
```

What happens when you load this app in your browser? You can use a browser extension to check the actual request sent to GeoServer.

 Firebug is a powerful extension for FireFox, and with Chrome, you can use the developer console.

Using FireFox with Firebug, you should see a few requests upon loading the `ch01_wfsVersion.html` file. OpenLayers executes the `POST` WFS request with our parameters; you can see that the version is 1.0.0, the operation is `GetFeature`, and there is a bounding box filter defined in GML 2:

Now, try to load the `ch01_wfsVersion110.html` file; the request is a little bit different. Of course, now the version is 1.1.0, but the filter looks different as well:

```
<ogc:Filter xmlns:ogc="http://www.opengis.net/ogc">
  <ogc:BBOX>
    <ogc:PropertyName>geom</ogc:PropertyName>
    <gml:Envelope xmlns:gml="http://www.opengis.net/gml"
      srsName="EPSG:4326">
      <gml:lowerCorner>-53.43796875 3.04921875</gml:lowerCorner>
      <gml:upperCorner>78.39796875 82.15078125</gml:upperCorner>
    </gml:Envelope>
  </ogc:BBOX>
</ogc:Filter>
```

You need to be aware that WFS 1.1.0 uses GML 3, which uses a different representation of geometry. In this case, OpenLayers hides the complexity of creating the correct geometry filter.

There's more...

You probably noted when downloading the Blue Marble dataset that the GeoTIFF file is quite a big file. To render this file, GeoServer must navigate the file contents and read blocks of pixels off the disk. To optimize data storage and enhance rendering speed, you can use GDAL tools to restructure the contents of the file for faster access.

If you have GDAL tools at your fingertips, you can check the metadata of the file:

```
:$ gdalinfo BlueMarbleNG-TB_2004-12-01_rgb_3600x1800.TIFF
...
Metadata:
  AREA_OR_POINT=Area
  TIFFTAG_RESOLUTIONUNIT=1 (unitless)
  TIFFTAG_XRESOLUTION=1
  TIFFTAG_YRESOLUTION=1
Image Structure Metadata:
  INTERLEAVE=PIXEL
...
```

Now, let's transform the file using a compression method to reduce the file size and tile the dataset for faster access:

```
:$ gdal_translate -of GTiff -co COMPRESS=DEFLATE -co TILED=YES
  BlueMarbleNG-TB_2004-12-01_rgb_3600x1800.TIFF blueMarble.tiff
```

Tiling organizes the file contents on disk into tiles, ideally locating blocks of pixels next to each other on disk. This optimization helps in performance when GeoServer is zoomed in to a small area of interest.

Then, we will add an overview to further hasten the data extraction:

```
:$ gdaladdo -r cubic -ro blueMarble.tiff 2 4 8 16 32 64
```

An overview creates a small *summary* image, which can be used by GeoServer when zoomed out. By drawing using the overview, GeoServer can read fewer pixels off disk and avoid having to sample through the entire file.

By executing the `gdalinfo` tool again, you can check that these have actually been applied successfully:

```
...
Metadata:
  AREA_OR_POINT=Area
  TIFFTAG_RESOLUTIONUNIT=1 (unitless)
  TIFFTAG_XRESOLUTION=1
  TIFFTAG_YRESOLUTION=1
Image Structure Metadata:
  COMPRESSION=DEFLATE
  INTERLEAVE=PIXEL
```

...

```
Band 1 Block=256x256 Type=Byte, ColorInterp=Red
  Overviews: 1800x900, 900x450, 450x225, 225x113, 113x57, 57x29
Band 2 Block=256x256 Type=Byte, ColorInterp=Green
  Overviews: 1800x900, 900x450, 450x225, 225x113, 113x57, 57x29
Band 3 Block=256x256 Type=Byte, ColorInterp=Blue
  Overviews: 1800x900, 900x450, 450x225, 225x113, 113x57, 57x29
```

Using WFS nonspatial filters

In the previous recipe, we just specified a layer to get features from. The OpenLayers strategy, BBOX, created a spatial filter to get only features intersecting the map extent. For common use, you may want to create filters yourself in order to extract specific sets of features from GeoServer.

In this recipe, we will build a map with four layers, each one containing countries according to their mean income. The data source for each layer is the countries' feature type, and we will apply different filters on them.

The resulting map looks like this:

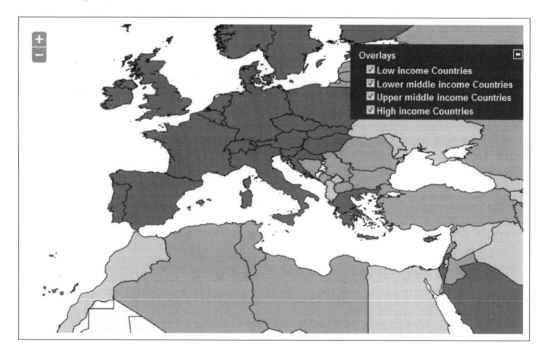

You can find the full source code for this recipe in the `ch01_wfsFilter.html` file.

How to do it...

1. Use the `ch01_wfsVersion.html` file of the previous recipe; rename it as `wfsFilter.html` in the same folder. Then, edit the JavaScript part as shown in the following code:

```
<script type="text/javascript">
  function init() {
    map = new OpenLayers.Map({
      div: "myMap",
      allOverlays: true,
```

2. Remove the Blue Marble layer; we will have only WFS layers here:

```
layers: [
  new OpenLayers.Layer.Vector("Low income Countries",
    {
    strategies: [new OpenLayers.Strategy.BBOX()],
    protocol: new OpenLayers.Protocol.WFS({
      url: "http://localhost/geoserver/wfs",
      featureType: "countries",
      featureNS: "http://www.naturalearthdata.com/",
      geometryName: "geom"
    }),
```

3. Change the style for the first request; the features will be drawn with a pale brown fill and a dark outline:

```
styleMap: new OpenLayers.StyleMap({
  strokeWidth: 3,
  strokeColor: "#000000",
  strokeWidth: 1,
  fillColor: "#ffffcc",
  fillOpacity: 1
}),
```

4. Now, add a filter to only have low income countries in this layer:

```
filter: new OpenLayers.Filter.Logical({
  type: OpenLayers.Filter.Logical.AND,
  filters: [
    new OpenLayers.Filter.Comparison({
      type:
        OpenLayers.Filter.Comparison.EQUAL_TO,
```

```
        property: "income_grp",
        value: "5. Low income"
      }),
    ]
  })
}),
```

5. We will repeat the previous steps for three other layers. Name the first as `Lower middle income Countries`:

```
new OpenLayers.Layer.Vector("Lower middle income
    Countries", {
```

6. The source of the layer is obviously the same; change the style with a fill as shown in the following line of code:

```
fillColor: "#c2e699",
```

7. Then, change the filter to extract countries with a proper value:

```
new OpenLayers.Filter.Comparison({
    type:
      OpenLayers.Filter.Comparison.EQUAL_TO,
    property: "income_grp",
    value: "4. Lower middle income"
}),
```

8. Now, add a new layer for the upper-middle income countries; the only modified line of code is shown here:

```
new OpenLayers.Layer.Vector("Upper middle income
    Countries", {
...
    fillColor: "#78c679",
...
    new OpenLayers.Filter.Comparison({
        type:
          OpenLayers.Filter.Comparison.EQUAL_TO,
        property: "income_grp",
        value: "3. Upper middle income"
    }),
```

9. Eventually, add a last layer for high income countries:

```
new OpenLayers.Layer.Vector("High income
    Countries", {
...
    fillColor: "#238443",
```

10. The `Filter` is a bit more complex as we have two different values for high income countries:

```
filter: new OpenLayers.Filter.Logical({
   type: OpenLayers.Filter.Logical.OR,
   filters: [
     new OpenLayers.Filter.Comparison({
       type:
         OpenLayers.Filter.Comparison.EQUAL_TO,
       property: "income_grp",
       value: " 1. High income: OECD"
     }),
     new OpenLayers.Filter.Comparison({
       type:
         OpenLayers.Filter.Comparison.EQUAL_TO,
       property: "income_grp",
       value: " 2. High income: nonOECD"
     })
   ]
})
```

11. Save the file and point your browser to it. You should get a map that looks like the one shown in the introduction to this recipe.

How it works...

The first part of the script is quite similar to that used in the previous recipe. We create a `Map` object and start adding layers to it.

To have the first layer containing only low income countries, we need to set a filter:

```
filter: new OpenLayers.Filter.Logical({
```

The filter might contain more criteria, so we need to specify a logical operator to join more criteria. This is required only with a single-criteria filter, as shown in the following code:

```
type: OpenLayers.Filter.Logical.AND,
```

Then, we set the filter type. In this case, an equality type, that is, only records with the value we specify, will be selected:

```
filters: [
   new OpenLayers.Filter.Comparison({
     type: OpenLayers.Filter.Comparison.EQUAL_TO,
```

Eventually, we need to set the attributes on which the filter will be applied and the value to use for filtering records:

```
        property: "income_grp",
        value: "5. Low income"
    }),
   ]
})
```

To create the other three layers, we clone the same filter by setting a different value. We create four different layers from the same feature type.

Of course, we need to set a different style for each layer to have a proper distinct representation.

Using WFS spatial filters

Filtering alphanumerical attributes is quite a common task. However, in a GIS application, you may also want to filter features according to geometric properties.

WFS includes a few spatial relationships that you can use to create a spatial filter. From a general point of view, you need an input shape, a relationship to be checked, and some target shapes to be filtered.

In this recipe, we use the DWITHIN spatial relationship to filter countries that are within a circular buffer.

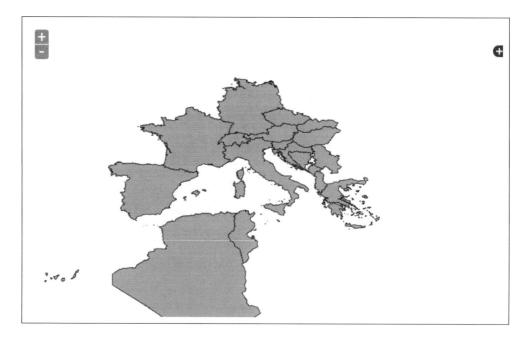

> You can find the full source code for this recipe in the code bundle available from the Packt site for this book. Look for the `ch01_wfsSpatialFilter.html` file.

How to do it...

1. Copy the file used in the first recipe to the `wfsSpatialFilter.html` file in the same folder. Then, alter the JavaScript part as shown in the following code:

```
<script type="text/javascript">
  function init() {
    map = new OpenLayers.Map({
      div: "myMap",
      allOverlays: true,
      layers: [
        new OpenLayers.Layer.Vector("Filtered Countries", {
          strategies: [new OpenLayers.Strategy.Fixed()],
          protocol: new OpenLayers.Protocol.WFS({
            url: "http://localhost/geoserver/wfs",
            featureType: "countries",
            featureNS: "http://www.naturalearthdata.com/",
            geometryName: "geom"
          }),
          styleMap: new OpenLayers.StyleMap({
            strokeWidth: 3,
            strokeColor: "#000000",
            strokeWidth: 1,
            fillColor: "#78c679",
            fillOpacity: 1
          }),
```

2. Insert a spatial filter, as shown in the following code:

```
          filter: new OpenLayers.Filter.Logical({
            type: OpenLayers.Filter.Logical.AND,
            filters: [
              new OpenLayers.Filter.Spatial({
                type: OpenLayers.Filter.Spatial.DWITHIN,
                value: new OpenLayers.Geometry.Point(12,
                  42),
                distance: 8
              })
            ]
          })
        })
```

```
        ],
        center: [12.48, 42.60],
        zoom: 4
    });
    map.addControl(new OpenLayers.Control.LayerSwitcher());
    }
</script>
```

3. Save the file and point your browser to it. You should get a map that looks like the one shown in the introduction to this recipe.

How it works...

Not surprisingly, the code contained in the file is not so different from that used in the previous recipe. Indeed, we are performing the same task, which is filtering data, but now we want to use a different filter: a spatial filter.

You set a logical filter with an AND logical join:

```
        filter: new OpenLayers.Filter.Logical({
            type: OpenLayers.Filter.Logical.AND,
```

Then, you add a `Filter.Spatial` class. This is the magic of this recipe. The value parameter lets you choose the spatial relationship; in this case, we use DWITHIN, that is, all features within a specific distance from the source geometry will be selected:

```
        filters: [
            new OpenLayers.Filter.Spatial({
                type: OpenLayers.Filter.Spatial.DWITHIN,
```

The source geometry is a point feature created with an `OpenLayers` class and specifies the latitude and longitude values:

```
            value: new OpenLayers.Geometry.Point(12, 42),
```

Then, you have to set a distance. Please note that you can also set zero as a distance value; in this case, if you have a polygon geometry, only the feature that is contained in the polygon will be selected:

```
            distance: 8
            })
        ]
    })
```

GeoServer lets you use a few spatial filters: `Disjoint`, `Equals`, `DWithin`, `Beyond`, `Intersect`, `Touches`, `Crosses`, `Within`, `Contains`, `Overlaps`, and `BBOX`. For more details about them, point to `http://www.opengeospatial.org/standards/filter`.

Using WFS vendor parameters

The previous recipes used standard WFS requests. GeoServer also supports a few optional parameters that you can include in your requests. In this recipe, we will see how to ask GeoServer, which is reprojecting the data from the native SRS to another SRS, to use a vendor parameter.

Reprojection of data is a part of WFS 1.1.0 and 2.0.0, and GeoServer has provided support since 1.0.0 so that you can use it with any WFS version. The following screenshot is what we're targeting in this recipe:

 You can find the full source code for this recipe in the code bundle available from the Packt site for this book; look for the `ch01_wfsReprojection.html` file.

How to do it...

1. Copy the file used in the first recipe to the `wfsReprojection.html` file in the same folder. Insert a new parameter for the `Map` object:

   ```
   projection: "EPSG:3857",
   ```

2. Then, alter the JavaScript part when creating the WFS layer:

   ```
   new OpenLayers.Layer.Vector("countries", {
       strategies: [new OpenLayers.Strategy.BBOX()],
       protocol: new OpenLayers.Protocol.WFS({
           url: "http://localhost/geoserver/wfs",
           featureType: "countries",
           featureNS: "http://www.naturalearthdata.com/",
           geometryName: "geom",
   ```

3. Add a parameter to request data reprojection:

   ```
   srsName: new OpenLayers.Projection("EPSG:3857"),
   srsNameInQuery: true
   }),
   ```

4. Save the file and point your browser to it. You should get a map that looks like the one shown in the introduction to this recipe.

How it works...

Using a vendor parameter is really straightforward; you just add it to your request. In our recipe, we want to use the countries' data that is stored in the EPSG:4326 projection, which is the geographical coordinates, and in EPSG:3857, which is the planar coordinates. First of all, we set the spatial reference system for the map:

```
map = new OpenLayers.Map({
    div: "myMap",
    allOverlays: true,
    projection: "EPSG:3857",
```

Then, we create the WFS request for data by inserting the `srsName` parameter and assigning it the same projected coordinate system used for the map. The Boolean parameter `srsNameInQuery` is really important, as it defaults to false. If you don't set it, OpenLayers will not ask for reprojection when using WFS 1.0.0:

```
srsName: new OpenLayers.Projection("EPSG:3857"),
srsNameInQuery: true
```

Let's see what happens when you load the page in your browser and the `OpenLayers` framework creates the WFS request. Use Firebug to capture the XML code sent to GeoServer with the `GetFeature` request. The `Query` element contains the `srsName` parameter that forces GeoServer to project data:

```
<wfs:Query typeName="feature:countries_1" srsName="EPSG:3857"
  xmlns:feature="http://www.naturalearthdata.com/">
  <ogc:Filter xmlns:ogc="http://www.opengis.net/ogc">
    <ogc:BBOX>
      <ogc:PropertyName>geom</ogc:PropertyName>
      <gml:Box xmlns:gml="http://www.opengis.net/gml"
        srsName="EPSG:3857">
        <gml:coordinates decimal="." cs="," ts=" ">-
          13325909.428711,-3545545.6572266
          16025909.428711,14065545.657227</gml:coordinates>
      </gml:Box>
    </ogc:BBOX>
  </ogc:Filter>
</wfs:Query>
```

Filtering data with CQL

Another vendor parameter is `cql_filter`. It allows users to add filters to requests using **Extended Common Query Language** (**ECQL**).

In the previous recipes, you created filters using the OGC filter XML standard. ECQL lets you create filters in an easier text format and in a much more compact way. A CQL filter is a list of phrases similar to the `where` clauses in SQL, each separated by the combiner words AND or OR.

CQL was originally used for catalog systems. GeoServer uses an extension for CQL, allowing the full representation of OGC filters in the text form. This extension is called ECQL.

ECQL lets you use several operators and functions. For more information, you can read the documents available at the following URLs:

- `http://docs.geoserver.org/stable/en/user/filter/ecql_reference.html#filter-ecql-reference`

- `http://docs.codehaus.org/display/GEOTOOLS/ECQL+Parser+Design`

In this recipe, we will create a map with a filter on `income_grp`, which is very similar to the previous one. Your result should look like the following screenshot:

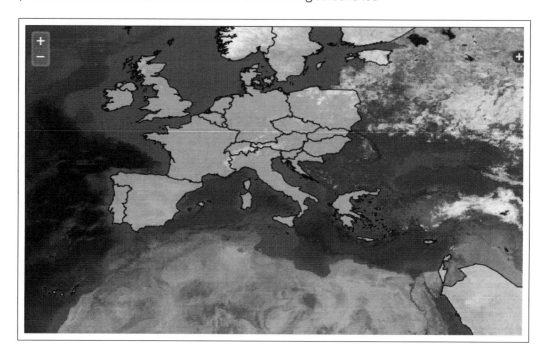

 You can find the full source code for this recipe in the `ch01_wmsCQLFilter.html` file.

How to do it...

1. Copy the file used in the first recipe to a new file and name it `wfsCQLFilter.html` in the same folder. Insert a new `sld` variable and populate it as shown in the following lines:

```
<script type="text/javascript"
  src="http://openlayers.org/api/2.13.1/OpenLayers.js">
  </script>
<script type="text/javascript">
  function init() {
    var sld = '<StyledLayerDescriptor version="1.0.0">';
    sld+= '<NamedLayer>';
    sld+= '<Name>NaturalEarth:countries</Name>';
    sld+= '<UserStyle>';
    sld+= '<IsDefault>1</IsDefault>';
    sld+= '<FeatureTypeStyle>';
```

```
sld+= '<Rule>';
sld+= '<PolygonSymbolizer>';
sld+= '<Stroke>';
sld+= '<CssParameter
    name="stroke">#000000</CssParameter>';
sld+= '<CssParameter name="stroke-
    width">1</CssParameter>';
sld+= '</Stroke>';
sld+= '<Fill>';
sld+= '<CssParameter name="fill">#FFFFCC</CssParameter>';
sld+= '<CssParameter name="fill-
    opacity">0.65</CssParameter>';
sld+= '</Fill>';
sld+= '</PolygonSymbolizer>';
sld+= '</Rule>';
sld+= '</FeatureTypeStyle>';
sld+= '</UserStyle>';
sld+= '</NamedLayer>';
sld+= '</StyledLayerDescriptor>';
```

2. After the Blue Marble layer, add a new WMS layer:

```
new OpenLayers.Layer.WMS("countries",
  "http://localhost/geoserver/wms",{
    layers: "NaturalEarth:countries",
    format: "image/png",
    transparent: true,
    CQL_FILTER: "income_grp = '1. High income: OECD'
      OR income_grp ='2. High income: nonOECD'",
    sld_body: sld
    })
```

3. Save the file and point your browser to it. You should get a map that looks like the one shown in the introduction to this recipe.

How it works...

As with the vendor parameter for reprojection, the use of CQL filters is really easy. You can add one when you create the Layer object and insert the textual representation of the filter, that is, a string. In this filter, we want to select high income countries; two different values match the condition, so we use the logical operator OR to join them:

```
CQL_FILTER: "income_grp = '1. High income: OECD' OR income_grp
  ='2. High income: nonOECD'",
```

Then, we add an `sld_body` parameter and assign the content of the variable `sld` to it. This is not a filter requirement; we just want to override the default style for the countries' layers, so we use the WMS option to send a **Styled Layer Descriptor** (**SLD**) description of drawing rules to GeoServer:

```
sld_body: sld
```

Of course, we need to create an actual SLD document and insert it into the `sld` variable before creating the countries layer. We do this by adding a well-formed XML code line by line to the `sld` variable. You will note that we're creating exactly the same symbology used in the *Using WFS spatial filters* recipe:

```
var sld = '<StyledLayerDescriptor version="1.0.0">';
...
sld+= '<PolygonSymbolizer>';
sld+= '<Stroke>';
sld+= '<CssParameter name="stroke">#000000</CssParameter>';
sld+= '<CssParameter name="stroke-width">1</CssParameter>';
sld+= '</Stroke>';
sld+= '<Fill>';
sld+= '<CssParameter name="fill">#FFFFCC</CssParameter>';
sld+= '<CssParameter name="fill-opacity">0.65</CssParameter>';
sld+= '</Fill>';
sld+= '</PolygonSymbolizer>';
...
```

This is just a small peek at SLD. If you are curious about the standard, you can find the official papers for SLD at `http://portal.opengeospatial.org/files/?artifact_id=22364` and the XSD schemas at `http://schemas.opengis.net/sld/`.

Filtering data with CQL spatial operators

ECQL does not only let you create readable and powerful filters on feature attributes; obviously, it also lets you filter out geometric properties.

There are a few spatial operators that you can use in a CQL filter: `EQUALS`, `DISJOINT`, `INTERSECTS`, `TOUCHES`, `CROSSES`, `WITHIN`, `CONTAINS`, `OVERLAPS`, `RELATE`, `DWITHIN`, and `BEYOND`. With all these operators at your fingertips, you can really build complex filters.

In this recipe, we will use the BEYOND operator that is the inverse of DWITHIN, which we used in the recipe *Using WFS spatial filters*. With the filter, we will select the populated places located at least 1,000 km away from Rome, Italy. The result is shown in the following screenshot:

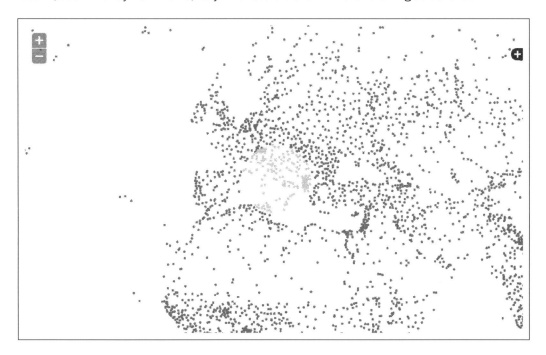

 You can find the full source code for this recipe in the ch01_wmsCQLSpatialFilter.html file.

How to do it...

1. Create a projected table with populated places in PostGIS:

   ```
   gisdata=> CREATE TABLE populatedplaceswm AS SELECT name,
     ST_Transform(geom,3857) AS geom FROM populatedplaces;

   gisdata=> CREATE INDEX populatedplaceswm_0_geom_gist ON
     populatedplaceswm USING gist(geom);
   ```

2. Have a look at the latitude and longitude values for Rome using the following lines of code:

```
gisdata=> select ST_AsText(geom) from populatedplaces where
  name = 'Rome';
------------------------------------------
  POINT(12.481312562874 41.8979014850989)
```

3. Copy `wmsCQLFilter.html` to `wmsCQLSpatialFilter.html` and edit the JavaScript code. Change `sld` to `PointSymbolizer` with a red fill for points outside the buffer:

```
sld+= '<PointSymbolizer>';
sld+= '<Graphic>';
sld+= '<Mark>';
sld+= '<WellKnownName>circle</WellKnownName>';
sld+= '<Fill>';
sld+= '<CssParameter name="fill">#FF0000</CssParameter>';
sld+= '</Fill>';
sld+= '</Mark>';
sld+= '<Size>3</Size>';
sld+= '</Graphic>';
sld+= '</PointSymbolizer>';
```

4. Add an `sld2` variable that holds drawing rules for points contained in the buffer area. You can reuse the code for the `sld` variable, changing the fill color to green:

```
sld2+= '<PointSymbolizer>';
sld2+= '<Graphic>';
sld2+= '<Mark>';
sld2+= '<WellKnownName>circle</WellKnownName>';
sld2+= '<Fill>';
sld2+= '<CssParameter name="fill">#00FF00</CssParameter>';
sld2+= '</Fill>';
sld2+= '</Mark>';
sld2+= '<Size>3</Size>';
sld2+= '</Graphic>';
sld2+= '</PointSymbolizer>';
```

5. Set the SRS for the map to `EPSG:3857`:

```
map = new OpenLayers.Map({
  div: "myMap",
  allOverlays: true,
  projection: "EPSG:3857",
  maxExtent: new OpenLayers.Bounds(-20037508, -20037508,
    20037508, 20037508.34),
  maxResolution: 156543.0339,
  units: 'm',
```

6. Add a layer with a `cql` filter for points located outside a 1,000-kilometre circular buffer from Rome:

```
new OpenLayers.Layer.WMS("Far away places",
   "http://localhost/geoserver/wms",{
      layers: "NaturalEarth:populatedplaceswm",
      format: "image/png",
      transparent: true,
      cql_filter: "BEYOND(geom,POINT(1389413
         5145697),1000000,meters)",
      sld_body: sld,
```

7. Add a layer with a `cql` filter for points located inside a 1,000-kilometre circular buffer from Rome:

```
new OpenLayers.Layer.WMS("Near places",
   "http://localhost/geoserver/wms",{
      layers: "NaturalEarth:populatedplaceswm",
      format: "image/png",
      transparent: true,
      cql_filter: "DWITHIN(geom,POINT(1389413
         5145697),1000000,meters)",
      sld_body: sld2,
```

8. Save the file and point your browser to it. Your map will show a set of green points around Rome. As shown in the previous image, Rome is surrounded by red points.

How it works...

Using spatial operators in `cql_filter` is not really different than filtering other attributes. We used a map in a planar coordinate, in this case, the Web Mercator projection, because of an issue within GeoServer. Although you can define units that will be used to calculate distance in the `BEYOND` and `DWITHIN` operators, the interpretation depends on the data store (see `http://jira.codehaus.org/browse/GEOS-937` for a detailed discussion). In PostGIS, the distance is evaluated according to the default units for the native spatial reference system of the data.

A **spatial reference system** (**SRS**) is a coordinate-based local, regional, or global system used to locate geographical entities. SRS defines a specific map projection as well as transformations between different SRS.

We need to create a new table with points projected in a planar coordinate. Then, we create an `OpenLayers` map object and set it to `EPSG:3857`. When using a projected SRS, we also need to set the map extent, resolution, and units:

```
projection: "EPSG:3857",
maxExtent: new OpenLayers.Bounds(-20037508, -20037508, 20037508,
   20037508.34),
maxResolution: 156543.0339,
units: 'm',
```

We then add two layers pointing to the same feature type, `populatedplaceswm`, and using two different spatial filters. The first one uses the `BEYOND` operator, passing it the coordinates of Rome expressed in meters, a 1000-kilometer distance, and the units:

```
cql_filter: "BEYOND(geom,POINT(1389413 5145697),1000000,meters)",
```

 Although the units are not evaluated when filtering features, the parameter is mandatory. Hence, you have to insert it, but you need to be aware of the native SRS of the data and calculate a proper value for the distance

To override the default rendering of features, we set `sld_body` for the request to the SLD created in the JavaScript code:

```
sld_body: sld,
```

To represent features inside the buffer, we create a similar layer, filtering features with the `DWITHIN` operator. The syntax is pretty similar to `BEYOND`; please ensure that you set the same point and distance to build the buffer area:

```
cql_filter: "DWITHIN(geom,POINT(1389413 5145697),1000000,meters)",
```

Then, we set a different `sld_body` value to represent features with a different symbol:

```
sld_body: sld2,
```

Creating a SQL view

You probably know how to create a SQL view. Using views lets you represent data in different ways, extracting and transforming the data and avoiding data duplication.

With RDBMS, you can store views inside the database. In this case, a view is just a feature type for GeoServer, just like for a table.

You can also use a different approach with GeoServer, storing the SQL code inside your GeoServer configuration. This way, SQL views allow the execution of a custom SQL query on each request to the layer. This avoids the need to create a database view for complex queries.

We use PostGIS in this book. While it is one of the most powerful spatial databases available, not to mention that it is free to use, you may need to use other databases. GeoServer also supports Oracle, SQL Server, and MySQL with extension modules. You can use the recipes in this book with any of them; you only need to be careful with the SQL code. Code inserted in this book uses the ST_* functions that may have different syntax or be unavailable in other databases than PostGIS.

How to do it...

1. We will build a view that contains only European countries. Open your GeoServer web interface and switch to **Layers**:

    ## Layers

    Manage the layers being published by GeoServer
    - Add a new resource
    - *Remove selected resources*

2. Select **Add a new resource**, and from the dropdown list, select the data store pointing to your RDBMS, PostGIS in our case. Instead of selecting a table from the list, select the **Configure new SQL view...** link:

    Add layer from NaturalEarth:PostGISLocal ▼

    You can create a new feature type by manually configuring the attribute names and types. Create new feature type...
    On databases you can also create a new feature type by configuring a native SQL statement. Configure new SQL view...
    Here is a list of resources contained in the store 'PostGISLocal'. Click on the layer you wish to configure

3. In the form, insert EuropeanCountries as **View Name** and the following code as the SQL statement:

```
SELECT
  ADMIN,
  ST_UNION(COUNTRIES_EXP.GEOM) AS GEOM
FROM
  (SELECT
     ADMIN,
     (ST_DUMP(GEOM)).geom as geom
   FROM
     COUNTRIES
   WHERE
     REGION_UN = 'Europe') COUNTRIES_EXP
```

```
WHERE
    ST_Intersects(COUNTRIES_EXP.GEOM,
        ST_GeomFromText('POLYGON((-11 37.40, -11 73.83, 27.28
        73.83, 27.28 37.40, -11 37.40))',4326)) = TRUE
GROUP BY ADMIN
```

4. Move to the bottom of the screen and select the **Guess Geometry type and srid** checkbox and click on **Refresh**. The **4326** EPSG code is properly detected, but you have to manually select **MultiPolygon** to avoid detecting the value of the polygon instead:

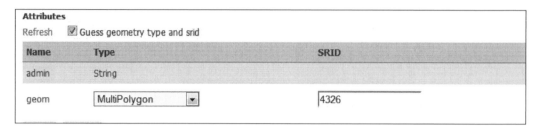

5. Click on **Save**, and you will be brought to the publish layer form. Click on the button to calculate the native data extent and click on **Publish**. Move to **Layer Preview** and select the **EuropeanCountries** layer; your map should look like this one:

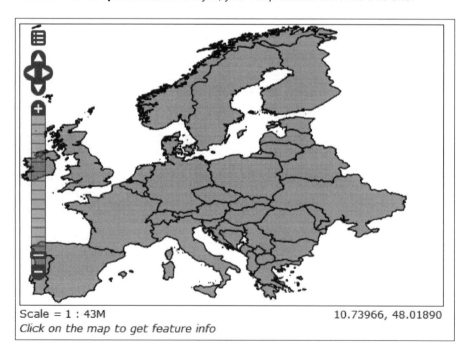

How it works...

Creating a SQL view in GeoServer is not different from creating one in an RDBMS. You just have to build proper SQL code to filter and transform the feature.

It is not mandatory that source tables for your view are already published in GeoServer. You only need to have a data store properly configured to an RDBMS; you can't use a SQL view against a shapefile or other file-based stores.

As you can see in the SQL code for this recipe, you can use any combination of the standard SQL and vendor extension. GeoServer does not evaluate the code, but it demands parsing and evaluation to the RDBMS.

You can use the aggregation and transformation function as we did. You need to return at least a proper geometrical field so that GeoServer can evaluate it and use it to configure a layer.

There's more...

The view created from GeoServer is not stored inside your RDBMS. This may sound odd if you're used to creating views in a database. Indeed, GeoServer views are a sort of virtual table. You can check this inside the data directory. Look for the workspace and find the `featuretype` definition, which is in the `featuretype.xml` file. You will find that your SQL query is just stored inside it:

```
<metadata>
  <entry key="JDBC_VIRTUAL_TABLE">
    <virtualTable>
      <name>EuropeanCountries</name>
      <sql>SELECT &#xd;
ADMIN,&#xd;
ST_UNION(COUNTRIES_EXP.GEOM) AS GEOM&#xd;
FROM &#xd;
  (SELECT &#xd;
     ADMIN, &#xd;
     (ST_DUMP(GEOM)).geom as geom&#xd;
   FROM &#xd;
     COUNTRIES &#xd;
   WHERE &#xd;
     REGION_UN = &apos;Europe&apos;) COUNTRIES_EXP &#xd;
WHERE &#xd;
  ST_Intersects(COUNTRIES_EXP.GEOM,
    ST_GeomFromText(&apos;POLYGON((-11 37.40, -11 73.83, 27.28
    73.83, 27.28 37.40, -11 37.40))&apos;,4326)) = TRUE &#xd;
GROUP BY ADMIN</sql>
```

```
<escapeSql>false</escapeSql>
<geometry>
  <name>geom</name>
  <type>MultiPolygon</type>
  <srid>4326</srid>
</geometry>
</virtualTable>
</entry>
</metadata>
```

Creating a parametric view

A parametric SQL view is based on a SQL query containing the named parameters with values provided dynamically in WMS and WFS requests.

How to do it...

1. We will now create a new view by extending the code of the previous step. What if you want to have a dynamic view that works for each continent? You need to start the same way as we did previously: select **Add a new resource** from the **Layer** menu.

2. Select the data store pointing to PostGIS or your preferred RDBMS. Instead of selecting a table from the list, select the **Configure new SQL view...** link:

3. In the form, insert ContinentView as **View Name** and the following code as the SQL statement:

```
SELECT
  ADMIN,
  GEOM
FROM
  COUNTRIES
WHERE
  CONTINENT = '%continent%'
```

4. Go to the **SQL view parameters** section and click on the **Guess parameters from SQL** link. Insert Africa as the default value.

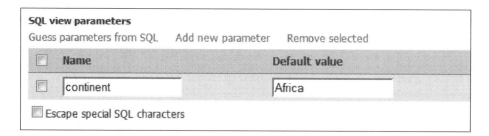

5. At the bottom of the page, select the **Guess Geometry type and srid** checkbox and click on **Refresh**. The **4326** EPSG code is properly detected, but you have to manually select **MultiPolygon** instead of the detect value of **Polygon**.

6. Click on **Save**, and you'll be taken to the publish the layer form. Click on the button to calculate the native data extent, and then click on **Publish**. Move to **Layer Preview** and select the **ContinentView** layer. Your map now looks like this one:

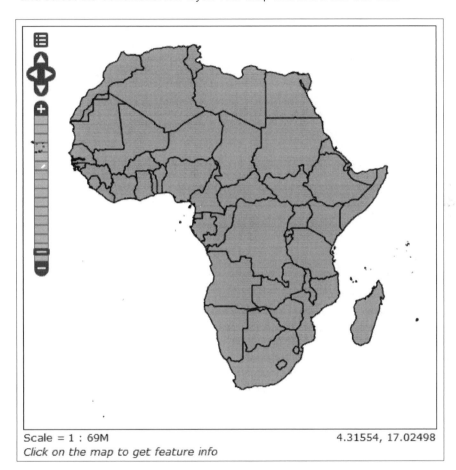

Scale = 1 : 69M   4.31554, 17.02498
Click on the map to get feature info

7. The preview map shows you the result of filtering with default values. Add `&viewparams=continent:Europe` to your request URL and reload the map. You should now see a different map:

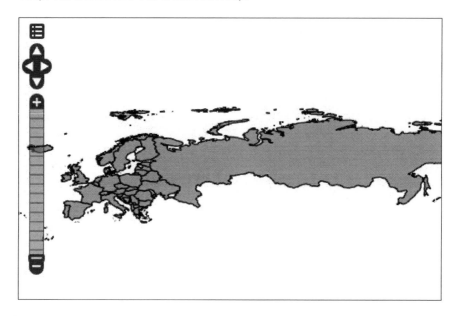

How it works...

A parametric view lets you define one or more filtering parameters at request time. In this recipe, instead of building five different views (one for each continent), we have a single view, and the calling app can define which continent is relevant in the request.

Building a parametric view is not different from a standard SQL view. You can start creating the code without any parameters to check that you have no syntax or logical errors.

Once you are done with the code, you can select which field should become a parameter. To let GeoServer recognize the parameters, you simply enclose them within % characters, as shown in the following code:

```
WHERE CONTINENT = '%continent%'
```

GeoServer recognizes the parameters and lets you set an optional default value. Please note that if you don't set a default value, you always need to set a value for parameters when sending a request to GeoServer.

At run time, you set values for each parameter, adding the `viewparams` option to your request. As per the value of the option, you insert a set of `params-value` couples.

Improving performance with pregeneralized features

The feature type may contain a lot of coordinates. Also, if it's not a really big data, the simple vector datasets we use in this recipe contain a large number of vertices:

```
gisdata=> select sum(ST_NPoints(geom)) from countries;
sum
--------
548604
```

When you're creating a small-scale map, that is, a continent view, it does not make sense to have the GeoServer process all this data to output a really simplified rendering of the shapes. You are just wasting CPU time and degrading the performance of your server.

Having a simplified version of your data for general representation would be more practical, but you also want to have a detailed version of the data when your map goes to middle or large scale.

The idea behind the pregeneralized features module is to combine more versions of a feature type so that users of GeoServer can choose the one that is the best for each scale, while the user continues to use it as if it was a single feature type.

> Pregeneralized features are supported by an extension module. If you want to use this feature, you need to download the optional module. Please note that any extension module will follow the version of GeoServer. Installation is quite easy. Download the archive from `http://geoserver.org/release/stable/` and extract the two JAR files into the `WEB-INF/lib` directory of the GeoServer installation.

How to do it...

1. Start creating three generalized versions of countries for use in this recipe. The following instructions work for PostGIS:

    ```
    gisdata=> create table countries_0 as select admin, geom from
      countries;
    ```

    ```
    gisdata=> CREATE INDEX countries_0_geom_gist ON countries_0
      USING gist(geom);
    ```

    ```
    gisdata=> create table countries_01 as select admin,
      ST_SimplifyPreserveTopology(geom,0.01) as geom from
      countries;
    ```

```
gisdata=> CREATE INDEX countries_01_geom_gist ON countries_01
  USING gist(geom);

gisdata=> create table countries_05 as select admin,
  ST_SimplifyPreserveTopology(geom,0.05) as geom from
  countries;

gisdata=>CREATE INDEX countries_05_geom_gist ON countries_05
  USING gist(geom);

gisdata=>create table countries_1 as select admin,
  ST_SimplifyPreserveTopology(geom,0.1) as geom from
  countries;

gisdata=>CREATE INDEX countries_1_geom_gist ON countries_1
  USING gist(geom);
```

2. Create a new XML file, insert the following code snippet, and save it as `geninfo_postgis.xml`:

```xml
<?xml version="1.0" encoding="UTF-8"?>

<GeneralizationInfos version="1.0">

  <GeneralizationInfo dataSourceNameSpace="NaturalEarth"
  dataSourceName="PostGISLocal"
  featureName="GeneralizedCountries"
  baseFeatureName="countries_0" geomPropertyName="geom">

    <Generalization dataSourceNameSpace="NaturalEarth"
      dataSourceName="PostGISLocal"  distance="1"
      featureName="countries_01" geomPropertyName="geom"/>

    <Generalization dataSourceNameSpace="NaturalEarth"
      dataSourceName="PostGISLocal"  distance="5"
      featureName="countries_05" geomPropertyName="geom"/>

    <Generalization dataSourceNameSpace="NaturalEarth"
      dataSourceName="PostGISLocal"  distance="10"
      featureName="countries_1" geomPropertyName="geom"/>

  </GeneralizationInfo>

</GeneralizationInfos>
```

3. Go to the data store section of the GeoServer web interface, click on **Add new data store**, and then select **Generalizing data store**:

Vector Data Sources

📄 Directory of spatial files (shapefiles) - Takes a directory of shapefiles and exposes it as a data store
📄 Generalizing data store - Data store supporting generalized geometries
📄 PostGIS - PostGIS Database
📄 PostGIS (JNDI) - PostGIS Database (JNDI)

4. Input `GeneralizedCountries` as the name for the data store, and then point to the location of the `geninfo_postgis.xml` file. Change the `org.geotools` string to `org.geoserver` in the two textboxes and click on **Save**:

Connection Parameters

RepositoryClassName *

org.geoserver.data.gen.DSFinderRepository

GeneralizationInfosProviderClassName *

org.geoserver.data.gen.info.GeneralizationInfosProvide

GeneralizationInfosProviderParam

file:data/geninfo_postgis.xml

Namespace *

http://www.naturalearthdata.com/

5. You can now see the feature type you defined in the XML file and click on the **Publish** button. You are now done. Switch to the layer's preview to check whether GeoServer is properly visualizing the data.

How it works...

If you look at the layer preview, you will not see any difference from the countries' layers. You will observe a faster rendering; this is because GeoServer is indeed extracting geometries form the simplified table. Let's check what is happening behind the scenes.

Set the log detail in GeoServer to GEOTOOLS_DEVELOPER_LOGGING, and then open your GeoServer log with the `tail` command:

```
$: tail -f /opt/Tomcat7042/webapps/geoserver/data/logs/geoserver.log
```

Now open the preview for **GeneralizedCountries**. After the map is shown, you should see some rows that state **GeoServer first evaluates the geometry distance from the map's scale**. Select the table that is more appropriate to extract the features from:

```
INFO [org.geotools.data.gen] - Hint geometry distance:
   0.5681250333785898

INFO [org.geotools.data.gen] - Hint geometry distance:
   0.5681250333785898

INFO [org.geotools.data.gen] - Using generalizsation: PostGISLocal
   countries_1 geom 0.1
```

In the log, the actual query that is performed on the database is present, and you can check whether it is created on a simplified version of the countries. As you can see, it is indeed created on a simplified version of the countries. Actually, the version with a higher generalization degree, which contains the more simplified features, is used:

```
DEBUG [org.geotools.jdbc] - CREATE CONNECTION

DEBUG [org.geotools.jdbc] - SELECT
   encode(ST_AsBinary(ST_Force_2D("geom")),'base64') as "geom" FROM
   "public"."countries_1" WHERE  "geom" && ST_G

eomFromText('POLYGON ((-244.29375672340652 -121.77904978394649, -
   244.29375672340652 115.41315165161649, 244.29377198219652
   115.41315165161649, 244.29377198219652 -121.7

7904978394649, -244.29375672340652 -121.77904978394649))', 4326)

   [org.geotools.jdbc] - CLOSE CONNECTION
```

From the database, you can check the total number of features in this table:

```
gisdata=> select sum(ST_NPoints(geom)) from countries_1;
   sum
-------

44085
```

Now, zoom in to your map and check what GeoServer writes in the log. When your map is centered on Europe, the map scale triggers GeoServer to use another table. If you inspect the log, you can indeed observe that now GeoServer is using the table countries_05:

```
INFO [org.geotools.data.gen] - Using generalizsation: PostGISLocal
   countries_05 geom 0.05
```

Check the database again; the total number of features is higher. However, you are using a fraction of them, as only a portion of the Earth is represented on the map, so you get finer detail without a slow rendering. This is attained using the following lines of code:

```
gisdata=> select sum(ST_NPoints(geom)) from countries_05;

  sum

-------

 66042
```

Continue to zoom in until you see in the log that GeoServer is using the original table, `countries_0`. You are now using the entire detailed geometries, but in a relatively small area:

```
DEBUG [org.geotools.jdbc] - SELECT
  encode(ST_AsBinary(ST_Force_2D("geom")),'base64') as "geom" FROM
  "public"."countries_0" WHERE  "geom" && ST_G

eomFromText('POLYGON ((6.016917772920612 4.379043245570911,
  6.016917772920612 5.305575282428689, 7.925462806926788
  5.305575282428689, 7.925462806926788 4.37904324557091

1, 6.016917772920612 4.379043245570911))', 4326)
```

2
Working with Rasters

In this chapter, we will cover the following recipes:

- ► Getting coverages in different formats
- ► Using WCS vendor parameters
- ► Publishing a mosaic
- ► Using pyramids
- ► Adding GDAL formats
- ► Adding a PostGIS raster data source

Introduction

Working with raster data is a fundamental requirement when you are requested to build a spatial data infrastructure, which is a commonly used term today to define an information system using spatial data.

You are probably already skilled at using a simple raster format such as Geotiff. Configuring raster formats on GeoServer and querying the resulting layers with the WMS protocol is a common and pretty way to use them as base maps in your application.

In this chapter, we will focus on more advanced topics such as using raster in their native formats, not just as a map, and storing them in different ways. As usual, you are not requested to have any special prior knowledge, but a sound understanding of the difference between vector and raster data and how the latter is represented will help your journey through the recipes.

Getting coverages in different formats

WMS requests let you add vector and raster data to a map. This is very useful when your main purpose is data visualization. All the rendering work is on the server side, which means that it is performed by GeoServer, and your client application just has to properly show the final output to the users.

This model fails when your users want to manage the data represented on the map, for instance, to change a style or create derivative data with a processing tool.

In this case, the original data is needed. **Web Coverage Service** (**WCS**) is the equivalent of WFS to deliver original data. It is intended to get a raster dataset, or a subset of it, in its original form, without any rendering or other processing.

 WCS is of OGC standard, currently at Version 2.0.1; GeoServer supports versions ranging from 1.0.0 to the latest one.

For a detailed reference, you can consult the official documentation at `http://www.opengeospatial.org/standards/wcs`.

In this recipe, we will use QGIS as a WMS and WCS client. It is a powerful and open source tool. You can download it from `http://qgis.org/en/site/`.

How to do it...

1. Open the QGIS Desktop. From the toolbar, select the **Layer** menu and then click on the **Add WCS Layer...** voice:

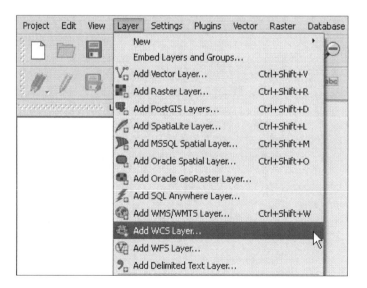

2. A connection window is shown. In the upper part, click on the **New** button to add a reference to your GeoServer instance:

3. Insert `localhost` as the connection name and `http://localhost:8080/ geoserver/ows?service=WCS&version=2.0.1&request=GetCapabilities` as the URL.

4. Click on **OK** to save the new connection. In the add layer window, click on the **Connect** button, after which a list of the available layers will be shown.

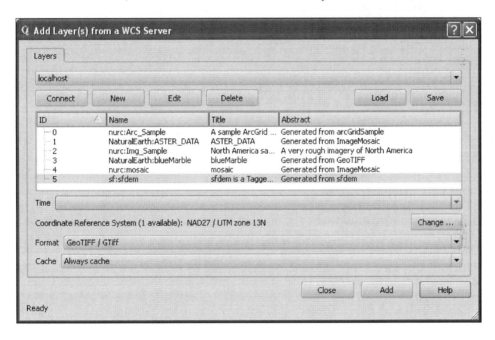

5. Select the **sf:dem** layer and go with the default values for all the other parameters. Then, click on **Add**. The coverage is downloaded and added to your map canvas.

6. Now repeat the procedure to add the same layer using the WMS protocol. From the toolbar, select the **Layer** menu and then click on the **Add WMS/WMTS Layer...** voice.

7. You need to add a connection to the server in a very similar way as you did previously for WCS. Use the following URL:

   `http://localhost:8080/geoserver/ows?service=wms&version=1.3.0&requ est=GetCapabilities`

8. After connecting to the localhost, select the `sf:dem` layer again. The default CRS is EPSG:4326. To avoid your client performing a reprojection of data, click on the **Change** button and select **EPSG:26713**:

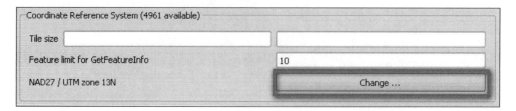

9. Click on the **Add** button and your layer will be loaded on the map on top of the previous layer.

How it works...

In this recipe, you added the same layer twice on the map. What is the purpose and what is the difference between them?

Also, if the original data is the same, what your client received from GeoServer is quite different in the two operations. The first hint may come from a look at the table of contents in QGIS:

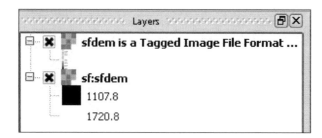

The layer on top is the result of the WMS request, while the other is a result of the WCS request. The first difference is in the symbology used to represent them. In a WMS request, the data is represented with a default style or a style provided within the request. So the data is transformed and represented as a picture.

WCS has no concept of style. It always delivers the original data, and a symbology is then applied from the client. In this case, QGIS uses a black to white color ramp stretched to the minimum/maximum range. If you open the layer properties window, you can see that style is not modifiable for the WMS layer while you can change it in the WCS layer.

Exporting the layer could help you better understand what you received. In the table of contents, right-click on the layer loaded with WMS and select the **Save As...** item.

Set the parameters as shown in the following screenshot and click on the **OK** button:

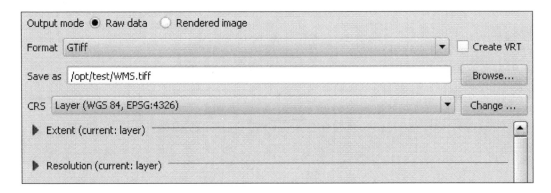

Repeat the process to save the layer obtained by the WCS request. Save the export in a file called WCS.tiff.

The first look at the file size shows a big difference, as the output from the WCS layer is way bigger than that from the WMS layer:

```
$ ls -lh
total 1.2M
-rw-r--r-- 1 root root 1.2M Jul 18 12:15 WCS.tiff
-rw-r--r-- 1 root root  22K Jul 18 12:15 WMS.tiff
```

Looking at the details with the gdalinfo utility shows a huge difference in the size and value contained:

```
$ gdalinfo -stats WCS.tiff
Driver: GTiff/GeoTIFF
Files: WCS.tiff
Size is 634, 477
...
Band 1 Block=634x3 Type=Float32, ColorInterp=Gray
  Minimum=1066.000, Maximum=1840.000, Mean=1353.669, StdDev=177.041
  NoData Value=-9.99999993381581251e+36
...
$ gdalinfo -stats WMS.tiff
Driver: GTiff/GeoTIFF
Files: WMS.tiff
Size is 100, 54
...
```

```
Band 1 Block=100x20 Type=Byte, ColorInterp=Red
  Minimum=0.000, Maximum=255.000, Mean=206.119, StdDev=67.776
...
Band 2 Block=100x20 Type=Byte, ColorInterp=Green
  Minimum=0.000, Maximum=255.000, Mean=171.005, StdDev=74.023
...
Band 3 Block=100x20 Type=Byte, ColorInterp=Blue
  Minimum=0.000, Maximum=63.000, Mean=13.006, StdDev=20.915
...
Band 4 Block=100x20 Type=Byte, ColorInterp=Alpha
  Minimum=0.000, Maximum=255.000, Mean=237.669, StdDev=64.179
...
```

As it is stated in the result, the output from the WCS layer is a single-band raster file with values ranging from 1,066 to 1,840, which are the elevation values of the area represented in dem. The output of the WMS file is an image with four bands whose values range from 0 to 255, which are indeed the expected values for an RGB-encoded picture. So if you're going to use the result of the WCS in QGIS, you might want to be sure that it is equivalent to using the original data.

A powerful option of WCS is the possibility to have the data in several different formats. If you connect again to GeoServer, you may see that in the window, QGIS lets you select what format you want to download the data in.

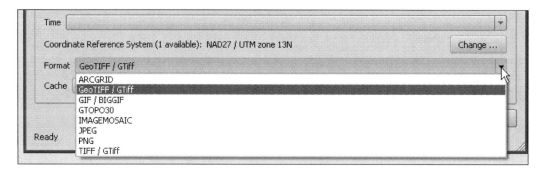

The nature and number of formats available depends on the server. QGIS merely shows you what GeoServer returns at its WCS DescribeCoverage request. You can check for yourself by inserting this URL in your browser:

```
http://localhost:8080/geoserver/wcs?service=WCS&version=1.0.0&request
=DescribeCoverage&Coverage=sf:sfdem
```

If your check the XML code, you will find the following supported formats:

```
<wcs:supportedFormats nativeFormat="GeoTIFF">
    <wcs:formats>ARCGRID</wcs:formats>
    <wcs:formats>GeoTIFF</wcs:formats>
    <wcs:formats>GIF</wcs:formats>
    <wcs:formats>GTOPO30</wcs:formats>
    <wcs:formats>IMAGEMOSAIC</wcs:formats>
    <wcs:formats>JPEG</wcs:formats>
    <wcs:formats>PNG</wcs:formats>
    <wcs:formats>TIFF</wcs:formats>
</wcs:supportedFormats>
```

You can control which formats are allowed on a per layer base. From the GeoServer web interface, open the **Layer** setting and go to the **Publishing** tab. There is a **Formats** section where you can choose which formats will be available for that layer.

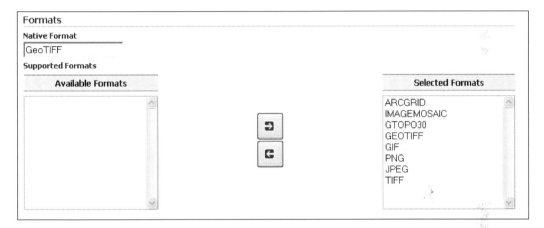

Using WCS vendor parameters

As with WFS, WMS, or WPS, vendors have the option of extending WCS capabilities with custom parameters. This way some extra functions can be delivered to users to help them manage their coverages.

In the case of WCS, GeoServer offers a basic customization; you can use a vendor parameter to filter out results according to a namespace.

How to do it...

1. Create a request for the WCS capabilities with cURL:

```
$ curl -u admin:geoserver -XGET -H 'Accept: text/xml' -G
  http://localhost:8080/geoserver/wcs \
 -d service=WCS \
 -d version=1.0.0 \
 -d request=GetCapabilities \
 -d namespace=NaturalEarth \
 -o coverages.xml
```

2. Now open the file that stores the results and check that only the coverages from the NaturalEarth namespace are listed:

```
...

<wcs:CoverageSummary>
    <ows:Title>blueMarble</ows:Title>
    <ows:Abstract>Generated from GeoTIFF</ows:Abstract>
    <ows:Keywords>
        <ows:Keyword>WCS</ows:Keyword>
        <ows:Keyword>GeoTIFF</ows:Keyword>
        <ows:Keyword>blueMarble</ows:Keyword>
    </ows:Keywords>
    <ows:WGS84BoundingBox>
        <ows:LowerCorner>-180.0 -90.0</ows:LowerCorner>
        <ows:UpperCorner>180.0 90.0</ows:UpperCorner>
    </ows:WGS84BoundingBox>
    <wcs:Identifier>blueMarble</wcs:Identifier>
</wcs:CoverageSummary>

...

<wcs:CoverageSummary>
    <ows:Title>colourRelief</ows:Title>
    <ows:Abstract>Generated from GeoTIFF</ows:Abstract>
    <ows:Keywords>
        <ows:Keyword>WCS</ows:Keyword>
        <ows:Keyword>GeoTIFF</ows:Keyword>
        <ows:Keyword>colourRelief</ows:Keyword>
    </ows:Keywords>
```

```
<ows:WGS84BoundingBox>
    <ows:LowerCorner>12.06486111111111
        42.033750000000005</ows:LowerCorner>
    <ows:UpperCorner>12.88375
        42.508472222222224</ows:UpperCorner>
</ows:WGS84BoundingBox>
<wcs:Identifier>colourRelief</wcs:Identifier>
</wcs:CoverageSummary>
...
```

How it works...

Unsurprisingly, the option is very easy to use. When adding the `namespace` parameter to the request, the coverages list is filtered. Using this option, you can split your data into logical groups. Be aware that using an incorrect namespace, one that doesn't exist in your GeoServer, does not return any error; you will simply obtain an empty list.

Publishing a mosaic

In the previous recipes, you used a single raster dataset. This is a common case when the datasets are not of a huge size. When your data covers a really big area or its resolution is high, that is, it contains a highly detailed representation of the measured parameter, a single dataset is not the best option, and in some cases is not an option at all.

The best approach is to create a mosaic of raster datasets. A mosaic is a collection of raster datasets that are virtually merged together to be used as a single dataset.

The virtual merging operation produces an index file that contains information on the extent of each raster dataset. Using this index file, GeoServer compares the area of each request and retrieves the granules of the mosaic that intersects it.

You may build this index file, which is actually a shapefile, with an external tool. GeoServer has a built-in plugin to create a new mosaic, which is the index file, and it works really well, making it the best option.

The plugin works with every raster format supported by GeoServer, such as Geotiffs, PNG, JPW with a world file, and so on.

There are some constraints that you should be aware of:

▶ All raster datasets in the mosaic must have the same coordinate reference system; no reprojection is performed

▶ All raster datasets must have the same ColorModel and SampleModel

▶ If you are going to use overviews to enhance performances of the raster dataset, all of them must have the same resolution

Getting ready

For this as well as the remaining recipes, we need a set of raster data. We will use data from an authoritative and open source agency, the **United States Geological Survey** (**USGS**). It offers a huge set of open data. We will select the global elevation data from **Advanced Spaceborne Thermal Emission and Reflection Radiometer** (**ASTER**).

ASTER is an instrument aboard of the satellite launched by NASA. NASA freely distributes ASTER data for public usage. For an introduction to it, take a look at:

http://en.wikipedia.org/wiki/Advanced_Spaceborne_
Thermal_Emission_and_Reflection_Radiometer

We also want to stress the fact that *ASTER GDEM is a product of METI and NASA*; if you plan to use it in your work, carefully read the license agreement and the citation constraint.

USGS offers several ways to search and download its data; a convenient and friendly tool is EarthExplorer. You will use it to download the data used in this recipe.

1. Using your preferred browser, open http://earthexplorer.usgs.gov/.

2. You may search the data anonymously, but in order to download it, you have to log in. If you already own an USGS account, click on the **Login** link and use it; otherwise, you should click on the **Register** button. The process is really simple and straightforward. After you receive the confirmation e-mail, you can log in.

3. Zoom into the map to locate the Italy peninsular area. Then, create a selection area like the one represented in the following screenshot. You can create the polygon by double-clicking on the map for each vertex:

4. Click on the **Data Sets** button. A list of the available datasets is shown. Browse for **ASTER GLOBAL DEM** and check the box to the left of it:

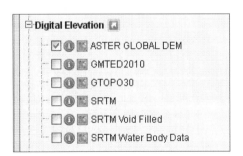

5. You may skip **Additional Criteria** and click on the **Results** button. A list of data is presented. You may use the footprint icon to see what the actual area is covered by each:

6. Check the box to the right of **Add All Results from Current Page to Bulk Download**. This prevents you from having to select the items individually, but will make you download items that cover a really small percentage of your selection area.

7. Click on the **View Item Basket** button.

8. Now click on the **Proceed to Checkout** button. Don't worry you will not be requested to use a credit card!

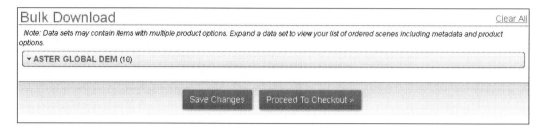

9. Click on the **Submit Order** button and then accept the End User License Agreement. A confirmation e-mail will be sent to you. The message contains links that you can use to download all the selected items.

10. You should end up with 10 ZIP files. Each ZIP file contains two TIFF files and a `readme.pdf` file. You only need the `_dem.tiff` files; extract them all in the same folder.

How to do it...

1. Locate the folder where you downloaded all the ZIP archives. Then, unzip them using the following command:

   ```
   $ for f in *.zip; do unzip $f '*dem.tif'; done
   ```

2. Open your browser and point to the GeoServer web interface.

3. From the left panel, select the **Stores** item in the **Data** section.

4. Click on the **Add new Store** link and you will find the list of Raster and Vector data sources supported. Find **Image Mosaic** in the **Raster** list and click on it.

5. Insert the values in the **Data Source Name** and **Description** fields, click on the **Browse...** link to the left of the textbox at the bottom of the screen, and locate the folder where you saved the ASTER TIFF files.

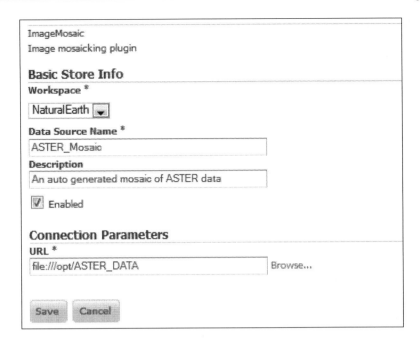

6. Click on the **Save** button and you will be prompted with the option to publish the mosaic. Click on the **Publish** link.

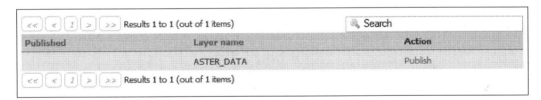

7. We can go with the default setting for now. Click on the **Save** button to publish the layer.

8. Take the ch02_aster.sld file from the code bundle accompanying this book and copy its content. Then, select **Styles** from the left panel of GeoServer web interface. Click on the **Add a new style** link. In the textbox, paste the content of the file previously copied and set **Name** to Aster_terrain. Click on the **Submit** button to save the new style.

9. Now, open the configuration for the `NaturalEarth:ASTER_DATA` layer and switch to the **Publishing** panel. Scroll down to the **WMS Setting** and select the previously created style. Then, click on the **Save** button.

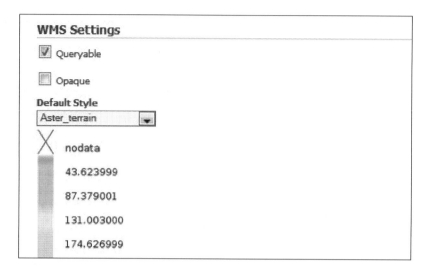

10. Go to the **Layers** preview section and open the **OpenLayers** preview for the `NaturalEarth:ASTER_DATA` layer.

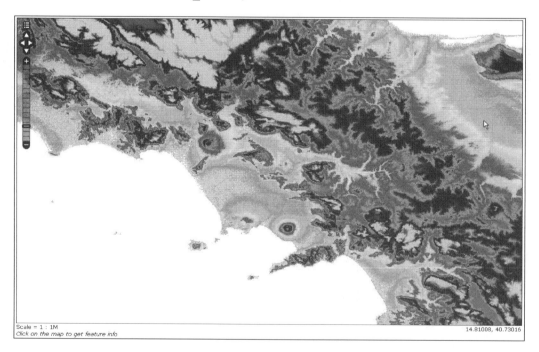

How it works...

You downloaded several TIFF files that are a part of the same layer and in fact, you published them as a single layer. This is quite a common situation when dealing with the raster data.

With vector data, you will have datasets covering a very wide area and containing features with high geometrical details that don't need to be split. In that case, you often store the vector data in an RDBMS, which is an efficient tool to store and retrieve huge amounts of data. We will see later that this approach could also be applied to raster data, but usually storing them in files is a more common and efficient approach.

How big can a file containing raster data be before it becomes unpractical to handle?

It depends on the binary format, the compression algorithm applied to the raster data, and also on the tools used to read them. With GeoServer and the TIFF format, the most used binary format; with it, you may have optimal performance up to a limit of 2 GB per file.

As you may have noted, the size of each file in this recipe is way less than the limit. This is due to a design choice by the provider USGS, because splitting the Earth's surface in tiles that are too big constrains users to download a lot of unnecessary data. However, you also have to remember that the size to consider is that of the uncompressed raster data. Take a file from those downloaded and transform it into a compressed flat TIFF file:

```
$ ls -l ASTGTM2_N40E013_dem.tif

-rw-r--r-- 1 stefano stefano 25963722 Mar 15  2011
  ASTGTM2_N40E013_dem.tif
$ gdal_translate -of GTiff -co COMPRESS=DEFLATE
  ASTGTM2_N40E013_dem.tif ASTGTM2_N40E013.tif
Input file size is 3601, 3601
0...10...20...30...40...50...60...70...80...90...100 - done.
$ ls -l ASTGTM2_N40E013.tif
-rw-rw-r-- 1 stefano stefano 249663 Jul 27 22:03 ASTGTM2_N40E013.tif
```

As you can see in this case, from 25 MB we compressed it to a 244 KB file!

This huge compression is because of the kind of data stored inside; this piece of the DEM is full of no data values as it mostly covers an offshore area.

To summarize, you should try to rearrange your data in the biggest tile you can handle and only then use a mosaic.

In this recipe, we used the automatic mode, made available by the Image Mosaic plugin, to produce the mosaic. Let's explore the folder where you stored your TIFF files to see what happened to them. Check the content of the folder where you stored the TIFF files:

```
$ ls -lh
total 248M
drwxr-xr-x 2 root   root     4.0K Jul 27 22:28 ./
drwxr-xr-x 5 root   root     4.0K Jul 27 22:25 ../
-rw-r--r-- 1 root   root     2.6K Jul 27 22:28 ASTER_DATA.dbf
-rw-r--r-- 1 root   root      133 Jul 27 22:28 ASTER_DATA.fix
-rw-r--r-- 1 root   root      335 Jul 27 22:28 ASTER_DATA.prj
-rw-r--r-- 1 root   root      294 Jul 27 22:28 ASTER_DATA.properties
-rw-r--r-- 1 root   root      100 Jul 27 22:28 ASTER_DATA.qix
-rw-r--r-- 1 root   root     1.5K Jul 27 22:28 ASTER_DATA.shp
-rw-r--r-- 1 root   root      180 Jul 27 22:28 ASTER_DATA.shx
-rw-r--r-- 1 root   root      25M Mar 15  2011 ASTGTM2_N40E013_dem.tif
-rw-r--r-- 1 root   root      25M Mar 15  2011 ASTGTM2_N40E014_dem.tif
-rw-r--r-- 1 root   root      25M Mar 15  2011 ASTGTM2_N40E015_dem.tif
-rw-r--r-- 1 root   root      25M Mar 15  2011 ASTGTM2_N41E012_dem.tif
-rw-r--r-- 1 root   root      25M Mar 15  2011 ASTGTM2_N41E013_dem.tif
-rw-r--r-- 1 root   root      25M Mar 15  2011 ASTGTM2_N41E014_dem.tif
-rw-r--r-- 1 root   root      25M Mar 15  2011 ASTGTM2_N41E015_dem.tif
-rw-r--r-- 1 root   root      25M Mar 15  2011 ASTGTM2_N41E016_dem.tif
-rw-r--r-- 1 root   root      25M Mar 15  2011 ASTGTM2_N42E014_dem.tif
-rw-r--r-- 1 root   root      25M Mar 15  2011 ASTGTM2_N42E015_dem.tif
-rw-r--r-- 1 root   root     1.8K Jul 27 22:28 sample_image
```

Some new files have been created. More specifically, you can see a shapefile, a properties file, and a PRJ file. What are they for?

The shapefile is used as an index to retrieve the raster that covers a specific area. It contains polygons that represent the spatial extents of each granule in the mosaic. Each feature contains an attribute that provides the location of the granule's file on the host filesystem. The location can be expressed either relative to the index file or as an absolute reference. Check the content with the `ogrinfo` utility as follows:

```
$ ogrinfo -al -ro ASTER_DATA.shp | more
INFO: Open of `ASTER_DATA.shp'
```

```
using driver `ESRI Shapefile' successful.


Layer name: ASTER_DATA
Geometry: Polygon
Feature Count: 10
Extent: (11.999861, 39.999861) - (17.000139, 43.000139)
Layer SRS WKT:
GEOGCS["WGS 84",
    DATUM["World Geodetic System 1984",
        SPHEROID["WGS 84",6378137.0,298.257223563,
            AUTHORITY["EPSG","7030"]],
        AUTHORITY["EPSG","6326"]],
    PRIMEM["Greenwich",0.0,
        AUTHORITY["EPSG","8901"]],
    UNIT["degree",0.017453292519943295],
    AXIS["Geodetic longitude",EAST],
    AXIS["Geodetic latitude",NORTH],
    AUTHORITY["EPSG","4326"]]
location: String (254.0)
OGRFeature(ASTER_DATA):0
  location (String) = ASTGTM2_N42E015_dem.tif
  POLYGON ((14.999861111111111 41.999861111111116,14.999861111111111
    43.000138888888891,16.000138888888888
    43.000138888888891,16.000138888888888
    41.999861111111116,14.999861111111111 41.999861111111116))
...
```

The projection file (`.prj`) provides the **Coordinate Reference System (CRS)** information for the mosaic. As you can see from the previous run of the `ogrinfo` utility, the CRS is obviously the same for all the TIFF files. This information is used by GeoServer when you publish a layer based on the mosaic and used as a native CRS.

The properties file (`.properties`) is the configuration file that provides information about the mosaic, such as the *x* and *y* cell size, and whether the file location attribute is absolute or relative:

```
$ cat ASTER_DATA.properties
#-Automagically created from GeoTools-
#Sun Jul 27 22:28:41 CEST 2014
Levels=2.77777777777778E-4,2.77777777777778E-4
```

```
Heterogeneous=false

AbsolutePath=false

Name=ASTER_DATA

TypeName=ASTER_DATA

Caching=false

ExpandToRGB=false

LocationAttribute=location

CheckAuxiliaryMetadata=false

LevelsNum=1
```

Each property has a specific meaning as is summarized in the following table:

Property	Description
Levels	This represents the resolutions for the various levels of the granules of the mosaic.
Heterogeneous	This determines whether the granules are all identical or not. If set to false, then the resolutions are not checked when creating the granules' index.
AbsolutePath	If set to false, then the value contained in the location attribute is evaluated as relative to the index path.
Name	This is the name of the mosaic that will be used.
Caching	If set to false, GeoServer will not cache the mosaic content.
ExpandToRGB	This determines whether to expand the color model from indexed to RGBA. There is a performance penalty using RGBA, so if all your granules are indexed color, then set this to false.
LocationAttribute	This is the name of the attribute that holds the location of a granule.
LevelsNum	This shows the number of reduced resolution layers available for each granule as an overview in GeoTIFF.

If you need to set custom properties for a mosaic, you can edit this file.

Using pyramids

Pyramids are a way to create overviews of your raster data. Overviews are really useful to enhance performance, especially when you have to serve a large amount of data. In this recipe, we will see how the plugin works and have a discussion about how GeoServer handles overviews.

How to do it...

1. GeoServer needs an extension plugin to be able to handle pyramids; hence, the first step is to download and install the plugin. As usual, you need to visit the download page and download the zip archive. Visit the following URL:

   ```
   http://geoserver.org/release/stable/
   ```

2. Get the archive by clicking on the **Image Pyramid** link in the **Coverage Formats** section, as shown in the following screenshot:

   ### Coverage Formats

   - GDAL
   - Image Pyramid
   - JPEG2K
   - JDBC Image Mosaic

   > Be sure to download the matching version of the plugin. If you're not using the latest stable release, instead of the previous URL, use the following URL and browse for your version folder:
   >
   > ```
   > http://geoserver.org/download/
   > ```

3. Extract the `.jar` files contained within the archive into the `WEB-INF/lib` folder of your GeoServer installation as follows:

   ```
   $ unzip geoserver-2.5.1- -pyramid-plugin.zip *.jar -d
   /opt/Tomcat7042/webapps/geoserver/WEB-INF/lib/
   ```

4. Now, merge the TIFF files into a single one:

   ```
   $ gdalbuildvrt aster.vrt *.tif
   $ gdal_translate -of GTiff -co COMPRESS=NONE aster.vrt
     ../pyramid_aster/aster.tif
   Input file size is 18001, 10801
   0...10...20...30...40...50...60...70...80...90...100 - done.
   $ ls -lh ../pyramid_aster/aster.tif
   -rw-r--r-- 1 root root 371M Jul 27 23:15
     ../pyramid_aster/aster.tif
   ```

   > Please note that the output folder for the TIFF file is a different one. This will avoid issues since the single TIFF files are yet to be published as a mosaic.

5. You can now build pyramids for the new TIFF as follows:

```
$ sudo mkdir pyramids
$ gdal_retile.py -r near -levels 6 -ps 2048 2048 -co TILED=YES
  -co COMPRESS=NONE -targetDir pyramids aster.tif
```

6. Now start GeoServer. On completion, open the web interface. On the left panel, locate **Stores** and click on it. Then, click on the **Add a new store** link. Now in the **Raster Data Sources** section, you may find a new format for image pyramids. Click on it.

7. Many more formats are available, as shown in the following screenshot:

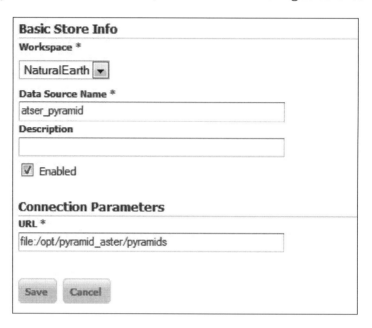

8. When requested, click on **Publish**. You will be presented with the usual form to define the layer properties. Use the same style you created in the *Publishing a mosaic* recipe. When you open the preview layer, you should see exactly the same data as shown in the screenshot in this recipe.

How it works...

When you add a new data store such as image pyramids, GeoServer creates some files on your filesystem:

```
$ ls pyramids/
0  1  2  3  4  5  6  pyramids.prj  pyramids.properties
```

The `pyramids.prj` file contains the CRS for your raster data and as in the previous recipes, this is EPSG:4326.

The `pyramids.properties` file describes the properties of the pyramid levels:

```
$ cat pyramids.properties
#Automatically generated
#Sun Jul 27 23:23:43 CEST 2014
Name=pyramids
Levels=2.777777777777778E-4,2.77777777777778E-4 5.555555555555556E-
   4,5.555555555555556E-4 0.0011111111111111111,0.0011111111111111111
   0.0022222222222222222,0.0022222222222222222
   0.0044444444444444444,0.0044444444444444444
   0.008888888888888889,0.008888888888888889
   0.017777777777777778,0.017777777777777778
LevelsNum=7
Envelope2D=11.999861,39.99986122222222 17.000138777777778,43.000139
LevelsDirs=0 1 2 3 4 5 6
```

It is quite similar to the properties file we saw when creating a mosaic. Levels contain the resolutions for *x* and *y* for each pyramid level.

You might know that overviews can also be created without the need for any GeoServer extension. Geotiff files support internal and external overviews and use standard tools such as `gdaladdo` provided by GDAL. You may create them very easily:

```
$ gdaladdo -r nearest -ro aster.tif 2 4 8 16 32 64
0...10...20...30...40...50...60...70...80...90...100 - done.
$ ls -alh aster*
-rw-r--r-- 1 root root 371M Jul 27 23:15 aster.tif
-rw-r--r-- 1 root root 129M Jul 27 23:40 aster.tif.ovr
```

These overviews can only be used by GeoServer when the Geotiff file size is less than 2 GB. So this plugin comes in need when you have to publish very large datasets.

Adding GDAL formats

GeoServer has a built-in support for several raster formats as you can check in the web interface section:

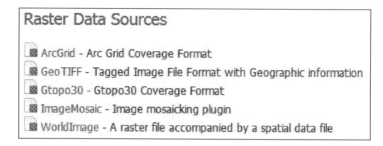

Although Geotiff is one of the best formats to publish raster data, you may need to have GeoServer using more formats. You may, for instance, want to avoid converting data to Geotiff.

In order to do this, we will install GDAL libraries on our server and then a specific GeoServer extension to include GDAL supported formats in GeoServer.

Getting ready

There are several ways to have GDAL libraries installed on your server. If the primary goal is to use them along with GeoServer, we recommend you use the binary archives from GeoSolutions, an Italian company that employs many core GeoServer developers. Using these artifacts, you can be sure to avoid compatibility issues among the GDAL version and the ImageIO plugin with Java bindings for the GDAL libraries. Installing GDAL is an easy task that we're going to execute with the following procedure:

1. Point your browser to the following URL:

   ```
   http://demo.geo-solutions.it/share/github/imageio-ext/
   releases/1.1.X/1.1.10/native/gdal/
   ```

2. Download the `gdal-data.zip` file and decompress it in a local folder on your server.

3. Now browse one of the two folders according to the operating system of your server and select a proper archive. If you are using Windows, one of the following should be a good choice:

⮐ Parent Directory		-
gdal-1.9.2-MSVC2010-x64.zip	11-Aug-2013 21:10	17M
gdal-1.9.2-MSVC2010.zip	11-Aug-2013 21:09	15M
gdal-19-1600-ecw.msi	11-Aug-2013 21:09	1.2M
gdal-19-1600-mrsid.msi	11-Aug-2013 21:10	2.3M
gdal-19-1600-x64-ecw.msi	11-Aug-2013 21:10	1.3M
gdal-19-1600-x64-mrsid.msi	11-Aug-2013 21:10	2.6M
msi-installer-license.txt	11-Aug-2013 21:10	1.1K

You just need the `gdal-1.9.2-MSVC20010.zip` or `gdal-1.9.2-MSVC2010-x64.zip` file to enable most of the GDAL formats. If you also need support for ECW and MrSID, you should get the additional `.msi` files. Be aware that both formats are proprietary and using them on a server requires a proper license to be acquired.

4. On Linux, select a proper file according to your architecture (32 bit or 64 bit) and Linux flavor.

⮐ Parent Directory		-
ECWEULA.txt	11-Aug-2013 21:11	21K
gdal192-CentOS5.8-gcc4.1.2-i386.tar.gz	11-Aug-2013 21:11	16M
gdal192-CentOS5.8-gcc4.1.2-x86_64.tar.gz	11-Aug-2013 21:11	16M
gdal192-Redhat6.0-gcc4.4.4-x86_64.tar.gz	11-Aug-2013 21:12	18M
gdal192-Ubuntu11-gcc4.5.2-i386.tar.gz	11-Aug-2013 21:12	17M
gdal192-Ubuntu11-gcc4.5.2-x86_64.tar.gz	11-Aug-2013 21:11	17M
gdal192-Ubuntu12-gcc4.6.3-i386.tar.gz	11-Aug-2013 21:11	17M
gdal192-Ubuntu12-gcc4.6.3-x86_64.tar.gz	11-Aug-2013 21:12	18M
notes_on_ECW_and_JP2ECW.txt	11-Aug-2013 21:12	612

5. Decompress the archive on a folder on your server. Now, you can open a command-line window to check whether the installation was successful. Change the current directory to the folder where you decompressed the GDAL archive and write the following command:

```
$ gdalinfo --formats
Supported Formats:
  VRT (rw+v): Virtual Raster
  GTiff (rw+v): GeoTIFF
  NITF (rw+v): National Imagery Transmission Format
  RPFTOC (rov): Raster Product Format TOC format
  ECRGTOC (rov): ECRG TOC format
  HFA (rw+v): Erdas Imagine Images (.img)
  AIG (rov): Arc/Info Binary Grid
  AAIGrid (rwv): Arc/Info ASCII Grid
  ...
```

How to do it...

1. Now that you have GDAL installed and configured on your system, we can get the GeoServer plugin to complete the installation.

2. As usual, you need to visit the download page and download the zip archive. Visit the following URL:

   `http://geoserver.org/release/stable/`

3. Get the archive by clicking on the **GDAL** link in the **Coverage Formats** section, as shown in the following screenshot:

   ### Coverage Formats

   - GDAL
   - Image Pyramid
   - JPEG2K
   - JDBC Image Mosaic

Be sure to download the matching version of the plugin. If you're not using the latest stable release, instead of the previous URL, use the following URL and browse for your version folder:

`http://geoserver.org/download/`

4. Extract the `.jar` files contained within the archive into the `WEB-INF/lib` folder of your GeoServer installation as follows:

```
$ unzip geoserver-2.5.1-gdal-plugin.zip *.jar -d
  /opt/Tomcat7042/webapps/geoserver/WEB-INF/lib/
```

5. Edit the startup file for your tomcat, probably something similar to `/etc/init.d/tomcat`, to add two new environmental variables pointing to the libraries and the data you installed previously:

```
export GDAL_DATA=/opt/gdal192/gdal-data
export LD_LIBRARY_PATH=/opt/gdal192
```

6. Now start GeoServer, then open the web interface. On the left panel, locate **Stores** and click on it. Then, click on the **Add a new store** link. Now in the **Raster Data Sources** section, you may find a lot more formats available as shown in the following screenshot:

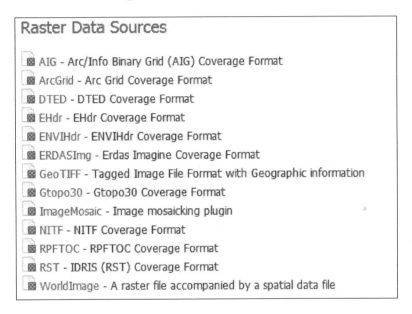

How it works...

GDAL is a powerful set of tools and libraries to manage raster data. Using them, you can open several different formats, convert them, and also process transformation on raster data.

If you compare the output of the `gdalinfo --formats` tool with the list showed by GeoServer, you may note that just a subset is available.

In fact, in order for a format to be available in GeoServer, the plugin should contain specific code to use it and make it accessible to the core modules. Developers concentrated on the formats mostly used and for which there is a need to publish them in the native format.

If your raster data is not available among those listed by GeoServer, you can always use the standard GDAL tool to convert them in a suitable format, for instance, the widely used and eclectic Geotiff.

Adding a PostGIS raster data source

In an earlier recipe, we served the raster data as a mosaic with pyramids. Another GeoServer extension offers the option to store all the tiles in an RDBMS. In this recipe, we will use PostgreSQL as a repository and will publish them on GeoServer.

How to do it...

1. In order to enable GeoServer to access tiles stored in PostgreSQL, you need an extension. As usual, you need to visit the download page and download the zip archive. Visit the following URL:

    ```
    http://geoserver.org/release/stable/
    ```

2. Get the archive by clicking on the **JDBC Image Mosaic** link in the **Coverage Formats** section.

     Be sure to download the matching version of the plugin. If you are not using the latest stable release, instead of the previous URL, use the following URL and browse for your version folder:

    ```
    http://geoserver.org/download/
    ```

3. Extract the .jar files contained within the archive into the WEB-INF/lib folder of your GeoServer installation:

    ```
    $ unzip geoserver-2.5.1-imagemosaic-jdbc-plugin.zip *.jar -d
      /opt/Tomcat7042/webapps/geoserver/WEB-INF/lib/
    ```

4. Open a command-line session on your server and locate the folder where you stored the ASTER dem file. Then, merge them in a virtual mosaic using the GDAL utility gdalbuildvrt:

    ```
    $ gdalbuildvrt aster.vrt *.tif
    ```

5. Now, we will create tiles and pyramids for the mosaic using another GDAL utility, `gdal_retile.py`. You first need to create the destination folder for the tiles:

   ```
   $ mkdir tiles
   ```

   ```
   $ gdal_retile.py -co TFW=YES -r near -ps 256 256 -of GTiff -
     levels 6 -targetDir tiles aster.vrt
   ```

6. Create a new file, call it `aster.postgis.xml`, insert the following code snippet, and then save it in the `<GEOSERVER_DATA_DIR>/coverages` folder:

   ```xml
   <?xml version="1.0" encoding="UTF-8" standalone="no"?>
   <!DOCTYPE ImageMosaicJDBCConfig [
       <!ENTITY mapping PUBLIC "mapping"
         "mapping.postgis.xml.inc">
       <!ENTITY connect PUBLIC "connect"
         "connect.postgis.xml.inc">
   ]>
   <config version="1.0">
       <coverageName name="aster"/>
       <coordsys name="EPSG:4326"/>
       <scaleop  interpolation="1"/>
       <verify  cardinality="false"/>
         &mapping;
         &connect;
   </config>
   ```

7. Create a new file, call it `connect.postgis.xml`, insert the following code snippet, and then save it in the `<GEOSERVER_DATA_DIR>/coverages` folder:

   ```xml
   <connect>
       <dstype value="DBCP"/>
       <username value="gisuser"/>
       <password value="gisuser"/>
       <jdbcUrl value="jdbc:postgresql:
         //localhost:5432/gisdata"/>
       <driverClassName value="org.postgresql.Driver"/>
       <maxActive value="10"/>
       <maxIdle value="0"/>
   </connect>
   ```

8. Create a new file, call it `mapping.postgis.xml`, insert the following code snippet, and then save it in the `<GEOSERVER_DATA_DIR>/coverages` folder:

```xml
<spatialExtension name="postgis"/>
<mapping>
    <masterTable name="mosaic" >
      <coverageNameAttribute name="name"/>
      <maxXAttribute name="maxx"/>
      <maxYAttribute name="maxy"/>
      <minXAttribute name="minx"/>
      <minYAttribute name="miny"/>
      <resXAttribute name="resx"/>
      <resYAttribute name="resy"/>
      <tileTableNameAtribute  name="tiletable" />
      <spatialTableNameAtribute name="spatialtable" />
    </masterTable>
    <tileTable>
      <blobAttributeName name="data" />
      <keyAttributeName name="location" />
    </tileTable>
    <spatialTable>
      <keyAttributeName name="location" />
      <geomAttributeName name="geom" />
      <tileMaxXAttribute name="maxx"/>
      <tileMaxYAttribute name="maxy"/>
      <tileMinXAttribute name="minx"/>
      <tileMinYAttribute name="minx"/>
    </spatialTable>
</mapping>
```

9. Execute the following command to create a SQL DDL script:

```
$ java -jar /opt/Tomcat7042/webapps/geoserver/WEB-INF/lib/gt-
  imagemosaic-jdbc-11.1.jar ddl -config
  /opt/data_dir_geoserver/coverages/aster.postgis.xml -
  spatialTNPrefix aster -pyramids 6 -statementDelim ";" -srs
  4326 -targetDir sqlscripts

23-Jul-2014 16:00:21 org.geotools.gce.
  imagemosaic.jdbc.DDLGenerator writeCreateMeta

INFO: createmeta.sql generated

23-Jul-2014 16:00:21 org.geotools.gce.imagemosaic.
  jdbc.DDLGenerator writeDropMeta

INFO: dropmeta.sql generated

23-Jul-2014 16:00:21
  org.geotools.gce.imagemosaic.jdbc.DDLGenerator generate
```

```
INFO: sqlscripts/add_aster.sql generated

23-Jul-2014 16:00:21
  org.geotools.gce.imagemosaic.jdbc.DDLGenerator generate

INFO: sqlscripts/remove_aster.sql generated
```

10. Four scripts are created. Connect to the database and execute two of them to create the metadata and spatial tables:

    ```
    $ psql -U gisuser -d gisdata -f createmeta.sql
    $ psql -U gisuser -d gisdata -f add_aster.sql
    ```

11. Copy the `jdbc` JAR file to connect to PostgresSQL from the GeoServer folder to the JRE folder:

    ```
    $ cp /opt/Tomcat7042/webapps/geoserver/WEB-INF/lib/
    postgresql-8.4-701.jdbc3.jar /usr/lib/jvm/jre1.6.0_37/lib/ext/
    ```

12. Connect to the database with the `postgres` account, or whatever username you used during installation, and execute the following command:

     If you used a packaged binary to install PostgreSQL, your instance owner is `postgres`; if you installed by compiling from source, it is the owner of the installation folder.

    ```
    $ psql -U postgres -d gisdata -f createmeta.sql

    gisdata=# ALTER DATABASE gisdata SET bytea_output TO 'escape';

    ALTER DATABASE

    gisdata=#
    ```

13. Execute the following command to import the tiles into PostGIS:

    ```
    $ java -jar /opt/Tomcat7042/webapps/geoserver/WEB-INF/lib/gt-
      imagemosaic-jdbc-11.1.jar import -config /opt/
      data_dir_geoserver/coverages/aster.postgis.xml -
      spatialTNPrefix aster -tileTNPrefix aster -dir
      tiles -ext tif

    ...

    INFO: FINISHED
    ```

14. The execution will take some time. After it shows you the last message, all of your tiles are loaded into PostGIS.

15. Open the GeoServer web interface, go to **Stores**, and click on the **Add new Store** link. From the **Raster Data Source** list, select **ImageMosaicJDBC**. Then, insert the following properties:

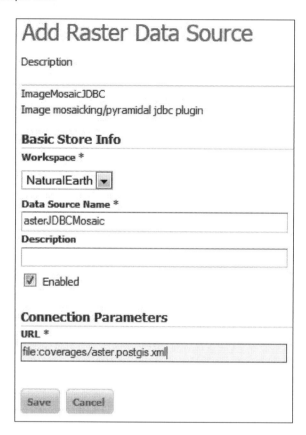

16. Click on the **Save** button and publish the mosaic as you did in the *Publishing a mosaic* recipe, choosing the same style. When you open the preview layer, you should see exactly the same data as shown in the screenshot in that recipe.

How it works...

As you may have noted, the process of preparing the data was very similar to what we did when using the Image pyramid plugin. We again used the `gdal_retile.py` command:

```
$ gdal_retile.py -co TFW=YES -r near -ps 256 256 -of GTiff -levels 6
  -targetDir tiles aster.vrt
```

Also, the output tiles are very similar. The big difference is that in this case, we are going to store the tiles inside a database, so we need some additional configuration files. The three XML files contain this information.

The `aster.postgis.xml` file contains information about the CRS and the interpolation algorithm to be used when resampling the tiles. The two links `&mapping` and `&connect` are references to the other two files. The following syntax forces the XML parser to include the external content:

```
<config version="1.0">
    <coverageName name="aster"/>
    <coordsys name="EPSG:4326"/>
    <!-- interpolation 1 = nearest neighbour, 2 = bipolar, 3 =
      bicubic -->
    <scaleop  interpolation="1"/>
    <verify  cardinality="false"/>
    <!-- axisOrder ignore="false"/-->
      &mapping;
      &connect;
</config>
```

The `connect.postgis.xml.inc` file describes parameters mandatory to create a connection to the database.

The other file, `mapping.postgis.xml.inc`, describes where the metadata is restored inside the database. GeoServer uses this information as an index to retrieve the tiles necessary to compose the map on each request.

We could go with just a single file, but the information contained in the two that we gave the .inc extension is common to any coverage you want to store in the database. We created three files because you can avoid redundancy of the common configuration parameters.

3

Advanced Styling

In this chapter, we cover the following recipes:

- ► Installing the CSS module
- ► Creating a simple polygon style with CSS
- ► Adding filters to your style
- ► Adding labels with CSS
- ► Creating scale-dependent rules
- ► Rendering transformations for raster data
- ► Creating a dot density chart

Introduction

Maps are a powerful representation of data. To produce a beautiful map, very often, you need to use a lot of symbols. For instance, dashing lines for roads under construction, lines with hatching for railroads, appropriate filling for swamps, and points for caves and mines. A map can contain dozens of different symbols; it's your way of expressing your idea of a part of the world to other people.

A standard way to produce maps with GeoServer is using WMS configured with appropriate styles.

 WMS lets you define styles with **Styled Layer Descriptor** (**SLD**); see http://en.wikipedia.org/wiki/Styled_Layer_Descriptor.

While SLD is a powerful tool and enables you to create complex and pretty rendering of data, it is also famous for being quite hard to write and understand for humans.

Cascading Style Sheets (CSS) (see http://en.wikipedia.org/wiki/CSS) is a convenient and easier replacement alternative to long SLD documents. When using CSS, you must be aware that this is GeoServer specific.

While SLD is a standard approach that can be reused with other WMS implementations or a desktop application such as QGIS, CSS is a GeoServer-specific module. For instance, you can't use the CSS syntax with MapServer, but you can, of course, reuse the styles on another GeoServer WMS server, assuming that layers with similar details are published on them.

> MapServer, not to be confused with the general term map server, is an open source software pretty similar to GeoServer. It lets you publish spatial data with OGC standards like WMS.
>
> You will find more information on this at the following URL:
>
> http://mapserver.org/

Indeed, the CSS module does not really replace SLD. The CSS syntax is used to generate the SLD styles and these are saved in that format in the GeoServer data directory. When a map is produced, GeoServer uses the SLD files to render maps, not the CSS ones.

The CSS module basically lets you use a simple human-readable syntax to quickly create drawing rules, taking care of translating your ideas into the XML format according to the SLD standard.

CSS styles can easily be read by humans and are easy to use and modify with a simple text editor. SLD styles are generated for use by the WMS rendering engine.

Installing the CSS module

The CSS module started as a community module, that is, an unofficial set of features that are not fully supported by the official releases and may or may not work. The CSS extension is an example of a successful community module that grew fast and has recently graduated as a formal extension.

> Extensions are an optional GeoServer functionality that are held to the same quality control and documentation standards as WMS and WFS.

Extensions

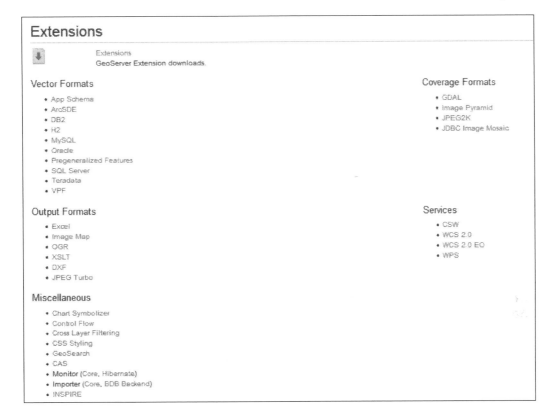

Extensions
GeoServer Extension downloads.

Vector Formats

- App Schema
- ArcSDE
- DB2
- H2
- MySQL
- Oracle
- Pregeneralized Features
- SQL Server
- Teradata
- VPF

Output Formats

- Excel
- Image Map
- OGR
- XSLT
- DXF
- JPEG Turbo

Miscellaneous

- Chart Symbolizer
- Control Flow
- Cross Layer Filtering
- CSS Styling
- GeoSearch
- CAS
- **Monitor** (Core, Hibernate)
- **Importer** (Core, BDB Backend)
- INSPIRE

Coverage Formats

- GDAL
- Image Pyramid
- JPEG2K
- JDBC Image Mosaic

Services

- CSW
- WCS 2.0
- WCS 2.0 EO
- WPS

The GeoServer download page offers several extensions. Some focus on data access, providing support for the new format for feature and raster data; others add new functionality. The CSS extension is listed under the **Miscellaneous** category in the GeoServer download page (`http://geoserver.org/release/stable/`). Please ensure that you download a version of the extension that exactly matches the GeoServer version you are using.

How to do it...

1. Download the ZIP archive. Please verify that the version number in the filename is the same as the GeoServer WAR file you installed.

 If you don't remember your GeoServer release, you can look for it in the web admin interface. Go to `http://localhost/geoserver/web/?wicket:bookmarkablePage=:org.geoserver.web.AboutGeoServerPage`.

2. Stop your GeoServer instance and extract the contents of the ZIP archive into the `/WEB-INF/lib/` directory in the GeoServer web app. For example, if you have deployed the GeoServer WAR file, you should place the CSS extension's JAR files in `CATALINA_HOME/webapps/geoserver/WEB-INF/lib/`.

3. After extracting the extension, restart GeoServer in order for the changes to take effect. Your module is installed and running and you may check that a new item is now shown on the left pane of the admin interface.

> **CSS Styles**
>
> **Demos**
>
> **Tools**

How it works...

Enabling the CSS module is a really easy task. The developer team packed it into a couple of JAR files that contain all the code for the logic and the user interface. From a user's point of view, you get a new form on the web interface where you can create rendering rules with the CSS syntax, try them out, and eventually generate them as SLD styles to be stored in your GeoServer configuration.

In the upper part of the interface, you can see a text line informing you what styles you are editing and which layer you're using to preview the style. Just under the line, you can find four links that let you change the style and/or the layer to work with. You can also create a totally new style.

> # CSS Styles
>
> Create and modify CSS styles. This is an alternative to editing SLD styles.
>
> Currently editing style **population** and previewing with data from **states**. Edit the style here, or:
> * Edit a different style.
> * Choose a different layer to preview this style.
> * Create a new style and preview with this layer.
> * Change layer associations for this style.

There is a textbox under these options. This is the place where you write the CSS code that will build your style. This is a dynamic textbox; as you insert the code, the module performs a syntax check and will highlight any errors. When you are happy with the CSS code, you can click on the **Submit** button and the module will translate your CSS code in to an XML SLD style.

The bottom part of the page contains a tabbed form with four sections. The first section lets you preview the XML code generated. The tab named **Map** is obviously a quick preview of your data represented with the rules you are coding.

The **Data** tab contains a list of fields in your layer, such as a field name, data type, and a sample value (as shown in the following screenshot). You may also calculate the maximum and minimum values by pressing the link in the **Compute stats** column. This will prove quite useful when you're creating a thematic map and need to define class breaks or discrete values to render.

Generated SLD	Map	Data	CSS Reference

For reference, here is a listing of the attributes in this data set.

Name	Type	Sample value	Min	Max	Compute stats
the_geom	MultiPolygon	MULTIPOLYGON (((-88.071564 37.51099000000001, -88.087883 37.476273000000006, -88.311707 37.442852, -88.359177 37.40930899999999, -88.419853 37.420292, -88.467644 37.400757, -88.511322 37.296852, -8...			Compute
STATE_NAME	String	Illinois			Compute
STATE_FIPS	String	17	01	56	Compute
SUB_REGION	String	E N Cen			Compute
STATE_ABBR	String	IL	AL	WY	Compute
LAND_KM	Double	143986.61	159.055	688219.07	Compute
WATER_KM	Double	1993.335	17.991	30456.797	Compute
PERSONS	Double	1.1430602E7	453588.0	2.9760021E7	Compute

The last tab points to the online help for the CSS module. You may find a brief tutorial there and also an almost complete reference for CSS coding.

Creating a simple polygon style with CSS

We're assuming that you already know how to make WMS GetMap requests to GeoServer and you have already played with simple SLD styles. Now, you'll start creating your first simple style using the CSS syntax. For this recipe, you'll use the countries feature type you published in *Chapter 1, Working with Vectors*.

 The entire CSS style for the recipe is located in the `GeneralizedCountries.css` file.

How to do it...

1. Open the **CSS Style** section from the GeoServer web interface. Then, select the link **Choose a different layer**. From the list of layers, select **PostGISLocal:GeneralizedCountries**.

2. Select the **Create a new style** link. In the form, select the **NaturalEarth** workspace and insert the style name, as shown in the following screenshot:

3. GeoServer inserts a short template for you:

```
* { fill: lightgrey; }
```

4. Replace the code in the textbox with the following rules:

```
* {
  fill: #8FBC8F;
  fill-opacity: 0.7;
}
* {
  stroke: #000000;
  stroke-opacity: 0.7;
}
```

5. Press the **Submit** button and scroll down to the **Map** preview. You should see that the new rules are applied to your data.

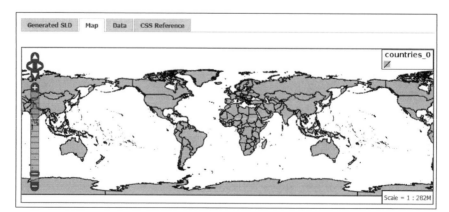

How it works...

The style you created is very simple. It is just composed of two rules: one used for the fill and the other for the outline. Let's see how the CSS code works.

On the first line, you have the * character. This is a reference to the feature to which the rule will be applied. The * character stands for all features; in this simple recipe, we're applying the same symbol to all countries.

The first element, which can be a reference to just a set of features, is called a selector. After that, you inserted two lines to define the properties used to draw the selected features of the filling:

```
* {
  fill: #8FBC8F;
  fill-opacity: 0.7;
}
```

The key property `fill` defines the color to be used for drawing polygon features. In this case, it is expressed as a hexadecimal value. You can also define colors using RGB decimal values or well-known names.

 For a full list of well-known names, you can take a look at `http://www.w3.org/TR/SVG/types.html#ColorKeywords`.

Indeed, all the following lines are equivalent ways to define the same color:

- `fill: #8FBC8F`
- `fill: rgb(143, 188, 143)`
- `fill: darkseagreen`

The property `fill-opacity` sets the transparency for the filling. This is quite useful if you need to compose more layers in your map. The value ranges from 0 (totally transparent) to 1 (solid fill).

The key property `fill` is mandatory to render polygons; the property `fill-opacity` used on its own will have no effect.

What happens to your code when you press the **Submit** button? The CSS module takes this simple text code and translates it into a standard SLD style. The generated XML file is compliant to SLD schemas. For the simple rule you inserted, here is the result:

```
<?xml version="1.0" encoding="UTF-8"?>
<sld:UserStyle xmlns="http://www.opengis.net/sld"
    xmlns:sld="http://www.opengis.net/sld"
    xmlns:ogc="http://www.opengis.net/ogc"
    xmlns:gml="http://www.opengis.net/gml">
    <sld:Name>Default Styler</sld:Name>
    <sld:FeatureTypeStyle>
        <sld:Name>name</sld:Name>
        <sld:Rule>
            <sld:PolygonSymbolizer>
                <sld:Fill>
                    <sld:CssParameter name="fill">#8FBC8F</sld:CssParameter>
                    <sld:CssParameter name="fill-
                        opacity">0.699999988079071</sld:CssParameter>
                </sld:Fill>
            </sld:PolygonSymbolizer>
        </sld:Rule>
    </sld:FeatureTypeStyle>
</sld:UserStyle>
```

It looks a bit more complicated than the code you inserted, doesn't it? However, if you look at it, the properties and values you typed are there, just in a different syntax.

To have the outline drawn on your polygons, you insert another rule.

The selector * is used to apply the properties to all features. The properties used are quite similar to the ones used for the filling and for setting the color and transparency. The key property `stroke` is used to indicate that we want an outline. The property `stroke-opacity` provides additional information on how we want the outline drawn.

When you translate the code to XML, note that `LineSymbolizer` is generated with our transparency parameter. This is because black is the default value for the `Stroke` color. Even though black is the default color for SLD, we still need to use the key property `stroke:black` in our CSS to request the generation of `LineSymbolizer`, as shown in the following code:

```
...
        <sld:LineSymbolizer>
            <sld:Stroke>
                <sld:CssParameter name="stroke-
                    opacity">0.699999988079071</sld:CssParameter>
            </sld:Stroke>
        </sld:LineSymbolizer>
...
```

As per our two rules, use the same selector; they can be combined and will produce exactly the same SLD document. Try this yourself:

```
* {
  fill: #8FBC8F;
  fill-opacity: 0.7;
  stroke: #000000;
  stroke-opacity: 0.7;
}
```

This rule uses the `*` selector and is applied to all features. The two key properties `fill` and `stroke` generate a `PolygonSymbolizer` and `LineSymbolizer` XML, respectively. The properties `fill-opacity` and `stroke-opacity` are used to fine-tune the appearance.

Adding filters to your style

Having a map with a single symbol (that is, the same appearance for all features) is not very common. This approach is useful, and it can be used when building an index map to provide a reference showing you which part of the world is represented in the main map.

The real power of styling comes from the representation of features according to their properties, geometrical or nongeometrical. A map created to show attribute values is a thematic map. To create a thematic map, we will need to use filters to select content based on an attribute value.

In this recipe, you will build a map of countries grouped according to the continent they belong.

The full CSS style for the recipe is located in the `continent.css` file.

How to do it...

1. Open the **CSS Style** section from the GeoServer web interface. Then, select the **Choose a different layer** link. From the list of layers, select **PostGISLocal:Countries**.

2. Select the **Create a new style** link. In the form, select the **NaturalEarth** workspace and insert **Continents** as the style name.

3. Replace the code in the textbox with the following snippet:

```
/* @title outline */
* {
    stroke: #000000;
    stroke-width: 0.1;
}

/* @title North America */
[continent = 'North America']
* { fill: #66C2A5;}
```

4. Press the **Submit** button and look at your map. It should show all countries with a thin black outline and the North American countries with a color fill.

5. Add filling for other continents, as shown in the following code snippet:

```
/* @title Europe */
[continent = 'Europe']
* { fill: #8DA0CB; }

/* @title Oceania */
[continent = 'Oceania']
* { fill: #E78AC3; }

/* @title Asia */
[continent = 'Asia']
* { fill: #A6D854; }

/* @title Africa */
[continent = 'Africa']
* { fill: #FFD92F; }

/* @title Antartica */
[continent = 'Antarctica']
* { fill: #E5C494; }

/* @title South America */
[continent = 'South America']
* { fill: #FC8D62; }
```

6. Press the **Submit** button. Your map should look like the following screenshot:

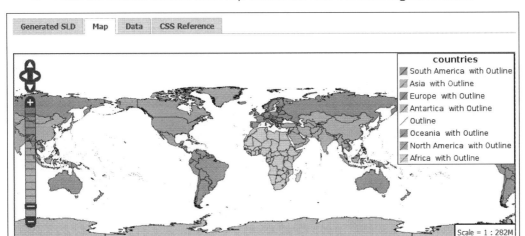

How it works...

This time, you created a style with a few more rules. You may have noted in the previous screenshot that the CSS module creates a simple **table of contents (TOC)** for you with elements describing symbols used in the style and a label for each symbol.

You gave directions to GeoServer with the `@title` marker:

```
* @title outline */
```

In this case, you are defining the symbol for the outline. So, you typed the word `outline` after the marker. The label is free text, so you can insert anything and use more than a word. You must have guessed from the * selector that the outline is applied to all features.

We use the key property `stroke` to generate a line and `stroke-width` for a thin black line:

```
* {
    stroke: #000000;
    stroke-width: 0.1;
}
```

Next, you create a filter for countries belonging to North America. To group them, we use the `continent` field attribute, that is, an attribute of the countries layer, and of course, we define a very simple filter that selects just features that hold the `North America` value in that field:

```
/* @title North America */
[continent = 'North America']
* { fill: #66C2A5; }
```

We use the key property `fill` to ask these features to be drawn as a polygon.

We use the `@title` marker again to define a label. Please note that when more than one rule applies to a feature, the corresponding label is the merger of all the strings:

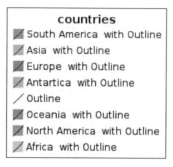

We then inserted similar filters for all remaining continents. The code is very easy; just copy and paste and change the color codes, labels, and filter values.

When we submit our code that is just 26 lines, including labels, the resulting XML is a bit more complex. It is translated into 194 lines of XML code. If you're curious about it, you can switch to the **Generated SLD** tab in the CSS panel. This shows you the XML code formatted according to the SLD syntax.

Here is a fragment that is the corresponding code for the `North America` filter shown previously:

```
<sld:Rule>
  <sld:Title>North America  with Outline</sld:Title>
  <ogc:Filter>
    <ogc:PropertyIsEqualTo>
      <ogc:PropertyName>continent</ogc:PropertyName>
      <ogc:Literal>North America</ogc:Literal>
    </ogc:PropertyIsEqualTo>
  </ogc:Filter>
  <sld:PolygonSymbolizer>
    <sld:Fill>
      <sld:CssParameter name="fill">#66C2A5</sld:CssParameter>
    </sld:Fill>
  </sld:PolygonSymbolizer>
  <sld:LineSymbolizer>
    <sld:Stroke>
      <sld:CssParameter name="stroke-width">0.1</sld:CssParameter>
    </sld:Stroke>
  </sld:LineSymbolizer>
</sld:Rule>
<sld:Rule>
```

Isn't the CSS syntax far more simple and readable?

Adding labels with CSS

As you probably already guessed, CSS can also handle properties for label placement and rendering. Labels are quite useful in maps. They are there to help you understand what places you're looking at, or just to identify the place you were searching for hours! Yes, I know what you're thinking—this must've been before the age of smartphones!

To work with labels, we will use an expression to access the feature attribute values. This results in a dynamic style that changes for each feature!

To practice with labels, you'll use the populated place layers created in *Chapter 1, Working with Vectors*. The target is to create a map of capitals.

[A full CSS style for the recipe is located in the `Capitals.css` file.]

How to do it...

1. Open the **CSS Style** section from the GeoServer web interface. Then, select the link **Choose a different layer**. From the list of layers, select **PostGISLocal:PopulatedPlaces**.

2. Select the link **Create a new style**. In the form, select the **NaturalEarth** workspace and insert `Capitals` as the style name.

3. Replace the code in the textbox with the following code snippet:

```
[megacity = 1] {
    mark: symbol(square);
    mark-size: 4px;
    label: [name];
    font-fill: black;
    font-family: DejaVu
    font-style: bold;
    font-size: 10;
    label-anchor: 0.5 0;
    label-offset: 0 3;
}

:mark {
    fill: #2CA25F;
    stroke: black;
    stroke-width: 1px;
}
```

4. Press the **Submit** button, switch to the map preview, and zoom in on West Europe. Your map should look like the following screenshot:

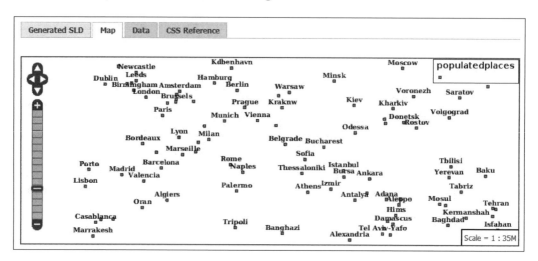

How it works...

The first part of the CSS code defines the rule for selecting features containing 1 in the `megacity` field. This is not really an equivalent of `Capitals`, that is, the place that is the center of government of a country as formally defined. However, let's filter out most of the points from the map and produce a representation of the most important cities.

We use the key property `mark` to draw each location as a square. The property `mark-size` is used to provide a symbol size in pixels.

The key property `label` is used to generate labels. This also shows the use of an expression to access feature attributes. You select a simple marker, a square, and a symbol size. You also set the field, `name` in this case, where GeoServer should search for text values to print as a label near each marker:

```
[megacity = 1] {
    mark: symbol (square);
    mark-size: 4px;
    label: [name];
```

Then you set the printing properties; black for the text and the `DejaVu` font. Please note that you can use any font available on your system (or in the GeoServer styles folder). The DejaVu font may not be available on Windows machines. If this is your case, please change this recipe according to a font available on your system. After selecting a font size, you set the distance and the bearing of a label placement:

```
font-fill: black;
font-family: DejaVu;
font-size: 10;
label-anchor: 0.5 0;
label-offset: 0 3;
```

Did you note that nothing about the color for the marker was included in the previous lines of code?

Indeed, we now use a reference to the marker and set the color and stroke for it:

```
:mark {
    fill: #2CA25F;
    stroke: black;
    stroke-width: 1px;
}
```

Creating scale-dependent rules

Most maps contain more than one layer—each one styled with one or more symbols according to its complexity and the map purpose.

When you browse interactive maps with many layers, you can see that the map changes its style according to the zoom level. When your view on the data is a portrait of the entire world, symbols are simple and there are a few features drawn on the map. As you get closer, you can see more labels, major roads change their symbols, and minor roads appear.

This approach lets you insert a large quantity of information on a web map while avoiding producing an almost unreadable jumble of labels and symbols.

How can you do a similar map with CSS code? It's again a matter of creating filters. This time, you should not only create filters that apply symbols according to the features' attributes, but you should also insert a constraint on the map scale to have GeoServer select the features that have to be drawn.

In this recipe, you will use the global roads dataset—again from the Natural Earth collection of open data.

Just go to http://www.naturalearthdata.com/downloads/10m-cultural-vectors/ and download the roads dataset. Then, load it in PostGIS and publish it with the road's name in the **NaturalEarth** workspace. Isn't it as simple as ready, steady, go?

 The entire CSS style for the recipe is located in the WorldRoad.css file.

How to do it...

1. Open the **CSS Style** section from the GeoServer web interface. Then, select the link **Choose a different layer**. From the list of layers, select **PostGISLocal:Roads**.

2. Select the link **Create a new style**. In the form, select the **NaturalEarth** workspace and insert WorldRoads as the style name.

3. Replace the code in the textbox with the following snippet:

```
[@scale < 5000000]
{
  label: [label];
  font-fill: black;
}
/* @title Road */
[type = 'Road'] [@scale < 5000000]
{
  stroke: #000000, #FFFF00;
  stroke-width: 4, 2;
  z-index: 0, 1;
}
/* @title Major Highway */
[type = 'Major Highway'] [@scale > 10000000]
{
  stroke: red;
  stroke-width: 1;
}
/* @title Major Highway */
[type = 'Major Highway'] [@scale < 10000000]
{
  stroke: black, red, black;
  stroke-width: 7, 3, 1;
  z-index: 0, 1, 2;
}
/* @title Secondary Highway */
[type = 'Secondary Highway'] [@scale < 5000000]
{
```

```
    stroke: #808080, #FF7F00;
    stroke-width: 4, 2;
    z-index: 0, 1;
}
/* @title Ferry Route */
[type = 'Ferry Route'] [@scale < 5000000]
{
    stroke: #6699CD;
    stroke-width: 1;
    stroke-dasharray: 6 2;
}
/* @title Track */
[type = 'Track'] [@scale < 5000000]
{
    stroke: #808080;
    stroke-width: 2;
    stroke-dasharray: 15 10;
}
/* @title Ferry, seasonal */
[type = 'Ferry, seasonal'] [@scale < 5000000]
{
    stroke: blue;
    stroke-width: 1;
    stroke-dasharray: 6 2;
}
```

4. Press the **Submit** button, switch to the map preview, and zoom in on West Europe. Your map should look like the following screenshot.

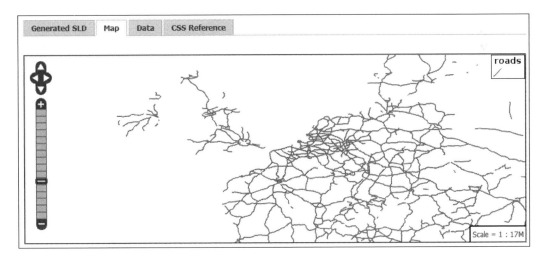

5. Now zoom in to have a closer look at the area containing London and the channel. You can see that other items appear in the TOC and the way the roads are drawn on the map is quite more complex.

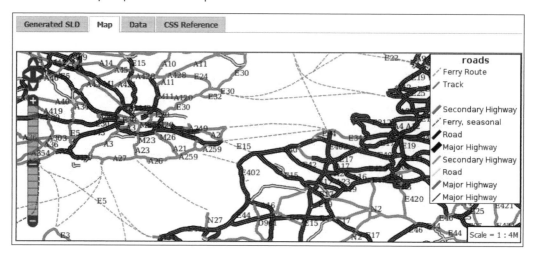

How it works...

You probably noticed a new element inside the code. On the very first line of the CSS file, there is the `@scale` selector, which is used to define a rule that only applies when the map scale fits the constraint you inserted. In this case, you just want GeoServer to draw labels when the map scale is lower than 5 million. The rule properties just set the field expression used to access text, where it can be found, and the color for its labels:

```
[@scale < 5000000]
{
   label: [label];
   font-fill: black;
}
```

As you probably guessed, the first rule applies to all features, as there is no selector apart from the map scale.

When you first open the map, there is only one symbol for all roads drawn; if you look for it in the code, you can find that the following lines set the filter for the maps with a scale higher than 10 million:

```
/* @title Major Highway */
[type = 'Major Highway'] [@scale > 10000000]
{
   stroke: red;
   stroke-width: 1;
}
```

At that scale, you just want GeoServer to show major highways, so you set a filter on the type field and create a very simple red thin line symbol for them.

What happens for a scale under 10 million? Again, you have the same set of roads drawn, but you use a complex ticker symbol. It is in fact composed of three overlaid lines: a black one (which is 7-pixels thick), a red one (3-pixels wide), and eventually a black thin line with a width of just 1 pixel:

```
/* @title Major Highway */
[type = 'Major Highway'] [@scale < 10000000]
{
    stroke: black, red, black;
    stroke-width: 7, 3, 1;
    z-index: 0, 1, 2;
}
```

The result is shown in the following screenshot:

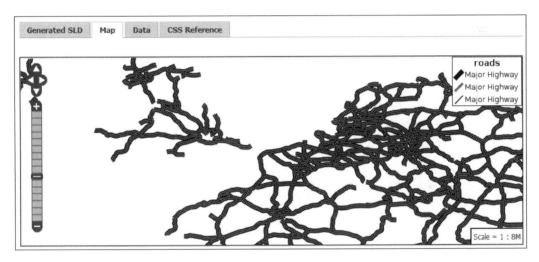

Until your map's scale goes under 5 million, you don't see anything else; then suddenly, all other roads are drawn. So, in the code snippet, you set four other filters for secondary highways, roads, tracks, and ferry routes. The logic is always the same. Let's have a look at how it works for secondary highways:

```
/* @title Secondary Highway */
[type = 'Secondary Highway'] [@scale < 5000000]
{
    stroke: #808080, #FF7F00;
    stroke-width: 4, 2;
    z-index: 0, 1;
}
```

Obviously, your filter uses the `type` attribute to select a different value to be searched and sets the scale. This symbol is composed of two overlapping lines; the `stroke` element accepts two colors for the two lines and so does `stroke-width`. Pay attention to the `z-index` element where you set the drawing order of the lines. While the sequence *0,1, ... n* is probably more clear and understandable, you can set it in whatever order you need.

Rendering transformations for raster data

Since the first recipe of the chapter, we've been working with vector data; of course, GeoServer is also there to serve raster data. Moreover, while you may think that raster data doesn't need a style, this is only true for a small set of them. Most people think of raster data as aerial imagery, where the surface of the Earth is represented with true colors. In fact, this paradigm has been greatly enforced by the huge popularity web mapping applications have gained in the last decade.

However, there is a great variety of different raster data containing data about any parameter a sensor can measure, from elevation to temperature to satellite radar scenes and so on. Visualization of all this data makes more sense when you classify them and choose a set of colors. You will apply this technique to elevation data in this recipe.

For this recipe, we need a **Digital Elevation Model** (**DEM**). As usual, we will use freely available open source data. Go to `https://lpdaac.usgs.gov/products/aster_products_table/astgtm`, the main page for an archive of high resolution DEMs provided by **United States Geological Survey** (**USGS**). Here, you will find a lot of data. For this recipe, you will need just a small portion of the data, which is provided to you with the code bundle of this book. At `http://reverb.echo.nasa.gov/reverb`, you will find an interactive map where the area was selected and downloaded. After signing in, you can search for data in other areas and experiment yourself with GeoServer, as shown in the following screenshot:

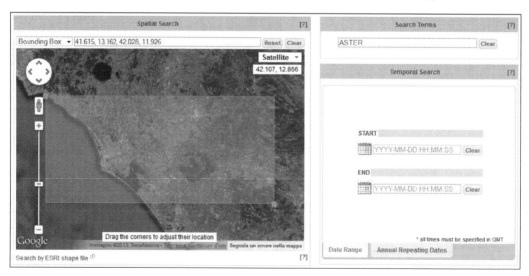

The entire CSS style for the recipe is located in the `Dem.css` file.

How to do it...

1. Open the **CSS Style** section in the GeoServer web interface. Then, select the link **Choose a different layer**. From the list of layers, select the DEM file you loaded previously.

2. Select the link **Create a new style**. In the form, select the **NaturalEarth** workspace and insert `Dem` as the style name.

3. Replace the code in the textbox with the following snippet:

```
* {
        raster-channels: auto;
        raster-color-map:
                color-map-entry(#2E9A58,  9)
                color-map-entry(#AAFF7F,  180)
                color-map-entry(#FDFF7F,  350)
                color-map-entry(#FFAA00,  500)
                color-map-entry(#F47221,  600)
                color-map-entry(#C83737,  1100)
                color-map-entry(#D7F4F4,  1300)
}
```

4. Press the **Submit** button and switch to the map preview. Your map should look like the following screenshot:

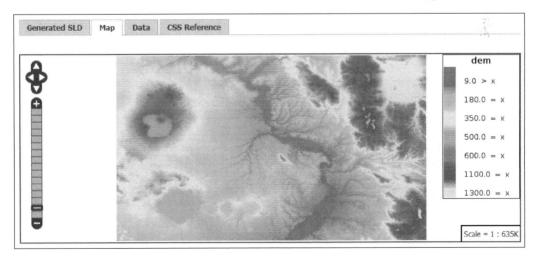

How it works...

The CSS code in this recipe is fairly simple. In the first line, you find the * selector as the classification that will apply to all the data. To display raster data, the key property raster-channels is used. The following lines select the band we want to be represented. The value auto lets GeoServer select the appropriate band.

In this case, we're working with a raster with just one band, so GeoServer has an easy job of finding the proper one to represent. In scientific datasets, some rasters may contain tens of bands, so you need to manually select which ones you want to represent in the map. This is shown in the following lines of code:

```
* {
    raster-channels: auto;
```

Then, you use the color-map element to create a color ramp to render the data. To build it, you enter several color-map-entry elements—each one with two values. The first one is the color, defined as a hexadecimal value or by well-known color names, and the second element represents the value of your data to which the color applies. GeoServer automatically creates a continuous ramp among two different entries in the ramp. The code is as follows:

```
raster-color-map:
        color-map-entry(#2E9A58,  9)
        color-map-entry(#AAFF7F,  180)
        color-map-entry(#FDFF7F,  350)
        color-map-entry(#FFAA00,  500)
        color-map-entry(#F47221,  600)
        color-map-entry(#C83737,  1100)
        color-map-entry(#D7F4F4,  1300)
}
```

 There are several resources that will help you select nice color ramps. One popular resource is http://colorbrewer2.org/, which was created by Cynthia Brewer of Penn State University. You may use it with the example data or also upload your data. Then, select the number of classes you need and the color ramp.

There is also a third optional value that you can set. It's the transparency value, which is by default equal to 1, that is, totally opaque. The result, shown in the previous screenshot, is quite nice. Compare it with the default representation of the data when you don't set any style, as shown in the following screenshot:

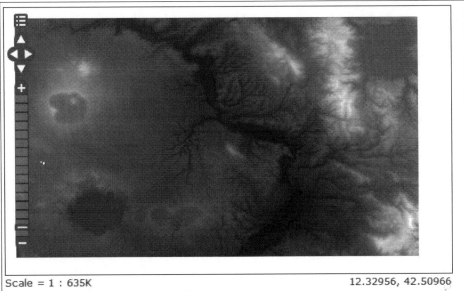

Scale = 1 : 635K   12.32956, 42.50966
Click on the map to get feature info

Creating a dot density chart

In the *Using WFS spatial filters* recipe, *Chapter 1, Working with Vectors*, you created a thematic map by classifying the features contained in the countries layer according to the continent they belong. You used an opaque fill for this map.

However, when dealing with statistical data, it is more appropriate to use a dot density chart.

 A dot density chart is an often used way to represent data on a map. For a general introduction, have a look at http://en.wikipedia. org/wiki/Dot_distribution_map.

You will again use the countries layer and will classify features according to population.

 The entire CSS style for this recipe is located in the DotDensity.css file.

How to do it...

1. Open the **CSS Style** section from the GeoServer web interface. Then, select the **Choose a different layer** link. From the list of layers, select the **countries** layer.

2. Select the link **Create a new style**. In the form, select the **NaturalEarth** workspace and insert `DotDensity` as the style name.

3. Replace the code in the textbox with the following snippet:

```
* {
  fill: symbol("circle");
  stroke: black;
  -gt-fill-random: grid;
  -gt-fill-random-tile-size: 100;
}

:fill {
  size: 2;
  fill: brown;
}

[pop_est < 10E7] {
   -gt-fill-random-symbol-count: 50;
}

[pop_est >= 10E7] [pop_est < 10E8] {
   -gt-fill-random-symbol-count: 350;
}

[pop_est >= 10E8] [pop_est < 50E8] {
   -gt-fill-random-symbol-count: 700;
}

[pop_est >= 50E8] {
   -gt-fill-random-symbol-count: 1000;
}
```

4. Press the **Submit** button and switch to the map preview. Your map should look like the following screenshot:

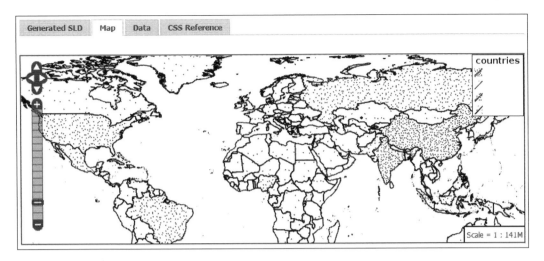

How it works...

The first part of the CSS code uses the ∗ selector to select all features and set a filling with a common marker, the circle. If you set the color of the outline to black, then two new element properties to discuss appear.

The -gt-fill-random property defines the distribution of the circles inside the polygons. The possible values are none, free, and grid. None disables random distribution, free generates a completely random distribution, and grid generates a regular grid of positions to a grid.

The -gt-fill-random-tile-size property defines the tile size for the texture of the filling, as shown in the following code:

```
* {
  fill: symbol("circle");
  stroke: black;
  -gt-fill-random: grid;
  -gt-fill-random-tile-size: 100;
}
```

These two properties are vendor-specific parameters that are available only in the GeoServer rendering engine. Vendor-specific parameters start with -gt-, allowing easy identification of special effects that are not available in other systems.

Then, you set the size and color for the circles that will be drawn inside the polygons:

```
:fill {
  size: 2;
  fill: brown;
}
```

After this, you start defining the classes for your map. For the first one, you select the countries with a population lower than 10 million. The number of circles to be drawn in a tile, in this case, is 50. The code is as follows:

```
[pop_est < 10E7] {
    -gt-fill-random-symbol-count: 50;
}
```

For the next class, you select countries with a population among 10 and 100 million. For them, you want 350 circles to be drawn in each tile. The code is as follows:

```
[pop_est >= 10E7] [pop_est < 10E8] {
    -gt-fill-random-symbol-count: 350;
}
```

Similarly, the other two classes are also composed. To fully understand the tile-size concept, try to zoom in on your map as in this screenshot:

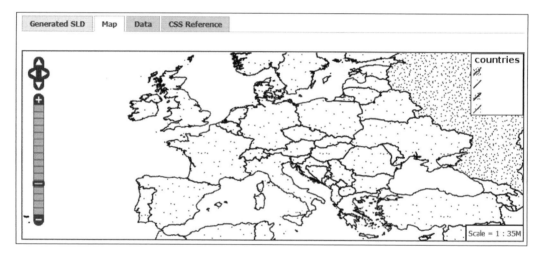

Look at countries like Spain or Ireland, which had just one circle inside their boundaries in the previous screenshot. As the scale changes, the portion of the tile occupied by a country is higher and it has the opportunity to reach its limit. By playing with the tile-size value, you can reach the desired representation.

 The code in this recipe uses vendor options only available since the GeoServer 2.4.2 release. If things on your side do not work, check the version before anything else.

4
Geoprocessing

In this chapter, we will cover the following recipes:

- ▶ Installing the WPS module
- ▶ Using the WPS process builder
- ▶ Chaining process – selecting features contained in a polygon
- ▶ Chaining process – building your own task

Introduction

Apart from requesting map and data, GeoServer has another great feature: it can be used as a geoprocessing server. Geoprocessing lets the user perform operations on data, transform them, and also produce new datasets. The general concept is that the user creates a task by selecting the input data and operations to be performed on them.

Geoprocessing is a traditional concept in desktop GIS; in fact, this type of software is created to process spatial data. Later, geoprocessing was migrated to the server side; there are now several ways a user can ask a server to process a task on data. As with producing maps and delivering data, GeoServer implements geoprocessing referring to a standard, the WPS standard defined by OGC.

The **OpenGIS® Web Processing Service** (**WPS**) interface standard provides rules to standardize how inputs and outputs (requests and responses) for geospatial processing services, such as polygon overlay. The WPS standard also defines how a client can request the execution of a process and how the output from the process is handled. WPS defines an interface that facilitates the publishing of geospatial processes and clients' discovery and binding to those processes. The data required by the WPS can be delivered across a network or they can be referenced to data already available on the server.

WPS is a rather detailed standard. If you are curious about it and want to learn more, have a look at the official documentation:

`http://www.opengeospatial.org/standards/wps`

In practice, WPS is similar to **Simple Object Access Protocol (SOAP)** or **XML Remote Procedure Call** (**XMLRPC**). The key benefit of WPS is the ability to respect spatial data types such as GML and handle the large data volumes associated with spatial data.

Refer to the 1.0.0 release, which is the current standard and the version supported by GeoServer.

Installing the WPS module

Unlike the WFS, WMS, and WCS connectors, WPS is not available with the base installation of GeoServer. You have to download and install it. So, as in the first recipe, you will set up our GeoServer instance with the WPS module. Please ensure that you download a version of the extension that exactly matches the GeoServer version you are using.

How to do it...

1. Point your browser to the download page (`http://geoserver.org/release/stable/`) and get the archive. Please verify that the version number in the filename is the same as the GeoServer WAR you installed.

In case you don't remember your GeoServer's release, you can look for it in the web admin interface. Go to `http://localhost/geoserver/web/?wicket:bookmarkableP age=:org.geoserver.web.AboutGeoServerPage`.

About GeoServer

General information about GeoServer

Build Information

Version

2.5.2

Git Revision

878d05129d090db388d1717ec136010ce104b2e3

Build Date

22-Jul-2014 09:05

GeoTools Version

11.2 (rev 59edb005ac690fabd8a0e02b898a82fac1618468)

GeoWebCache Version

1.5.3 (rev 1.5.x/a648922b85343e01811131725764da833997ffa9e)

2. Stop your GeoServer instance and extract the contents of the ZIP archive into the `/WEB-INF/lib/` directory in the GeoServer webapp. For example, if you have deployed the GeoServer WAR file, you should place the WPS extension's JAR files in `CATALINA_HOME/webapps/geoserver/WEB-INF/lib/`.

3. After extracting the extension, restart GeoServer in order for the changes to take effect. Your module is now installed. You can check that a new item is now shown in the **Service Capabilities** list in the right-hand side pane:

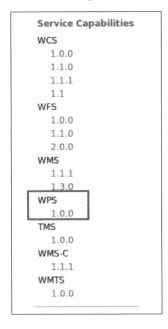

Service Capabilities

WCS
    1.0.0
    1.1.0
    1.1.1
    1.1
WFS
    1.0.0
    1.1.0
    2.0.0
WMS
    1.1.1
    1.3.0
WPS
    1.0.0
TMS
    1.0.0
WMS-C
    1.1.1
WMTS
    1.0.0

How it works...

As with the CSS module in the previous chapter, the installation of WPS is really easy. Do you wonder what changes were applied to your GeoServer? Apart from the capabilities list, which is now showing the new operations supported, there is also another important change in the GeoServer user interface. If you go to the **Demos** section, you will find a new item: **WPS request builder**.

GeoServer Demos

Collection of GeoServer demo applications

- Demo requests Example requests for GeoServer (using the TestServlet).
- SRS List List of all SRS known to GeoServer
- Reprojection console Simple coordinate reprojection tool
- WCS request builder Step by step WCS GetCoverage request builder
- WPS request builder Step by step WPS request builder

The request builder is a very useful tool to practice and debug WPS requests; we will use it extensively in this chapter.

WPS request builder

Step by step WPS request builder.
Choose process

Choose One

Authentication

☐ Authenticate (will run the request as anonymous otherwise)

Execute process   Generate XML from process inputs/outputs

Using the WPS process builder

In the previous recipe, you installed the WPS module. It's now time to have a look at what it offers you and what can be done with its operations. As it is the easiest way, we will use the WPS request builder to explore geoprocessing operations.

How to do it...

1. Open the GeoServer administrative interface and open the WPS process builder page.

2. The first control in the page is a list containing all processes published by the WPS to you. If you open it and scroll down, you will see that it is a very long list and there are several different process grouped in categories.

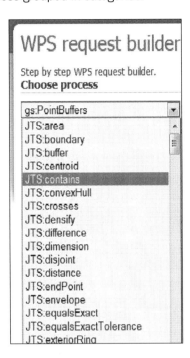

3. Select the **JTS:buffer** item. The page loads some controls where you can input the operation's parameters. The first one is about the geometry on which you want to apply the buffer operation. Leave the **TEXT** type in the first list and select the **application/wkt** in the other list. This will allow you to insert geometry in a simple and well readable format. Insert a point geometry, as shown in the following screenshot:

Process inputs

geom* - Geometry
Input geometry

TEXT	application/wkt

```
POINT(12.33 42.24)
```

4. Now switch to distance and insert `0.01`. As stated by the **Help** option, the units have to be the same you used when specifying the geometry. In this example, you're using decimal degrees.

distance* - Double
Distance to buffer the input geometry, in the units of the geometry
```
0.01
```

5. Leave the other parameters unchanged, scroll down to the bottom of the page, and press the **Execute Process** button. GeoServer will show you the result in a new panel.

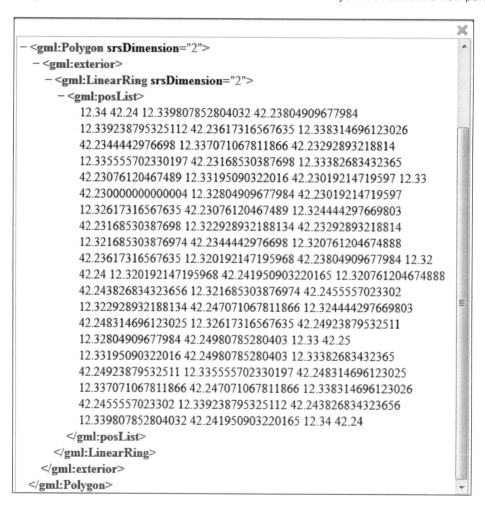

```xml
- <gml:Polygon srsDimension="2">
  - <gml:exterior>
    - <gml:LinearRing srsDimension="2">
      - <gml:posList>
          12.34 42.24 12.339807852804032 42.23804909677984
          12.339238795325112 42.23617316567635 12.338314696123026
          42.2344442976698 12.337071067811866 42.23292893218814
          12.335555702330197 42.23168530387698 12.33382683432365
          42.23076120467489 12.33195090322016 42.23019214719597 12.33
          42.230000000000004 12.32804909677984 42.23019214719597
          12.32617316567635 42.23076120467489 12.324444297669803
          42.23168530387698 12.322928932188134 42.23292893218814
          12.321685303876974 42.2344442976698 12.320761204674888
          42.23617316567635 12.320192147195968 42.23804909677984 12.32
          42.24 12.320192147195968 42.241950903220165 12.320761204674888
          42.243826834323656 12.321685303876974 42.2455557023302
          12.322928932188134 42.247071067811866 12.324444297669803
          42.248314696123025 12.32617316567635 42.24923879532511
          12.32804909677984 42.24980785280403 12.33 42.25
          12.33195090322016 42.24980785280403 12.33382683432365
          42.24923879532511 12.335555702330197 42.248314696123025
          12.337071067811866 42.247071067811866 12.338314696123026
          42.2455557023302 12.339238795325112 42.243826834323656
          12.339807852804032 42.241950903220165 12.34 42.24
        </gml:posList>
      </gml:LinearRing>
    </gml:exterior>
  </gml:Polygon>
```

How it works...

The WPS process builder is an easy way to use geoprocessing operations. It builds the XML requests for you. This is very useful not only to learn but also to build requests that you may use in another application.

How does the process builder work? It parses the WPS capabilities and renders the information contained in it to a form human-readable. Point your browser to `http://localhost/geoserver/ows?service=wps&version=1.0.0&request=GetCapabilities`, and you will see a long XML containing all the operations supported. The following fragment shows the basic operations and the info for `JTS:buffer`:

```
<ows:OperationsMetadata>
  <ows:Operation name="GetCapabilities">
    <ows:DCP>
      <ows:HTTP>
        <ows:Get xlink:href="http://localhost/geoserver/wps"/>
        <ows:Post xlink:href="http://localhost/geoserver/wps"/>
      </ows:HTTP>
    </ows:DCP>
  </ows:Operation>
  <ows:Operation name="DescribeProcess">
    <ows:DCP>
      <ows:HTTP>
        <ows:Get xlink:href="http://localhost/geoserver/wps"/>
        <ows:Post xlink:href="http://localhost/geoserver/wps"/>
      </ows:HTTP>
    </ows:DCP>
  </ows:Operation>
  <ows:Operation name="Execute">
    <ows:DCP>
      <ows:HTTP>
        <ows:Get xlink:href="http://localhost/geoserver/wps"/>
        <ows:Post xlink:href="http://localhost/geoserver/wps"/>
      </ows:HTTP>
    </ows:DCP>
  </ows:Operation>
</ows:OperationsMetadata>
...
<wps:Process wps:processVersion="1.0.0">
  <ows:Identifier>JTS:buffer</ows:Identifier>
  <ows:Title>Buffer</ows:Title>
  <ows:Abstract>Returns a polygonal geometry representing the
    input geometry enlarged by a given distance around its
    exterior.</ows:Abstract>
</wps:Process>
...
```

So when you select `JTS:buffer` from the list, a `DescribeProcess` request is created and forwarded to GeoServer:

```
http://localhost/geoserver/ows?service=wps&version=1.0.0&request=Desc
ribeProcess&Identifier=JTS:buffer
```

The WPS process builder receive an XML like the following and it parses it to build the interface to populate processing parameters:

```
...
<ows:Identifier>JTS:buffer</ows:Identifier>
  <ows:Title>Buffer</ows:Title>
  <ows:Abstract>Returns a polygonal geometry representing the
    input geometry enlarged by a given distance around its
    exterior.</ows:Abstract>
  <DataInputs>
    <Input maxOccurs="1" minOccurs="1">
      <ows:Identifier>geom</ows:Identifier>
      <ows:Title>geom</ows:Title>
      <ows:Abstract>Input geometry</ows:Abstract>
      <ComplexData>
        <Default>
          <Format>
            <MimeType>text/xml; subtype=gml/3.1.1</MimeType>
          </Format>
        </Default>
        <Supported>
          <Format>
            <MimeType>text/xml; subtype=gml/3.1.1</MimeType>
          </Format>
          <Format>
            <MimeType>text/xml; subtype=gml/2.1.2</MimeType>
          </Format>
          <Format>
            <MimeType>application/wkt</MimeType>
          </Format>
          <Format>
            <MimeType>application/gml-3.1.1</MimeType>
          </Format>
          <Format>
            <MimeType>application/gml-2.1.2</MimeType>
          </Format>
        </Supported>
      </ComplexData>
    ...
```

The described process response contains all information needed to build a proper `Process` request. If your input is correct, when you press the **Execute Process** button, the WPS process builder sends a `POST` request with a body similar to this one:

```
<?xml version="1.0" encoding="UTF-8"?>
<wps:Execute version="1.0.0" service="WPS"
  xmlns:xsi="http://www.w3.org/2001/XMLSchema-instance"
  xmlns="http://www.opengis.net/wps/1.0.0"
  xmlns:wfs="http://www.opengis.net/wfs"
  xmlns:wps="http://www.opengis.net/wps/1.0.0"
  xmlns:ows="http://www.opengis.net/ows/1.1"
  xmlns:gml="http://www.opengis.net/gml"
  xmlns:ogc="http://www.opengis.net/ogc"
  xmlns:wcs="http://www.opengis.net/wcs/1.1.1"
  xmlns:xlink="http://www.w3.org/1999/xlink"
  xsi:schemaLocation="http://www.opengis.net/wps/1.0.0
  http://schemas.opengis.net/wps/1.0.0/wpsAll.xsd">
    <ows:Identifier>JTS:buffer</ows:Identifier>
    <wps:DataInputs>
        <wps:Input>
            <ows:Identifier>geom</ows:Identifier>
            <wps:Data>
                <wps:ComplexData mimeType="application/wkt">
                    <![CDATA[POINT(12.33 42.24)]]>
                </wps:ComplexData>
            </wps:Data>
        </wps:Input>
        <wps:Input>
            <ows:Identifier>distance</ows:Identifier>
            <wps:Data>
                <wps:LiteralData>0.01</wps:LiteralData>
            </wps:Data>
        </wps:Input>
    </wps:DataInputs>
    <wps:ResponseForm>
        <wps:RawDataOutput mimeType="text/xml; subtype=gml/3.1.1">
            <ows:Identifier>result</ows:Identifier>
        </wps:RawDataOutput>
    </wps:ResponseForm>
</wps:Execute>
```

The result of this operation is the XML showed in the previous screenshot.

Chaining process – selecting features contained in a polygon

In the previous recipe, you started working with geoprocessing requests. Looking at the supported operations, you see that it is a very long one. There are several different operations you can perform on the data. Most of these operations are quite simple, while in a real-world use case, you often need more complex ones. So, how can you translate a real-world use case into a task that GeoServer is able to execute? The elegant and efficient answer is chaining processes.

WPS lets you use the result of an operation as an input to another operation. While this may seem very simple, it offers you an incredible flexibility and power. By using the built-in operations as building blocks, you can create very complex geoprocessing tasks. The WPS process builder will let us try out this powerful idea.

In this recipe, your target is to find all populated places located inside Switzerland.

How to do it...

1. Open the GeoServer administrative interface and open the WPS process builder page.

2. Select **gs:Clip** from the processes' list. The **Input feature collection** is the layer from where we want to extract the data, so select **NaturalEarth:populatedplaces**.

3. Scroll down to the section where you have to define the clipping geometry. This time, you won't input a geometry. You're going to use the result from another operation. To build the chain, select **SUBPROCESS** from the list.

4. Press the **Define/Edit** link; a new panel shows up where you can define the parameters for the new process that will be executed. Select the **gs:CollectGeometries** operation and again choose **SUBPROCESS** as the input for you operation.

5. You're at the last step of this geoprocessing task. Select **Define/Edit** and select **gs:Query** task. The input for this query is the **NaturalEarth.EuropeCountries** layer. In the filter section, you can choose the CQL syntax, which is easier to type. You will then apply filter on the **admin** field.

 CQL was originally used for catalog systems, GeoServer uses an extension to CQL allowing the full representation of OGC filters in text form. This extension is called **Extended Common Query Language** (ECQL).

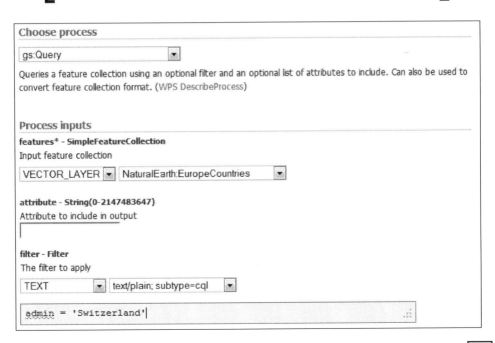

6. Now, press the **Apply** button to return to the previous operation. You will need to press it once more in order to apply all the chained operations. Eventually, you will land on the WPS process builder page with a huge XML code in the clip geometry textbox.

```
clip* - Geometry
Geometry to use for clipping (in same CRS as input features)

SUBPROCESS ▼  Define/Edit

http://schemas.opengis.net/wps/1.0.0/wpsAll.xsd">
  <ows:Identifier>gs:CollectGeometries</ows:Identifier>
  <wps:DataInputs>
    <wps:Input>
      <ows:Identifier>features</ows:Identifier>
      <wps:Reference mimeType="text/xml"
xlink:href="http://geoserver/wps" method="POST">
        <wps:Body>
          <wps:Execute version="1.0.0" service="WPS">
            <ows:Identifier>gs:Query</ows:Identifier>
            <wps:DataInputs>
              <wps:Input>
                <ows:Identifier>features</ows:Identifier>
```

7. Press the **Execute Process** button, a new panel shows and after a while, it is populated with the GML code for the populated places list. Your extraction was successful!

```
<wfs:FeatureCollection>
  <gml:boundedBy>
    <gml:Box srsName="http://www.opengis.net/gml/srs/epsg.xml#4326">
      <gml:coord>
        <gml:X>6.03000890974238</gml:X>
        <gml:Y>45.8999747915411</gml:Y>
      </gml:coord>
      <gml:coord>
        <gml:X>9.76670158807428</gml:X>
        <gml:Y>47.7504044790487</gml:Y>
      </gml:coord>
    </gml:Box>
  </gml:boundedBy>
  <gml:featureMember>
    <feature:populatedplaces fid="populatedplaces.106">
      <gml:name>Delemont</gml:name>
      <gml:boundedBy>
        <gml:Box srsName="http://www.opengis.net/gml/srs/epsg.xml#4326">
          <gml:coord>
            <gml:X>7.3449994876432925</gml:X>
            <gml:Y>47.36999712580081</gml:Y>
          </gml:coord>
          <gml:coord>
            <gml:X>7.3449994876432925</gml:X>
            <gml:Y>47.36999712580081</gml:Y>
          </gml:coord>
        </gml:Box>
```

How it works...

You created a relatively complex task by using three simple operations exposed by WPS.

Your target is to select all point features inside an area, that is, Switzerland. The first step is to set the geometry of Switzerland. You can input it by typing a WKT description, of course, but this may work only for a really simple and small geometry. In a real-world scenario, you'll have to type hundreds or thousands of vertices, which is also error-prone and time-consuming.

We already have a detailed representation of Switzerland boundaries in the **EuropeCountries** layer, so the first step is to filter it with the `gs:Query` operation.

The query made use of a CQL filter to select Switzerland and resulted in an XML document containing the description of the extracted feature. The XML included the values of geometrical and alphanumerical attributes.

You only need the geometry part and in a form suitable to work as an input for a `gs:Clip` operation. This transformation is what `gs:CollectGeometries` performs.

You can try to build a simpler task by just using the `gs:Query` and `gs:CollectGeometries` operations. The result is an XML fragment shown in the following snippet:

```
<gml:MultiPolygon
    srsName="http://www.opengis.net/gml/srs/epsg.xml#4326">
    <gml:polygonMember>
        <gml:Polygon>
            <gml:outerBoundaryIs>
                <gml:LinearRing>
                    <gml:coordinates>8.617437378000076,
                        47.757318624000085
                        8.62983972100005,47.76279632600007
                        ...
                        8.607618856000105,47.76225372300012
                        8.617437378000076,47.757318624000085
                    </gml:coordinates>
                </gml:LinearRing>
            </gml:outerBoundaryIs>
        </gml:Polygon>
    </gml:polygonMember>
</gml:MultiPolygon>
```

This is exactly the input that `gs:Clip` expects as clip geometry.

You can chain many different processes to fit your requirements. Of course, you can interact with WPS from an external app as we are going to see in the next recipe.

Chaining process – building your own task

You have seen how to send WPS request with the process builder, but what if you want to incorporate WPS capabilities in an external program?

In this recipe, you will create requests with XML and send them to GeoServer using the Python programming language and a shell utility cURL. Python is a programming language known for its simplicity and code readability, and is therefore very easy to use when creating small programs.

The cURL project is a library and a command-line tool that can easily be incorporated in simple shell scripts (it can also be used as a library by developers).

Both tools allow users to concentrate on what the program should do, rather than be distracted by a complex syntax.

In this chapter, it is assumed that you have a working installation of Python and cURL. If you are using a Linux box, it is quite probable you have both already installed and configured, or you can rely on your distribution package system to install a recent release.

For Windows, you can get Python from the project site at `http://python.org/`.

cURL is available as a source for those who are brave or as a binary packages from `http://curl.haxx.se/download.html`.

In order to make your experience with Python more smooth, you will use the `Requests` library. It is a powerful HTTP protocol library and you can use it inside any Python program, leveraging on its powerful objects to interact with the HTTP protocol.

`Requests` is an open source project started by Kenneth Reitz. You can download and use it in a very liberal way; it is released under the **Internet Software Consortium** (**ISC**) license used by OpenBSD. You can also fork `Requests` on GitHub if you wish to add features.

`http://docs.python-requests.org/en/latest/`

How to do it...

1. In the WPS request builder page, create a process to extract the road M11 data from the layer **NaturalEarth:roads**.

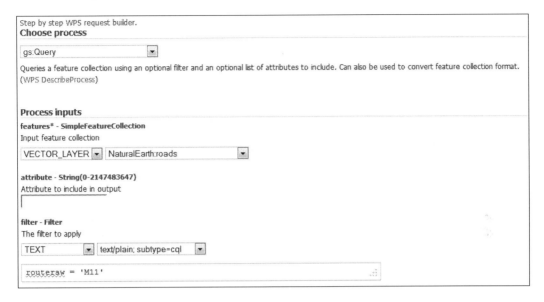

2. Now, instead of executing the request, press the button **Generate XML from process input/output**. A panel containing XML code for the request appears. Select the entire code snippet and save it in a file called `query.xml`.

3. Open a shell and go to the folder where you saved the `query.xml` file. Use cURL to send this request to GeoServer and save the result in an XML file called `results.xml`.

```
$ curl -XPOST -H 'Content-type: text/xml' -d @query.xml
  http://localhost/geoserver/wps -o results.xml
```

4. After a while, the operation terminates. Open the `results.xml` file with an editor and look at its content. It should be a GML containing a line feature for the M11 highway, as shown in the following fragment:

```
<feature:geom><gml:MultiLineString
  srsName="http://www.opengis.net/gml/srs/epsg.xml#4326">
  <gml:lineStringMember><gml:LineString><gml:coordinates>
  0.129189167383835,51.70460802098098
  0.14964133470251184,51.75797266063622
  0.16842512784744912,51.85780385442065
  0.17149353629286423,51.86688366002006
  0.19242696539243198,51.904635000808085
  0.1941740914939558,51.909010107907065
```

```
0.19534662019648152,51.91370313945523
0.19576663047798348,51.918463255978914
0.1954574562429876,51.92808265812053
0.19491494296271483,51.93195316953409
0.19387075073509408,51.93577117966247
0.17697408711884677,51.98231648571944
0.16511754688062297,52.04905728614528
0.16157954360658522,52.06182093192203
0.15678734296417218,52.07415581720307
0.15397560746856342,52.079397195507646
0.14318367662442455,52.09364837769804</gml:coordinates>
</gml:LineString></gml:lineStringMember>
</gml:MultiLineString></feature:geom>
```

5. Now, you will do the same with Python. Launch the Python interpreter and load the requests library, as shown in the following code:

```
$ python
Python 2.7.3 (default, Sep 26 2013, 20:03:06)
[GCC 4.6.3] on linux2
Type "help", "copyright", "credits" or "license" for more
  information.
>>> import requests
>>>
>>> myUrl = 'http://localhost/geoserver/wps'
>>> file = open('query.xml','r')
>>> payload = file.read()
>>> headers = {'Content-type': 'text/xml'}
>>> resp = requests.post(myUrl, auth=('',''), data=payload,
  headers=headers)
>>> resp.status_code
200
```

6. Nice! It succeeded, but what if you would like to extract the response body to list it or to save it in a file? The `response.text` method is what you are looking for, let's save the result in a file. The code is as follows:

```
>>> file = open('results.xml','w')
>>> file.write(resp.text)
>>> file.close()
```

7. Open the file and check whether the result is the same as with the cURL request.

How it works...

You have seen two examples on how to interact with WPS from an external application. For the sake of simplicity, we choose Python and cURL, but, of course, you can perform the same task from any programming or scripting language.

You always need to build an XML request, send it via HTTP to GeoServer, and then parse the result, which is usually again an XML file.

Some times, it is more useful to return the result in a different form, such as JSON for web development. Try, for instance, to execute a `gs:Query` operation and change the process output type to `application/zip`. You will be delivered a ZIP compressed archive containing a shapefile with the features extracted by your filter.

There is more...

You're not limited in the number of process that can be chained, so let's try a more complex task.

You want to find which features from the populated places layer that are within a 10-km distance from the M11 highway in England.

We already performed a similar process; this time we need to create a buffer geometry, which we'll use to select features within a distance from the specified road.

Let's start with it. You need to create a new XML file for the request. You will use again the process builder. What are the operations required?

The first one is `gs:Clip`, which extracts features from the `NaturalEarth:populatedplaces` layer. So, set the clip geometry to **SUBPROCESS** and select **JTS:Buffer**.

The input geometry for the buffer operation is `gs:CollectGeometries`.

The final operation is `gs:Query`, which will perform the extraction from the `NaturalEarth:roads` layer with the following `where` clause:

```
routeraw = 'M11'
```

Don't forget to set the distance for the buffer operation, both layers contain the `LAT-LONG` geometries, so set the distance to 0.3 degrees.

When you're done, you will have an XML file chaining all processes.

 If you need to check your result, the XML code for this operation is contained in the `buffer.xml` file in the code bundle of the book.

Save it in the `buffer.xml` file and execute the process using the following command:

```
$ curl -XPOST -H 'Content-type: text/xml' -d @buffer.xml http://
localhost/geoserver/wps -o results.xml
```

If you are successful, your `result.xml` file should contain several features in a form that looks like the following snippet:

```
<wfs:FeatureCollection xmlns:wfs="http://www.opengis.net/wfs"
  xmlns:feature="http://www.naturalearthdata.com/"
  xmlns:ogc="http://www.opengis.net/ogc"
  xmlns:gml="http://www.opengis.net/gml">
    <gml:boundedBy>
        <gml:Box srsName="http://www.opengis.net/gml/srs/epsg.
          xml#4326">
            <gml:coord>
                <gml:X>-0.118667702475932</gml:X>
                <gml:Y>51.5019405883275</gml:Y>
            </gml:coord>
            <gml:coord>
                <gml:X>0.11662308615098</gml:X>
                <gml:Y>52.2003912547825</gml:Y>
            </gml:coord>
        </gml:Box>
    </gml:boundedBy>
    <gml:featureMember>
...
            <feature:geom>
                <gml:Point>
                    <gml:coord>
                        <gml:X>0.11662308615098027</gml:X>
                        <gml:Y>52.20039125478246</gml:Y>
                    </gml:coord>
                </gml:Point>
            </feature:geom>
        </feature:populatedplaces>
    </gml:featureMember>
    <gml:featureMember>
...
</wfs:FeatureCollection>
```

5
Advanced Configurations

In this chapter, we'll cover the following recipes:

- ▶ Upgrading GeoServer
- ▶ Creating a script for automatic startup
- ▶ Optimizing Java
- ▶ Setting up a JNDI connection pool
- ▶ Working with CRS
- ▶ Using the reprojection console
- ▶ Overriding an official EPSG code
- ▶ Setting up GeoWebCache—how to make pre-rendered tiles for high availability
- ▶ Storing configurations in an RDBMS

Introduction

This chapter will introduce some less known features of GeoServer. When you have to deploy your server in production, a proper configuration is a crucial topic and sound knowledge of all features makes the difference between a sloppy map server and a fast and reliable one. Another crucial point is data optimization. In this chapter, we will explore recipes covering application server configuration and data handling.

For the first item, we will see how to properly configure database connections in an enterprise environment and how to plan a standard upgrade procedure for our GeoServer installation. Then, you will learn how to use cache to improve GeoServer capacity. GeoWebCache is a huge topic and we will explore its configuration in depth in the next chapter.

For data handling, we will focus on CRS. I hope you know what they are! However, in my years of GIS consulting, I am always asked about basic topics when the subject is **Coordinate reference system (CRS)**. GeoServer uses a standard approach and lets you use and transform data from any standard CRS or also create a custom one. You just need to learn how to control this power.

Upgrading GeoServer

At the time of writing this book, GeoServer is at its 2.5.0 release, and it's definitely a stable and mature project. It has a well-defined release schedule with major and minor versions released at regular intervals.

 For detailed and up-to-date information about the next releases, have a look at `http://blog.geoserver.org/2014/02/26/extended-release-schedule/`.

Upgrading frequently is a good thing; with any new release, you get many bugs fixed and new features included. Some experimental module, often from the community, may be included in the stable release. If you are running GeoServer in a production site, you have to choose between the benefits of upgrading it frequently and policies that your customer and/or system administrators may have enforced.

In any case, you need to fully understand what upgrading GeoServer means and its consequences on the following:

- Your service and data
- Establishing a standard procedure to upgrade your GeoServer installation

In this recipe, you will perform the simple steps required for upgrading.

Please note that in the following steps, I am assuming you are using GeoServer inside a Tomcat container, which is the most commonly used configuration for a production site.

How to do it...

1. Create a backup copy of your data folder. This is very important for an easy restore if something goes wrong with updating:

   ```
   $ sudo tar cvfz /opt/data_dir_geoserver.tar.gz
     /opt/data_dir_geoserver/*
   ```

2. Stop the GeoServer instance:

   ```
   $ sudo service tomcat stop
   ```

3. Create a backup copy of your Tomcat installation:

```
$ sudo tar cvfz /opt/Tomcat7042.tar.gz /opt/Tomcat7042/*
```

4. Restart GeoServer and undeploy GeoServer from Tomcat using the web interface:

```
$ sudo service tomcat start
```

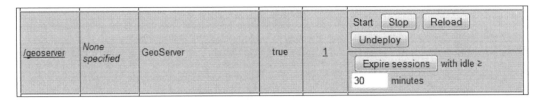

5. Now, you can deploy your new GeoServer to Tomcat:

```
$ sudo mv /download/geoserver.war /opt/tomcat7042/webapps/.
```

6. Check whether GeoServer is deployed safely by looking at the log and the web interface. If there is no critical error, you now have a standard installation pointing at the sample dataset. Stop Tomcat and edit the web.xml file to point it again to your custom data directory location:

```
$ sudo vi /opt/tomcat7042/webapps/geoserver/WEB-INF/web.xml
```

7. Find the section with the data directory configuration, uncomment it, and edit it according to your settings:

```
<context-param>
    <param-name>GEOSERVER_DATA_DIR</param-name>
    <param-value>/opt/data_dir_geoserver/</param-value>
</context-param>
```

8. Then download, unpack, and install any other plugin and community module you had in your old installation.

9. Now, you can start your GeoServer again. Check the log and the web interface for any error.

How it works...

If you followed the previous steps, you can guess that upgrading GeoServer is an easy task. In fact, it is usually a straightforward and simple operation.

Some problems may arise if you don't follow a regular upgrade process or you jump from a very old release to the latest one.

Detailed information about major changes in the data directory structure that you should be aware of are usually listed at `http://docs.geoserver.org/stable/en/user/datadirectory/migrating.html`.

GeoServer is quite a complex piece of software and sharing the same servlet container with other applications may result in out-of-memory issues or library conflicts.

The best option is to use a dedicated Tomcat for GeoServer. In some cases, you're not in control of the deployment environment, and you need to deploy it on the servlet container where other Java applications are hosted.

Also, for these complex configurations, you may follow the previous steps, but you need to modify them in order to avoid problems to other applications.

Also, consider that it is impossible to upgrade without an interruption of the service. So, we should accurately plan for the upgrade operation.

See also

▸ The *Storing configurations in an RDBMS* recipe

Creating a script for automatic startup

On a production server, we need to configure Tomcat as the system service, that is, a program running at boot without any users' action. If you install Tomcat on Windows, the installer creates the service for you and sets it for an automatic startup.

Are you wondering how to do it on Linux? In this recipe, we are going to configure your Linux box for automatic start of services. We will create a script and learn how it works.

How to do it...

1. Open your preferred editor and enter the following lines. Be sure to launch the editor with `sudo`, as we are going to create a file in a system folder:

```
#!/bin/sh
### BEGIN INIT INFO
# Provides:          tomcat
# Required-Start:    $local_fs $remote_fs $network $syslog
# Required-Stop:     $local_fs $remote_fs $network $syslog
# Default-Start:     2 3 4 5
# Default-Stop:      0 1 6
# Short-Description: Start/Stop Tomcat  v7.0.42
### END INIT INFO
```

```
#
#   /etc/init.d/tomcat
#
export JAVA_HOME=/usr/lib/jvm/jre1.6.0_37
export PATH=$JAVA_HOME/bin:$PATH
export CATALINA_HOME=/opt/tomcat7042
export JAVA_OPTS="-Djava.awt.headless=true"

case $1 in
    start)
        sh $CATALINA_HOME/bin/startup.sh
    ;;
    stop)
        sh $CATALINA_HOME/bin/shutdown.sh
    ;;
    restart)
        sh $CATALINA_HOME/bin/shutdown.sh
        sh $CATALINA_HOME/bin/startup.sh
    ;;
    *)
        echo "Usage: /etc/init.d/tomcat
          {start|stop|restart}"
        exit 1
    ;;
esac

exit 0
```

2. The preceding script is simple and contains all of the basic elements you will need to get going. Pay attention to the path; you should adjust your script according to your system settings.

3. Call the new file called `tomcat` and save it in the `/etc/init.d` folder.

4. Now, set the permissions for your script to make it executable:

    ```
    $ sudo chmod a+x /etc/init.d/tomcat
    ```

5. Let's try to call it and look for any problems:

    ```
    $ sudo service tomcat
    Usage: /etc/init.d/tomcat {start|stop|restart}
    ```

6. Try starting Tomcat with the following command:

    ```
    $ sudo service tomcat start
    ```

7. Using the following command lines, check whether Tomcat is running:

```
$ ps -ef | grep java
```

```
root      2813      1 99 19:06 pts/0    00:00:24 /usr/bin/java
  -Djava.util.logging.config.file=/opt/Tomcat7042/conf/
  logging.properties -Djava.util.logging.manager=org.apache.
  juli.ClassLoaderLogManager -Djava.endorsed.dirs=/opt/
  Tomcat7042/endorsed -classpath /opt/Tomcat7042/bin/
  bootstrap.jar:/opt/Tomcat7042/bin/tomcat-juli.jar -
  Dcatalina.base=/opt/Tomcat7042 -Dcatalina.home=/opt/
  Tomcat7042 -Djava.io.tmpdir=/opt/Tomcat7042/temp
  org.apache.catalina.startup.Bootstrap start
```

8. Now we will use the script to stop Tomcat:

```
$ sudo service tomcat stop
```

9. Now that you have a working script, the last step is adding to configured services; we will use `update-rc` as follows:

```
$ sudo update-rc.d tomcat defaults

 Adding system startup for /etc/init.d/tomcat ...
   /etc/rc0.d/K20tomcat -> ../init.d/tomcat
   /etc/rc1.d/K20tomcat -> ../init.d/tomcat
   /etc/rc6.d/K20tomcat -> ../init.d/tomcat
   /etc/rc2.d/S20tomcat -> ../init.d/tomcat
   /etc/rc3.d/S20tomcat -> ../init.d/tomcat
   /etc/rc4.d/S20tomcat -> ../init.d/tomcat
   /etc/rc5.d/S20tomcat -> ../init.d/tomcat
```

10. Reboot your system and check whether Tomcat is running.

How it works...

We created a shell script to start Apache Tomcat. Now, as you boot your Linux machine, Tomcat will be initialized and all the web application contained will be available for user requests. If you prefer to manually start and stop Tomcat, the script could be useful for you. Just create it as described and avoid the last step. You will use the script to start or stop Tomcat from the command line, that is, `sudo service tomcat start` or `sudo service tomcat stop`.

Optimizing Java

A crucial point to properly configure optimal performance is the GeoServer container, Tomcat, and its JVM setting. Tomcat's default startup script is configured for booting quickly, but, of course, it can't match all applications' requirements. Tuning your Java runtime parameters can greatly increase performance. There are many runtime parameters you can set at the JVM startup. In this recipe, you will set the most effective one on GeoServer performances. Note that values may vary according to the hardware configuration on your site.

Unfortunately, there is no way to cut corners on the path of tuning parameters for a Java application. While the options presented in this chapter have been widely tested on GeoServer and are recommended by core developers, you should note that best options may vary depending on your scenario. A value resource to understand how each parameter works is `http://www.oracle.com/technetwork/java/javase/tech/vmoptions-jsp-140102.html`.

How to do it...

In the previous recipe, we created a startup script for the automated startup of GeoServer on Linux. Now, you will edit the script with proper values for Java runtime parameters. Each parameter will be briefly described in the following steps:

1. Open the startup file we created in the previous recipe:

   ```
   $ sudo vi /etc/init.d/tomcat
   ```

`vi` is one the most famous editor on Linux. System administrators and developers often love it for its flexibility and power. On the other hand, it has a steep learning curve and newcomers may find its command mode / insert mode dual nature uncomfortable. On Debian distributions, such as Ubuntu or Mint, you may find nano a more user-friendly console editor. It goes without saying that you can use a powerful IDE such as gedit or jEdit if you can access a desktop environment.

2. Locate the following code line. If you didn't modify the script, it should be line number 15:

   ```
   export CATALINA_HOME=/opt/Tomcat7042
   ```

3. Insert the following lines of code after it:

   ```
   HEAP="-Xms2048m -Xmx2048m"

   NEW="-XX:NewSize=128m -XX:MaxNewSize=128m"
   ```

```
RMIGC="-Dsun.rmi.dgc.client.gcInterval=600000 -
   Dsun.rmi.dgc.server.gcInterval=600000"

PGC="-XX:+UseParallelGC"

PERM="-XX:PermSize=128m -XX:MaxPermSize=128m"

DEBUG="-verbose:gc -XX:+PrintTenuringDistribution"

DUMP="-XX:+HeapDumpOnOutOfMemoryError"

SERVER="-server"
```

4. Now go to the line, just after the ones you just inserted. We need to add all values you set in the JAVA_OPTS variable. JVM will read it at startup and use your values:

    ```
    export JAVA_OPTS="-Djava.awt.headless=true $HEAP $NEW
       $RMIGC $PGC $PERM $DEBUG $DUMP $SERVER"
    ```

5. Save the file and restart your Tomcat server.

How it works...

We inserted a few extra parameters to the script. This tunes the JVM environment and helps to increase your server's performance. Let's explore what we added and why it is important:

▶   HEAP: This parameter lets you reserve enough memory for GeoServer. It really depends on the memory availability on your system. 2 GB, as indicated, is a good figure. You may want to decrease it if you are hosting on a tiny cloud machine, where total memory size is limited:

    ```
    HEAP="-Xms2048m -Xmx2048m"
    ```

▶   NEWSIZE: This parameter lets you are reserve space for new objects created by GeoServer. This values shouldn't be more that a fourth of heap; reduce it proportionally if you need to reduce your heap:

    ```
    NEW="-XX:NewSize=128m -XX:MaxNewSize=128m"
    ```

▶   GARBAGE COLLECTOR: This parameter sets the frequency at which the Java garbage collector, which is used to destroy unused objects, should be run. Once every 10 minutes, as suggested in the recipe, should be more than enough:

    ```
    RMIGC="-Dsun.rmi.dgc.client.gcInterval=600000 -
       Dsun.rmi.dgc.server.gcInterval=600000"
    ```

▶   PGC: You should also add a line to use the parallel garbage collector, which enables multithreaded garbage collection. This improves performance if more than two cores are present:

    ```
    PGC="-XX:+UseParallelGC"
    ```

- PERM: This lets you increase the maximum size of permanent generation (or permgen) allocated to GeoServer. This is the heap portion where the class bytecode is stored. GeoServer uses lots of classes and it may exhaust that space quickly leading to out of memory errors. The code that let's you increase the size of permgen is as follows:

```
PERM="-XX:PermSize=256m -XX:MaxPermSize=256m"
```

- DEBUG: This parameter enables Java to perform tracing. This may greatly help if things go astray. The code for it is as follows:

```
DEBUG="-verbose:gc -XX:+PrintTenuringDistribution"
```

- DUMP: This parameter sets Java to create a dump of the memory state when your server ends in an **out of memory case** (**OOM**). It does not cost anything unless triggered, and may be useful to debug tricky bugs. The code that let's you achieve that is as follows:

```
DUMP="-XX:+HeapDumpOnOutOfMemoryError"
```

- SERVER: This parameter is used for forcing the server JVM. On most Linux systems, it is there by default. However, having it explicitly set doesn't harm. The code for it is as follows:

```
SERVER="-server"
```

Setting up a JNDI connection pool

Several recipes of this book use data stored in an RDBMS, in fact PostgreSQL, with the PostGIS spatial extension.

Configuring spatial data from a RDBMS in your GeoServer requires you to create a connection setting for several parameters from the admin web interface. Whatever database you are using, it may be useful to configure the connection using the **Java Naming and Directory Interface** (**JNDI**) standard.

For more information about JNDI, refer to the following websites:

- http://en.wikipedia.org/wiki/Java_Naming_and_Directory_Interface
- http://tomcat.apache.org/tomcat-7.0-doc/jndi-resources-howto.html
- http://docs.oracle.com/javase/jndi/tutorial/

How to do it...

1. Stop your Tomcat using the following command:

   ```
   $ sudo service tomcat stop
   ```

2. Move the JDBC PostgreSQL driver in the `lib` folder of Tomcat:

   ```
   $ cd /opt/Tomcat7042/webapps/geoserver/WEB-INF/lib
   $  sudo mv postgresql-8.4-701.jdbc3.jar /opt/Tomcat7042/lib/.
   ```

3. Now, edit the Tomcat configuration file in order to set up the connection pool:

   ```
   $ sudo vi /opt/Tomcat7042/conf/context.xml
   ```

4. Insert a new resource inside the `<Context>` tag:

   ```
   <Context>
     <Resource
       name="jdbc/postgis"
       auth="Container"
       type="javax.sql.DataSource"
       driverClassName="org.postgresql.Driver"
       url="jdbc:postgresql://127.0.0.1:5432/gisdata"
       username="gisuser"
       password="gisuser"
       maxActive="20"
       maxIdle="10"
       maxWait="-1"/>
   </Context>
   ```

5. Now edit the GeoServer `web.xml` file:

   ```
   $ sudo vi /opt/tomcat7042/webapps/geoserver/WEB-INF/web.xml
   ```

6. Insert a new reference into the JNDI resource, paste the following code snippet at the end of the file inside the `<web-app>` tag, and then save and close the `web.xml` file:

   ```
   <web-app>
     . . .
     <resource-ref>
       <description>PostGIS Datasource</description>
       <res-ref-name>jdbc/postgis</res-ref-name>
       <res-type>javax.sql.DataSource</res-type>
       <res-auth>Container</res-auth>
     </resource-ref>
   </web-app>
   ```

7. Start Tomcat.
8. Log in to the GeoServer web interface and create a new data store, select the **PostGIS (JNDI)** type, and populate the parameters according to following screenshot:

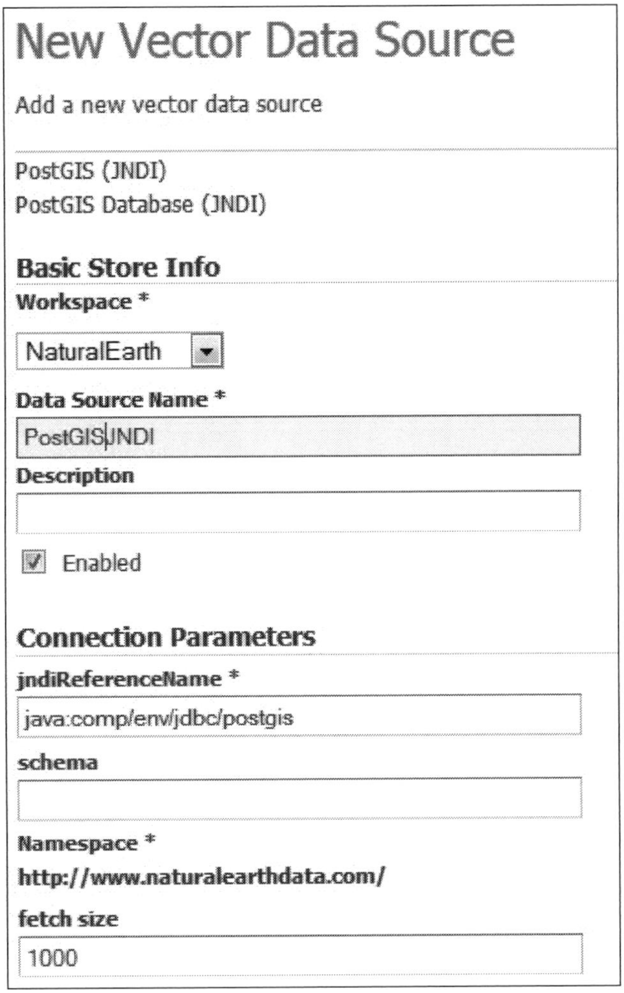

New Vector Data Source

Add a new vector data source

PostGIS (JNDI)
PostGIS Database (JNDI)

Basic Store Info

Workspace *

NaturalEarth

Data Source Name *

PostGISJNDI

Description

☑ Enabled

Connection Parameters

jndiReferenceName *

java:comp/env/jdbc/postgis

schema

Namespace *
http://www.naturalearthdata.com/

fetch size

1000

9. Leave the other parameters unchanged and then press the **Save** button. You will be presented with a list of spatial tables stored in the database for publishing them on GeoServer:

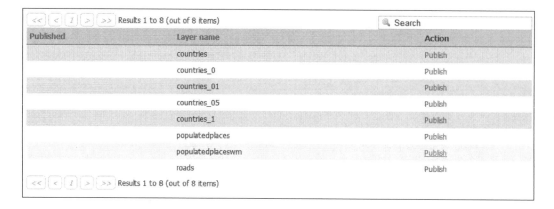

How it works...

JNDI allows GeoServer and any Java application in general to access data just using a predefined name.

In this recipe, you used JNDI to retrieve information about a JDBC data source from the servlet container.

Using JNDI you can store all configuration information in the container and also the connections are not replicated. This can prove very useful when you have multiple instances on GeoServer in the same container, or when GeoServer is deployed along to other applications that need to access the database. In this case, all the database connections are instantiated and managed by Tomcat to avoid having any component allocating resources to connect to the data.

Working with CRS

When working with spatial data, you should be aware of its features in order to avoid errors in its manipulation and representation. Among spatial data characteristics, a very important one is the **Coordinate Reference System** (**CRS**) that was originally used to define the data.

In this recipe, you will learn basic concepts about CRS and how to properly define them in GeoServer.

How to do it...

1. You need a new dataset for this recipe. We will use Texas counties' boundaries, freely available from U.S. Census Bureau. Go to `http://www.census.gov/cgi-bin/geo/shapefiles2013/main`, the main site to download the data from. Select the counties and click on the **submit** button.

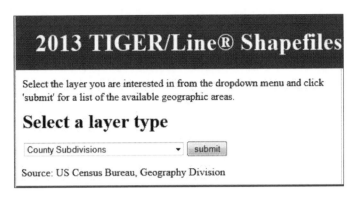

2. From the states' list, select **Texas** and click on the **Download** button. When prompted, select a proper location on the filesystem to save the archive.

3. Unzip the archive. You'll find five files; have a look at the `tl_2013_48_cousub.prj` file. It contains a **Well Known Text** (**WKT**) representation of CRS for the data:

```
GEOGCS["GCS_North_American_1983",DATA["D_North_American_19
   83",SPHEROID["GRS_1980",6378137,298.257222101]],
   PRIMEM["Greenwich",0],UNIT["Degree",
   0.017453292519943295]]
```

4. Now, create a new data store in GeoServer for the folder where you extracted the shapefile, then published it following the usual procedure.

5. In the publishing page, you can see that GeoServer marks the native CRS as unknown.

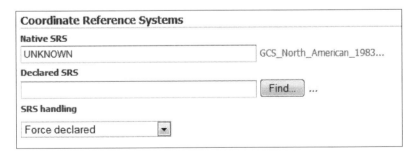

6. Type `EPSG:4269` in the **Declared SRS** textbox and leave the **SRS handling** option to **Force declared**. Compute the bounding boxes and then publish the layer.

How it works...

Coordinate systems build a frame of reference to place objects on earth's surface. There are two types of coordinate systems:

- Projected coordinate systems
- Geographic coordinate systems

Geographic coordinate systems use latitude and longitude as angles measured from the earth's center. A geographic coordinate system is substantially defined by the ellipsoid used to model the Earth, and the position of the ellipsoid positioned relatively to the center of the Earth (called **data**).

A projected coordinate system is defined on a flat two-dimensional surface. A projected coordinate system is always based on a geographic coordinate system. Hence, it uses an ellipsoid and its orientation, which is data.

Projected coordinate systems include a projection method to project coordinates from the Earth's spherical surface onto a two-dimensional Cartesian coordinate plane.

If you get back to the WKT definition, you can guess what type of CRS you're looking at:

```
GEOGCS["GCS_North_American_1983",DATA["D_North_American_1983",SPH
    EROID["GRS_1980",6378137,298.257222101]],
    PRIMEM["Greenwich",0],UNIT["Degree",0.017453292519943295]]
```

In fact, it is a geographic coordinate system and uses the North American data of 1983. So why does GeoServer complain about it being an unknown CRS?

A lot of different CRS exist and in order to properly identify them, standard codes and representation were established.

When you wrote EPSG:4269, you were using a **Spatial Reference System Identifier** (**SRID**). It is a code to easily reference a CRS. Another, more wordy, way of defining a CRS is a string containing parameters about projection, ellipsoid, and data. It can be defined using the OGC WKT representation. The CRS for the geographic NAD83 reference system is as follows:

```
GEOGCS["NAD83",
    DATA["North_American_Data_1983",
        SPHEROID["GRS 1980",6378137,298.257222101,
            AUTHORITY["EPSG","7019"]],
        AUTHORITY["EPSG","6269"]],
    PRIMEM["Greenwich",0,
        AUTHORITY["EPSG","8901"]],
    UNIT["degree",0.01745329251994328,
        AUTHORITY["EPSG","9122"]],
    AUTHORITY["EPSG","4269"]
```

The last line contains `4269`, the SRID uniquely identifying this CRS. The long form should also contain the authority, that is, EPSG:4269, but you will often find it indicated only by the number.

As you may have guessed, this string is a little bit different from the string contained in the `.prj` file. That is because the projection file uses a syntax from ESRI, which while widely adopted, does not strictly follow the standard rules.

While GeoServer manages to identify the CRS, in this case, and properly publish the data, some issues may arise when you need to convert the data to another CRS; for example, when you need to visualize data from different CRS in the same map. Whenever GeoServer fails to identify the CRS, you should always identify the standard code for your data and set it as `Declared CRS`.

European Petroleum Survey Group (**EPSG**) was founded in 1986 by several European oil companies to collect and maintain geodetic information. In 2005, EPSG was absorbed by OGP (an international forum of oil and gas producers) that formed the OGP Geomatics Committee. This committee maintains the registry and publishes it as a public web interface or a downloadable database. You can find its online reference at `http://epsg-registry.org/`.

An easier and accessible source of information can be found at `http://spatialreference.org/`.

See also

▶ The *Using the reprojection console* recipe

▶ The *Overriding an official EPSG code* recipe

Using the reprojection console

In the previous recipe, you learned that many CRS exist and data can be converted from one form to another.

In some cases, CRS, even if they are different, are really very similar. So, for general mapping purposes, you can consider them identical.

In this recipe, you'll discover a simple, yet very useful, tool that ships with GeoServer: the reprojection console. It lets you have a look at how coordinates change when you move data from an SRS to another one.

How to do it...

1. From the GeoServer Web admin interface, select the **Demos** link on the left panel.
2. From the list, select **Reprojection console**. A new interface is displayed.

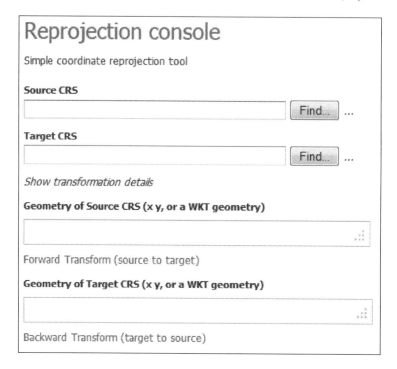

3. Insert EPSG:4326 in **Source CRS** and EPSG:4269 in **Target CRS**. Then, insert POINT(-98.5795 39.828175) in **Geometry of Source CRS**. Click on the **Forward Transformation** link; GeoServer calculates the new coordinates for you and fills the **Geometry of Target CRS** textbox.

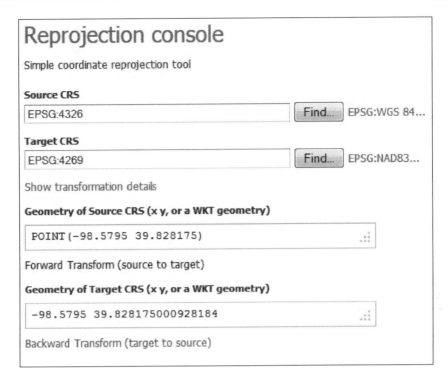

Reprojection console

Simple coordinate reprojection tool

Source CRS

| EPSG:4326 | | Find... | EPSG:WGS 84... |

Target CRS

| EPSG:4269 | | Find... | EPSG:NAD83... |

Show transformation details

Geometry of Source CRS (x y, or a WKT geometry)

POINT(-98.5795 39.828175)

Forward Transform (source to target)

Geometry of Target CRS (x y, or a WKT geometry)

-98.5795 39.828175000928184

Backward Transform (target to source)

You may be wondering how I chose the coordinates; well, they were not randomly selected. This point is known as the geometrical center of contiguous USA; for more information, have a look at `http://en.wikipedia.org/wiki/Geographic_center_of_the_contiguous_United_States`.

4. You may be surprised with values substantially equivalent after transformation, but there is a valid reason. I will explain what's happening in the *How it works...* section.

5. Now replace the value inside **Target CRS** with EPSG:4230 and insert
POINT(12.492269 41.890169) in the **Geometry of Source CRS** textbox. Again
click on the **Forward Transformation** link and look at the result of the transformation:

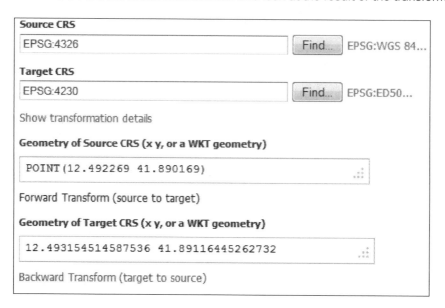

How it works...

Controls inside the **Reprojection console** are quite self-explanatory. Basically, you have to set
two CRS and geometry, and then you can transform the geometry from a CRS to another. As
you may have guessed, the function is reversible and almost all transformations do not have
a direction, so you can operate them both ways, for example, converting from WGS84 to ED50
or vice versa.

When you converted the value from WGS84 to NAD83, the values were
not changed, so was it GeoServer's fault?

In fact, the latitude value was very slightly different from the source, but
this was not really due to conversion. It was just a matter of the internal
representation of numbers.

To answer this question, you should understand how GeoServer transforms coordinates from a CRS to another. In the **Reprojection Console**, click on the link just to the right of the **Target CRS** textbox.

Source CRS		
EPSG:4326	Find...	EPSG:WGS 84...
Target CRS		
EPSG:4269	Find...	EPSG:NAD83...
Show transformation details		See the full definition of the coordinate system in WKT syntax

As the pop up suggests, a new window opens with the full description of the CRS.

Focus on the **TOWGS84** row. It contains the parameters to be used in transformation among **WGS84** and **NAD83**. There are different types of transformations and according to the type, this could require from a minimum of three to seven parameters. Anyway, in this case, all parameters are equal to zero. So, GeoServer considers **NAD83** and **WGS84** identical and no transformation is applied.

```
DATUM["North American Datum 1983",
    SPHEROID["GRS 1980", 6378137.0, 298.257222101, AUTHORITY["EPSG","7019"]],
    TOWGS84[0.0, 0.0, 0.0, 0.0, 0.0, 0.0, 0.0],
    AUTHORITY["EPSG","6269"]],
```

From a geodetic point of view, this isn't always correct; you may need more information about the data. Indeed, the first definition of **WGS84** and **NAD83** was fairly identical and differences among the two ellipsoids were under the meter accuracy, which is far less than the error introduced by transformations. If you are not going to deal with very accurate geodetic data, you can go with this simplification without any issue.

Now, check the same parameters for the **WGS84** to **ED50** transformation.

```
DATUM["European Datum 1950",
    SPHEROID["International 1924", 6378388.0, 297.0, AUTHORITY["EPSG","7022"]],
    TOWGS84[-116.641, -56.931, -110.559, 0.893, 0.921, -0.917, -3.52],
    AUTHORITY["EPSG","6230"]],
```

As you see, in this case, all seven parameters are populated and as you may expect, the transformation result is quite different.

Overriding an official EPSG code

In the previous recipe, you learned how to convert from one CRS to another. This transformation is also called a data shift operation, as the main difference among the two CRS is the data.

Performing a coordinate transformation is not always as simple as it was in the previous recipe. Let's dive into this new recipe to discover how things can quickly get far more complicated.

How to do it...

1. Open **Reprojection console** and insert EPSG:32632 for **Source CRS** and EPSG:3003 for **Target CRS**. Then, insert POINT(510071 4340827) in **Source Geometry** and click on the **Forward Transformation** link. The result is as follows:

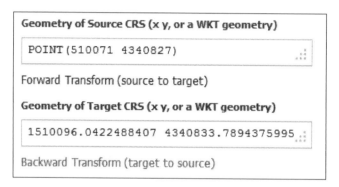

2. Take note of these values and open a console. Locate your data directory folder and switch to the user_projections directory. Create a new file and call it epsg_overrides.properties:

```
$ cd /opt/data_dir_geoserver/
$ cd user_projections/
$ sudo vi epsg_overrides.properties
```

3. Insert the following code inside epsg_overrides.properties and then save it:

```
3003=PROJCS["Monte Mario / Italy zone 1", GEOGCS["Monte
  Mario", DATA["Monte Mario", SPHEROID["International
  1924", 6378388.0, 297.0, AUTHORITY["EPSG","7022"]],
  TOWGS84[-168.6, -34, -38.6, -0.374, -0.679, -1.379, -
  9.48],AUTHORITY["EPSG","6265"]], PRIMEM["Greenwich", 0.0,
  AUTHORITY["EPSG","8901"]], UNIT["degree",
  0.017453292519943295], AXIS["Geodetic longitude", EAST],
  AXIS["Geodetic latitude", NORTH]],
  PROJECTION["Transverse_Mercator",
  AUTHORITY["EPSG","9807"]], PARAMETER["central_meridian",
```

```
9.0], PARAMETER["latitude_of_origin", 0.0],
PARAMETER["scale_factor", 0.9996],
PARAMETER["false_easting", 1500000.0],
PARAMETER["false_northing", 0.0], UNIT["m", 1.0],
AXIS["Easting", EAST], AXIS["Northing", NORTH],
AUTHORITY["EPSG","3003"]]
```

4. Restart GeoServer, go to **Reprojection console**, and insert the same values from step 1. Look at the result of the transformation:

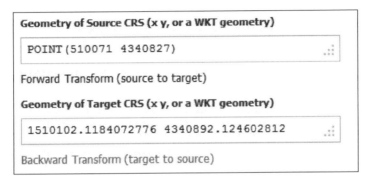

Geometry of Source CRS (x y, or a WKT geometry)

POINT (510071 4340827)

Forward Transform (source to target)

Geometry of Target CRS (x y, or a WKT geometry)

1510102.1184072776 4340892.124602812

Backward Transform (target to source)

How it works...

As you saw, there was a sensible distance between the two points. If you want to calculate it exactly, you can use the WPS Request builder, which was discussed in *Chapter 4, Geoprocessing*. The actual distance between the two points is around 59 meters, which is not acceptable in a simple map. What went wrong with one of the two transformations and what did you do to get the new one?

In fact, in many cases, there are several transformations among the two data and you have to select the proper one to use according to the area of the earth where your data is located.

In this recipe, you're transforming a point located in the area of Cagliari, Italy. The source coordinates are in the WGS84 data, while the target CRS is the Monte Mario, a local data widely used in Italy.

If you go to the official EPSG database, you will find that among WGS84 and Monte Mario, there are several different transformations. GeoServer alone, of course, cannot decide which transformation is the better one for any case. Hence, it always uses a default one. You should instead, as we're going to do, select the proper transformation according to the area where your data is located.

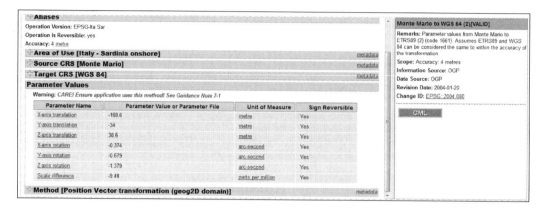

As you can see from the information in the preceding screenshot for Sardinia, a major Italian island where Cagliari is located, the best accuracy is delivered with a different set of parameters.

To force GeoServer, using these parameters, you can create a custom EPSG code or override an existing one.

In this recipe, we override the `3003` official EPSG code. To do this, we created a custom WKT definition and inserted them in the `epsg_overrides.properties` file. GeoServer checks whether this file exists at the start and gets any valid EPSG code that is there inside it, overriding the WKT to the one contained in the EPSG database.

You can insert the code you need here; just ensure that you delete the EPSG code inside the WKT for the element you are going to customize.

If you compare the original WKT for `3003` and the one you inserted in the overrides file, there are two differences: the `TOWGS84` parameters and the absence of the `AUTHORITY["EPSG","4265"]` identification for the geographic CRS Monte Mario.

If you want to add a custom code, you need to insert the same code in the `epsg.properties` file in the same folder. In this case, you can't use the `3003` code, but you have to define a custom code, for instance `103003`. Then, you can use your custom code in GeoServer as the official one.

Setting up GeoWebCache – how to make pre-rendered tiles for high availability

One of the main uses of GeoServer is that it acts as a map server. It gets your data, applies styles and other transformations, and outputs pretty maps.

Every time a client requests a map to visualize, GeoServer has to perform a complex set of operations, load data, apply styles, render the result to a bitmap, and push it back to the client who performed the request. As your web application gains popularity, more and more concurrent requests will add and you could run out of resource to satisfy them all.

Having to build the map from scratch every time seems like nonsense, especially if your web application does not offer the user the possibility to modify styles for layers. In many cases, the styles are defined once and never, or very rarely, updated. So, your GeoServer instance will render lots of identical maps.

Indeed, when you are requesting a map to GeoServer, the chances are that the same map was produced before. We need a procedure to store maps and to retrieve them when required and match them for equality. This is a more general problem and is not specifically linked to GeoServer. Several systems to implement map caching exist. Earlier, GeoServer releases didn't include any caching mechanism and you had to set a software in front of GeoServer intercepting map requests and forward only those that can't get a hit from the cache to GeoServer.

In this recipe, you will learn how to use the included GeoWebCache.

How to do it...

1. Locate your `webapps` folder inside the Apache Tomcat installation folder:

    ```
    $ cd /opt/Tomcat7042/webapps/
    ```

2. Go to the `geoserver/WEB-INF` folder:

    ```
    $ cd geoserver/WEB-INF/
    ```

3. Open the `web.xml` file and locate the line that contains the following code:

    ```
    <display-name>GeoServer</display-name>
    ```

4. There are several other parameters already defined. We will insert a new one to set the GeoWebCache folder location. You may enter the following code just after the previous line. The `param-value` is valorized with a folder path valid on Linux (use the appropriate syntax on Windows):

```
<!-- Setting GeoWebCache folder  -->
  <context-param>
    <param-name>GEOWEBCACHE_CACHE_DIR</param-name>
    <param-value>/opt/gwc</param-value>
  </context-param>
```

5. Save the file and close it. Now, go to the Tomcat manager application to reload GeoServer. All the parameters you changed from the web administration interface don't need to be reloaded to be effective. Instead, GeoServer reads the `web.xml` file on startup, so any change inside it is effective only after an application reload or a servlet container restarts.

6. Open your browser and go to `http://localhost:8080/manager/html/list`. Locate GeoServer in the application list and click on the **Reload** button on the left.

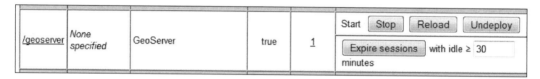

7. After a while, depending on the complexity of your configuration, a success message appears.

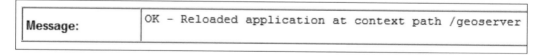

8. Now, go to the **Tile Layers** section on the **Administration** interface of GeoServer and browse the list to find the **NaturalEarth:populatedplaces** layer. From the drop-down list, select a combination of SRS and image format, for example, `EPSG:4326/jpeg`. A new map preview will show up in the browser window.

9. Navigate the map by panning and zooming. Each operation will request tiles to GeoWebCache; since this is the first time you use it, they have to be requested to GeoServer and stored for use in the future. Now, close the map and click on the **Tile Layers** link in the administration interface. When you go to the row showing the information for the layer, you can see that now there is a number showing the disk storage used by tiles.

		NaturalEarth:populatedplaces	N/A	4.33 MB	✓	Select One ▼	Seed/Truncate | Empty

How it works...

You configured the storage location for your tiles. By default, GeoWebCache stores them in the `temp` folder located inside the Tomcat installation location. For the production site, it is a good idea to use a folder on a different device. Also, try to avoid storing tiles on the same disk where the data is stored.

As map requests reach GeoServer, the size of the cache may grow very fast and can also fill your disk if you are caching a lot of layers. You may want to set a disk quota to avoid filesystem corruption.

You may also want to override the default setting of GeoServer that sets all layers to be cached. Cache is very useful with static data; if you have layers with data source updating very frequently, having them cached is a waste of time and may produce maps that do not reflect the actual state of the data.

There are several configuration parameters for GeoWebCache. We will explore them in detail in *Chapter 6, Automating GeoServer Configurations*.

Storing configurations in an RDBMS

Since the first few releases, GeoServer stores configuration data in a folder. This is the default way to persist information and is also the most used method. It allows you to configure a cluster configuration, with more than one GeoServer instance pointing at the same directory. In order to avoid data corruption, you just have to disable the integrated GeoWebCache and carefully avoid editing configuration from more than one GeoServer admin interface at the same time.

 For more information about how to configure GeoServer to run multiple instances in parallel, refer to my previous book, *GeoServer's Beginners Guide, Packt Publishing*.

Are you wondering whether there is a way to store configuration data in an RDBMS? Indeed, there is one option—a community module that you may add to your installation.

The JDBCConfig module lets you use a relational database, such as PostgreSQL, to store GeoServer configurations.

How to do it...

1. First of all, you need to download the JDBCConfig community module to enable GeoServer to store configurations in a database. Since it is not a released extension, you won't find it in the stable branch download page at `http://geoserver.org/release/maintain/`.

2. In fact, you have to go to the nightly build page at `http://ares.boundlessgeo.com/geoserver/` and select the branch for your version, 2.5.x for instance. Here, you will be pointed to a repository with the last builds.

Index of /geoserver/2.5.x/community-latest

Name	Last modified	Size	Description
Parent Directory		-	
geoserver-2.5-SNAPSHOT-aggregate-plugin.zip	14-Apr-2014 16:34	65K	
geoserver-2.5-SNAPSHOT-authkey-plugin.zip	14-Apr-2014 16:34	28K	
geoserver-2.5-SNAPSHOT-colormap-plugin.zip	14-Apr-2014 16:34	17K	
geoserver-2.5-SNAPSHOT-dds-plugin.zip	14-Apr-2014 16:34	6.1M	
geoserver-2.5-SNAPSHOT-ftp-plugin.zip	14-Apr-2014 16:34	868K	
geoserver-2.5-SNAPSHOT-geopkg-plugin.zip	14-Apr-2014 16:34	4.9M	
geoserver-2.5-SNAPSHOT-groovy-plugin.zip	14-Apr-2014 16:34	20M	
geoserver-2.5-SNAPSHOT-javascript-plugin.zip	14-Apr-2014 16:34	1.8M	
geoserver-2.5-SNAPSHOT-jdbcconfig-plugin.zip	14-Apr-2014 16:34	96K	
geoserver-2.5-SNAPSHOT-mbtiles-plugin.zip	14-Apr-2014 16:34	4.9M	

3. Select the `community-latest` folder and download the `geoserver-2.5-SNAPSHOT-jdbcconfig-plugin.zip` file.

4. After unpacking the archive, you'll find that it contains a `.jar` file. Move it to the `<GEOSERVER_HOME>/WEB-INF/lib` folder.

5. Now, restart your servlet container. After it restarts, you can find a new folder in the GeoServer data directory; it is called `jdbcconfig` and it contains three files:

```
-rw-r--r--  1 root root  506 jdbcconfig.properties
-rw-r--r--  1 root root 1.5K jdbcconfig.properties.h2
-rw-r--r--  1 root root 2.2K jdbcconfig.properties.postgres
drwxr-xr-x  2 root root 4.0K scripts/
```

6. Stop Tomcat and open the `jdbcconfig.properties.postgres` file. Inside, there are a lot of comments. You only need to set connection parameters according to your PostgreSQL instance:

```
enabled=true
initdb=true
initScript=${GEOSERVER_DATA_DIR}/jdbcconfig/scripts/initdb.
  postgres.sql
import=true
jdbcUrl=jdbc\:postgresql\://localhost\:5432/gscatalog
driverClassName=org.postgresql.Driver
username=postgres
password=postgres
```

7. Save the file and substitute it with the configuration file read by GeoServer:

```
$ mv jdbcconfig.properties jdbcconfig.properties.bck
$ mv jdbcconfig.properties.postgres jdbcconfig.properties
```

8. Restart GeoServer. It will now create the database structure and import configurations into it.

9. Now, check whether the `jdbcconfig.properties` file was changed by GeoServer. As GeoServer terminated, the import of your configuration changed the `initdb` and `import` parameters to false so that the database configuration won't be overwritten at the next restart:

```
enabled=true
initdb=false
import=false
```

10. You can also check whether all went well by logging in to the GeoServer admin interface and pointing at the main page. You should see a message similar to this one:

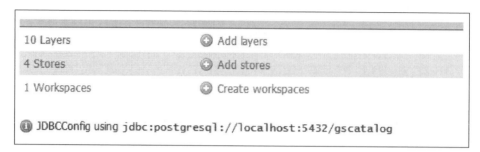

How it works...

You may be already familiar with the GeoServer data directory. It contains a structured set of XML files, grouped in folders, where all information about GeoServer configuration is stored.

When you installed the JDBCConfig module, the `initdb` was set to true. So GeoServer created a set of objects in the database, which are places for the configuration data to be stored inside. If you use a PostgreSQL client, such as pgAdmin, you may have a look at what was created inside the database.

pgAdmin is the most famous GUI interface to administer PostgreSQL. It is released under the open source license and you may find binaries for the main OS or source code to compile and build for yourself. Consult `http://www.pgadmin.org/` for more information.

If it seems an overkill to install a full admin client just to have a look at simple data, you may go with psql, the command-line client. It is shipped with PostgreSQL, so you can use it to avoid any extra installation.

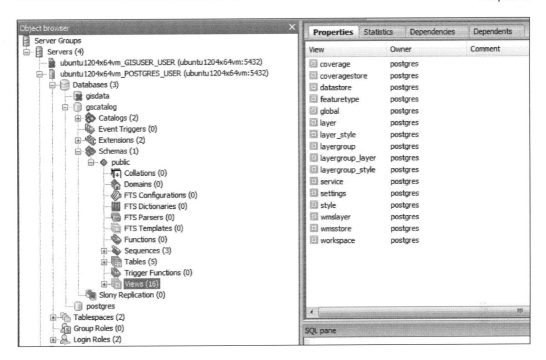

There are three tables where the data is really stored and 16 views that filter data according to homogeneous categories; layer view, for instance, lets you browse what layers are configured on your GeoServer:

```
$ psql -U postgres -d gscatalog
gscatalog=# select name, type, enabled, default_style from layer
  limit 3;
         name         |  type  | enabled | default_style
----------------------+--------+---------+---------------
 GeneralizedCountries | VECTOR | true    |      27
 roads                | VECTOR | true    |      21
 countries            | VECTOR | true    |      27
```

Try to change the default style or enabled property of some layers and check how the data gets updated in the database.

What does the value inside the default style field mean? Run another query:

```
gscatalog=# select name, filename from style where oid = 27;
   name    |        filename
-----------+----------------------
 polygon   | default_polygon.sld
```

So, it is pointing yet to a file that is not stored inside the database.

In fact, the module is at an early stage and while it lets you import a part of your configuration data, it will not leverage you by using the data directory folder where all information not stored in the database is actually stored.

6

Automating GeoServer Configurations

In this chapter, we will cover the following recipes:

- ▶ Managing workspaces with REST
- ▶ Creating and editing data stores with REST
- ▶ Managing layers with REST
- ▶ Uploading and updating styles with REST
- ▶ Managing layers with the GWC REST API
- ▶ Managing cache tiles with the GWC REST API

Introduction

So what is REST? The acronym stands for Representational State Transfer, which defines client-server interaction in terms of state transition. Each request from the client is a transition to a new state. The response sent by a server represents the application state after the transition.

Does it sound too complicated? If you are used to a stateful client server interaction, you will find REST unconventional. REST is stateless; once you get the general idea, you will discover it is very simple. A very important thing that you have to keep in mind is that each request is self-contained and you are never constrained to execute an operations chain or to open a session before making requests. That being said, it is always possible to create a complex workflow where several requests are chained to perform a task.

Although REST is commonly considered as a web interface, it is much more. The term REST was defined by Roy T. Fielding, one of the main people behind HTTP protocol design, in his PhD thesis. REST describes how clients and servers interact and do it abstracting from any communication protocol. You could also develop a REST interface without HTTP.

You can read the original work of Roy T. Fielding at `http://www.ics.uci.edu/~fielding/pubs/dissertation/top.htm`.

A more lightweight approach on REST can be found at `http://en.wikipedia.org/wiki/Representational_State_Transfer`.

The GeoServer REST interface uses HTTP and defines a set of operations and resources. Operations are derived from HTTP so you can perform the `GET`, `POST`, `PUT`, and `DELETE` operations. Resources are the building blocks of GeoServer configuration: workspaces, data stores, layers, and so on.

In the recipes of this chapter, we will use both cURL and Python to perform the same operations. Examples are showed in a Linux shell but cURL and Python syntax are identical in Windows shell.

REST defines a set of operations defined from the HTTP protocol, so how can you interact with it? Using a browser can be a common way to send HTTP requests to a server; you do it almost every day when you browse the Internet and you do it with the GeoServer web interface! However, using a browser is not a simple way to automate tasks; it requires human interaction. On the contrary, we need something that enables us to build small programs.

There are a lot of different tools that let you interact with REST. You can use programming languages such as Java or PHP or script languages such as PowerShell in Windows or any Linux shell. In this chapter, we will see examples in a programming language, Python, and with cURL. Python is a programming language that leverages on simplicity and code readability, and hence it is very easy to create small programs with it. cURL is a library and a command-line tool that can easily be incorporated in simple shell scripts. Both tools allow users to concentrate on what the program should do without being distracted by a complex syntax.

In this chapter, it is assumed that you have a working installation of Python and cURL. If you are using a Linux box, it is quite probable you have both already installed and configured, or you can rely on your distribution package system to install a recent release.

For Windows, you can get Python from the project site at `http://python.org/`.

cURL is available as a source, for the brave, or as binary packages from `http://curl.haxx.se/download.html`.

Managing workspaces with REST

Now that you are familiar with REST, it is time to get your hands on GeoServer and have a look at how its REST interface works.

Basically, it exposes operations to you so that you can manage all configurations' objects. You will find the same items, for example, layers and styles, which you are used to creating from the web interface.

In this first recipe, you will start with workspaces and namespaces, which are the logical groups that contain all other configuration's items.

Getting ready

We stated before that Python's main aims are simplicity and code readability; unfortunately, this is not always the case. Interacting with REST using standard Python libraries may be painful and very verbose. Luckily, there is an open source project that solves this problem. The project produced a library called `Requests` and I have to say, it is a really appropriate name.

`Requests` is an open source project started by Kenneth Reitz. You can download and use it liberally; it is released under the ISC license. You can also fork it on GitHub and add features. Refer to `http://docs.python-requests.org/en/latest/`.

Let's install it!

1. As the first step, you need to download the ZIP or TAR archive containing the library code:

   ```
   $ wget https://github.com/kennethreitz/requests/tarball/master
     -O master.tar.gz

   $ ls -al
   drwxrwxr-x 2 stefano stefano   4096 Oct 15 08:01 ./
   ```

```
drwxr-xr-x 9 stefano stefano   4096 Oct 15 07:41 ../
-rw-rw-r-- 1 stefano stefano 720204 Oct 15 08:02 master.tar.gz
```

2. Now extract the archive's content:

   ```
   $ tar xvfz master.tar.gz
   ```
   ...

3. Enter the new folder and install it in your site packages easily using the following command lines:

   ```
   $ cd kennethreitz-requests-07f9a7e
   $ sudo python setup.py install
   ```

4. The installation is now complete; check it by opening Python and importing the new library:

   ```
   $ python
   Python 2.7.3 (default, Feb 27 2014, 19:58:35)
   [GCC 4.6.3] on linux2
   Type "help", "copyright", "credits" or "license" for more
     information.
   >>> import requests
   >>> resp = requests.get
     ('http://geoserver.org/display/GEOS/License')
   >>> resp.text
   u'<!DOCTYPE html PUBLIC "-//W3C//DTD XHTML 1.0
     Transitional//EN" "http://www.w3.org/TR/xhtml1/DTD/xhtml1-
     transitional.dtd">    \n<html
     xmlns="http://www.w3.org/1999/xhtml" xml:lang="en"
     lang="en">\n<head>\n    <title>License - GeoServer</title> ...
   ```

You just installed the Requests library as a site package inside your Python installation. Furthermore, by asking for the license page on the GeoServer site, you also had your first taste of its power and simplicity. You can now use it inside any Python program, leveraging on its powerful objects to interact with the HTTP protocol.

 Please note that REST operations require authentication, so you need to supply the user ID and password for the GeoServer administrator or a user you defined and granted the admin role to. In these recipes, the default admin/geoserver values are used; replace them with proper values for your system.

How to do it...

1. Let's start by looking at which workspaces are defined in your GeoServer instance. This requires a GET operation. The following code snippet shows you the syntax:

```
$ curl -u admin:geoserver -v -XGET -H 'Accept: text/xml'
  http://localhost:8080/geoserver/rest/workspaces -o
  workspaces.xml
```

2. As you specified the verbose -v parameter on the command line, a lot of information is displayed. Note the line reporting the status code of operation to check whether it was successful:

```
> User-Agent: curl/7.22.0 (x86_64-pc-linux-gnu) libcurl/7.22.0
  OpenSSL/1.0.1 zlib/1.2.3.4 libidn/1.23 librtmp/2.3

> Host: localhost:8080

> Accept: text/xml

>

< HTTP/1.1 200 OK
```

3. As you can easily see, a new file was created in your local folder and named workspace.xml; check that its length is not equal to zero. The code is as follows:

```
$ ll

total 12K

drwxrwxr-x  2 stefano stefano 4.0K May  1 16:10 ./

drwxr-xr-x 20 stefano stefano 4.0K May  1 16:10 ../

-rw-rw-r--  1 stefano stefano  254 May  1 16:15 workspaces.xml
```

4. Before actually looking at what is inside it, we'll perform the analog operation using Python:

```
$ python

Python 2.7.3 (default, Feb 27 2014, 19:58:35)

[GCC 4.6.3] on linux2

Type "help", "copyright", "credits" or "license" for more
  information.

>>> import requests

>>> myUrl = 'http://localhost:8080/geoserver/rest/workspaces'

>>> headers = {'Accept': 'text/xml'}

>>> resp = requests.get(myUrl,auth=('admin','geoserver'),
  headers=headers)

>>> resp.status_code

200
```

5. Also, your Python code successfully retrieved information. Now, save it in a file so that you can compare it with that retrieved by cURL:

```
>>> file = open('workspaces_py.xml','w')
>>> file.write(resp.text)
>>> file.close()
```

6. Before opening the files and looking at the XML code, check whether there is any difference among them:

```
$ diff workspaces.xml workspaces_py.xml
$
```

7. As you probably guessed, the two files are identical. Now, open one of them and examine its content:

```
<workspaces>
  <workspace>
    <name>NaturalEarth</name>
    <atom:link xmlns:atom="http://www.w3.org/2005/Atom"
      rel="alternate" href="http://localhost:8080
      /geoserver/rest/workspaces/NaturalEarth.xml"
      type="application/xml"/>
  </workspace>
</workspaces>
```

8. Now retrieve details about the workspace with a new request using cURL:

```
$ curl -u admin:geoserver -XGET -H 'Accept: text/xml'
  http://localhost:8080/geoserver/rest/namespaces/NaturalEarth
  -o NaturalEarth.xml
```

9. To do the same with Python, you can reuse the previous code by just changing the URL to be requested and the file where the response will be saved:

```
...
>>> myUrl = 'http://localhost:8080/
  geoserver/rest/namespaces/NaturalEarth'
...
file = open('NaturalEarth_py.xml','w')
...
```

10. After examining the content, you will find the same information displayed in the web interface:

```
<namespace>
  <prefix>NaturalEarth</prefix>
  <uri>http://www.naturalearthdata.com/</uri>
  <featureTypes>
```

```
        <atom:link xmlns:atom="http://www.w3.org/2005/Atom"
            rel="alternate" href="http://localhost:8080/geoserver
            /rest/workspaces/NaturalEarth/featuretypes.xml"
            type="application/xml"/>
    </featureTypes>
</namespace>
```

11. You are now going to create a new workspace and define a URI for it. You need to create an XML file with the same structure as the previous response, as in this example:

```
<namespace>
    <prefix>MyOrganization</prefix>
    <uri>http://www.someone.org/</uri>
</namespace>
```

12. Now send the data to GeoServer using cURL:

```
$ curl -u admin:geoserver -XPOST -H 'Content-type: text/xml' -
d @MyOrganization.xml http://localhost:8080/
geoserver/rest/namespaces
```

13. You can do the same with Python; however, change the workspace to be created or you will receive an HTTP 500 for an internal server error. Indeed you can't create a duplicated namespace. The code is follows:

```
>>> myUrl =  'http://localhost:8080/geoserver/rest/namespaces'
>>> file = open('MyOrganization.xml','r')
>>> payload = file.read()
>>> headers = {'Content-type': 'text/xml'}
>>> resp = requests.post(myUrl, auth=('admin','geoserver'),
    data=payload, headers=headers)
>>> resp.status_code
201
```

How it works...

In this recipe, you learned how to manage workspaces and namespaces. In GeoServer, a workspace is a logical object that you can use to group together data stores, feature types, coverages, and styles.

What's the difference between a workspace and a namespace? You first queried GeoServer for the `NaturalEarth` workspace and obtained its properties, which is basically a name:

```
<name>NaturalEarth</name>
```

A namespace associated with a workspace that is in the form of a **Uniform Resource Identifier** (**URI**) and typically a URL always exists. Although you can insert any URL, it is usually a good choice to select something that is associated with your project.

Workspaces and namespace are very similar and, in fact, you created both by calling the namespace operation, perhaps with an added trailing identifier indicating the workspace.

The GeoServer REST interface exposes resources for each one of them; there are two resources that you can use to access these elements:

▸ `/workspaces`

▸ `/namespaces`

On both the resources, GET, POST, PUT, and DELETE operations are defined. This allows you to view, create, update, and delete workspaces and namespaces.

You have to use GET when you just want to retrieve information. If you want to create a new object, POST comes in handy. PUT is used to change properties of an existing item, while DELETE lets you remove items.

As GeoServer REST interface uses the HTTP protocol, you should always look for the return code. This lets you know whether your request was successfully implemented by the server or some errors arose.

> For a detailed list of operations supported and the HTTP status code expected, refer to the online GeoServer manual at `http://docs.geoserver.org/stable/en/user/rest/api/index.html`.

There's more...

If you changed your mind about the URI assigned to a namespace, you don't need to delete it. You can change it with a PUT request like this:

```
$ curl -u admin:geoserver -XPUT -H 'Content-type: text/xml' -H
  'Accept: text/xml' -d '<namespace><prefix>MyOrganization</prefix>
  <uri>http://about.me/geoserver</uri></namespace>'
  http://localhost:8080/geoserver/rest/namespaces/MyOrganization
```

Note that this time we didn't create a static file to submit information. In fact, the -d cURL parameter accepts the data on the command line as well. While this may be useful for less data, when your XML code grows, a file is a more appropriate approach.

Going to the web interface, you can see that the URI was actually changed.

Name

MyOrganization

Namespace URI

http://about.me/geoserver

The namespace uri associated with this workspace

The following Python code lets you perform the same operation:

```
>>> myUrl =  'http://localhost:8080/geoserver/rest/
  namespaces/MyOrganization'
>>> payload = '<namespace><prefix>MyOrganization</prefix>
  <uri>http://about.me/geoserver</uri></namespace>'
>>> headers = {'Content-type': 'text/xml'}
>>> resp = requests.put(myUrl, auth=('admin','geoserver'),
  data=payload, headers=headers)
>>> resp.status_code
200
```

To finish our tour of workspaces operations, we have to try the DELETE option. Let's remove the MyOrganization workspace:

```
$ curl -u admin:geoserver -XDELETE -H 'Accept: text/xml'
  http://localhost:8080/geoserver/rest/workspaces/MyOrganization
```

Here is the command to do so in Python:

```
>>> myUrl =  'http://localhost:8080/geoserver/rest/workspaces/
MyOrganization'
>>> headers = {'Accept': 'text/xml'}
>>> resp = requests.delete(myUrl, auth=('admin','geoserver'),
  headers=headers)
>>> resp.status_code
404
```

Can you guess why we got a 404 error?

404 stands for Not Found error (http://en.wikipedia.org/wiki/HTTP_404). You probably wondering whether the Python code contains an error.

This is not the case; it is just that we removed the workspace using cURL and obviously, you can't remove a nonexisting workspace. So, GeoServer complains when we try to remove it.

Creating and editing data stores with REST

Data stores connect GeoServer to your data. You can't use data that is not supported by GeoServer without a built-in connector or a plugin. Of course, the REST interface supports all operations on data stores. If you plan to automate GeoServer configurations, it is very important to understand how data stores can be created and edited.

The resource exposed is in the following form:

```
/workspaces/<ws>/datastores
```

Here, `ws` stands for the workspace on which the data store is linked.

How to do it...

1. As usual, you can use the GET operation to retrieve information about which data stores are available in the configuration for a specific workspace. Let's retrieve information in Python:

   ```
   >>> myUrl = 'http://localhost:8080/geoserver/rest/
   workspaces/NaturalEarth/datastores'
   >>> headers = {'Accept': 'text/xml'}
   >>> resp = requests.get(myUrl,auth=('admin','geoserver'),
   headers=headers)
   ```

2. Now do the same with cURL:

   ```
   $ curl -u admin:geoserver -XGET -H 'Accept: text/xml'
   http://localhost:8080/geoserver/rest/workspaces/
   NaturalEarth/datastores -o naturalEarthDataStores.xml
   ```

3. Let's look at the file content:

   ```
   <dataStores>
     <dataStore>
       <name>ShapeData</name>
       <atom:link xmlns:atom="http://www.w3.org/2005/Atom"
         rel="alternate" href="http://localhost:8080/
         geoserver/rest/workspaces/NaturalEarth/
         datastores/ShapeData.xml" type="application/xml"/>
     </dataStore>
     <dataStore>
       <name>GeneralizedCountries</name>
       <atom:link xmlns:atom="http://www.w3.org/2005/Atom"
         rel="alternate" href="http://localhost:8080
         /geoserver/rest/workspaces/NaturalEarth/
         datastores/GeneralizedCountries.xml"
         type="application/xml"/>
   ```

```
  </dataStore>
  <dataStore>
    <name>PostGISLocal</name>
    <atom:link xmlns:atom="http://www.w3.org/2005/Atom"
      rel="alternate" href="http://localhost:8080/
        geoserver/rest/workspaces/NaturalEarth/
        datastores/PostGISLocal.xml"
        type="application/xml"/>
  </dataStore>
</dataStores>
```

4. There are three data stores. Now, retrieve information about the PostGIS data source using cURL:

```
$ curl -u admin:geoserver -XGET -H 'Accept: text/xml'
  http://localhost:8080/geoserver/rest/
  workspaces/NaturalEarth/datastores/PostGISLocal -o
  PostGISLocal.xml
```

5. Next, retrieve information using Python:

```
>>> myUrl = 'http://localhost:8080/geoserver/rest/
  workspaces/NaturalEarth/datastores/PostGISLocal'

>>> headers = {'Accept': 'text/xml'}

>>> resp = requests.get(myUrl,auth=('admin','geoserver'),
  headers=headers)

>>> file = open(PostGISLocal_py.xml','w')

>>> file.write(resp.text)

>>> file.close()
```

6. Examine the content:

```
<dataStore>
  <name>PostGISLocal</name>
  <type>PostGIS</type>
  <enabled>true</enabled>
  <workspace>
    <name>NaturalEarth</name>
    <atom:link xmlns:atom="http://www.w3.org/2005/Atom"
      rel="alternate" href="http://localhost:8080
      /geoserver/rest/workspaces/NaturalEarth.xml"
      type="application/xml"/>
  </workspace>
  <connectionParameters>
    <entry key="Connection timeout">20</entry>
    <entry key="port">5432</entry>
    <entry key="passwd">crypt1:
      xbeWyWda+hqHCf456TK0Gg==</entry>
```

```
      <entry key="dbtype">postgis</entry>
      <entry key="host">localhost</entry>
      <entry key="validate connections">true</entry>
      <entry key="encode functions">false</entry>
      <entry key="max connections">10</entry>
      <entry key="database">gisdata</entry>
      <entry key="namespace">http://www.naturalearthdata.com/
        </entry>
      <entry key="schema">public</entry>
      <entry key="Loose bbox">true</entry>
      <entry key="Expose primary keys">false</entry>
      <entry key="Max open prepared statements">50</entry>
      <entry key="fetch size">1000</entry>
      <entry key="preparedStatements">false</entry>
      <entry key="Estimated extends">true</entry>
      <entry key="user">gisuser</entry>
      <entry key="min connections">1</entry>
    </connectionParameters>
    <__default>false</__default>
    <featureTypes>
      <atom:link xmlns:atom="http://www.w3.org/2005/Atom"
        rel="alternate" href="http://localhost:8080/
        geoserver/rest/workspaces/NaturalEarth/datastores/
        PostGISLocal/featuretypes.xml"
        type="application/xml"/>
    </featureTypes>
  </dataStore>
```

7. Prepare an XML file to create a new data store pointing to PostGIS in the new workspace created in the previous recipe:

```
<dataStore>
  <name>myPostGIS</name>
  <description>PostGIS local instance</description>
  <type>PostGIS</type>
  <enabled>true</enabled>
  <connectionParameters>
    <entry key="host">localhost</entry>
    <entry key="port">5432</entry>
    <entry key="database"> gisdata</entry>
    <entry key="schema">public</entry>
    <entry key="user">gisuser</entry>
    <entry key="passwd"> gisuser </entry>
    <entry key="dbtype">postgis</entry>
    <entry key="validate connections">true</entry>
    <entry key="Connection timeout">20</entry>
```

```
        <entry key="min connections">1</entry>
        <entry key="max connections">10</entry>
        <entry key="Loose bbox">true</entry>
        <entry key="fetch size">1000</entry>
        <entry key="Max open prepared statements">50</entry>
        <entry key="Estimated extends">true</entry>
    </connectionParameters>
    <__default>false</__default>
</dataStore>
```

8. Now use a cURL call to create your new PostGIS source:

    ```
    $ curl -u admin:geoserver -XPOST -d @postgis.xml -H 'Content-
    type: text/xml' -H 'Accept: text/xml' http://localhost:8080
    /geoserver/rest/workspaces/MyOrganization/datastores
    ```

9. Go to the web interface and you will find the new data store.

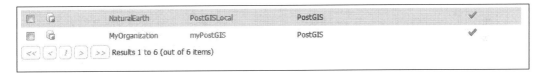

10. You can do the same using Python:

    ```
    >>> myUrl = 'http://localhost:8080/geoserver/rest
      /workspaces/MyOrganization/datastores'
    >>> file = open('postgis.xml','r')
    >>> payload = file.read()
    >>> headers = {'Content-type': 'text/xml','Accept':
      'text/xml'}
    >>> resp = requests.post(myUrl, auth=('admin','geoserver'),
      data=payload, headers=headers)
    >>> resp.status_code
    201
    ```

How it works...

The REST syntax is not different from that used in the previous recipe. What's changed is that the objects that you're using and data stores are more complicated objects than workspaces, so you found a lot of information in the XML file.

If you're wondering which request will get you a list of all data stores configured on GeoServer, I am sorry to tell you it does not exist. You have to query each workspace. You can request the workspace's list and iterate on items to retrieve all data stores.

You have to remember that data stores are heterogeneous. The connection parameter tag may contain very different elements, depending on the data store type, for example, a shapefile data store won't have a user ID, password, TCP port, and similar properties that only make sense when connecting to a database.

Try to query the BlueMarble data store we created in *Chapter 1, Working with Vectors*:

```
$ curl -u admin:geoserver -XGET -H 'Accept: text/xml'
  http://localhost:8080/geoserver/rest/workspaces
  /NaturalEarth/coveragestores/BlueMarble -o BlueMarble.xml
```

Please note that in the URL, we send the request to `coveragestores` and not `datastores`; the latter is only for vector data. The raster data stored in the filesystem is included in the `coveragestores` collection.

Examining the result, you can note that there is a reference to the actual raster file and its location:

```xml
<coverageStore>
  <name>BlueMarble</name>
  <type>GeoTIFF</type>
  <enabled>true</enabled>
  <workspace>
    <name>NaturalEarth</name>
    <atom:link xmlns:atom="http://www.w3.org/2005/Atom"
    rel="alternate" href="http://localhost:8080/geoserver/
    rest/workspaces/NaturalEarth.xml" type="application/xml"/>
  </workspace>
  <__default>false</__default>
  <url>file:data/blueMarble/blueMarble.tiff</url>
  <coverages>
    <atom:link xmlns:atom="http://www.w3.org/2005/Atom"
      rel="alternate" href="http://localhost:8080/
      geoserver/rest/workspaces/NaturalEarth
      /coveragestores/BlueMarble/coverages.xml"
      type="application/xml"/>
  </coverages>
</coverageStore>
```

There's more...

In this recipe, you created a data store for a PostGIS database; of course, you can also create it for a simple shapefile. In this case, you can also deliver the data with a REST operation.

We will use the coastline shapefile from the Natural Earth site; locate it at `http://www.naturalearthdata.com/downloads/110m-physical-vectors/`, save the ZIP file on your filesystem, and then execute the following Python code:

```
>>> myUrl =  'http://localhost:8080/geoserver/
  rest/workspaces/NaturalEarth/datastores/Coastline/file.shp'
>>> file = open('ne_110m_coastline.zip','rb')
>>> payload = file.read()
>>> headers = {'Content-type': 'application/zip'}
>>> resp = requests.put(myUrl, auth=('admin','geoserver'),
  data=payload, headers=headers)
>>> resp.status_code
201
```

You loaded the file and sent it to GeoServer, creating a new data store for it. Now look at the web interface and list the data stores; there is a new one.

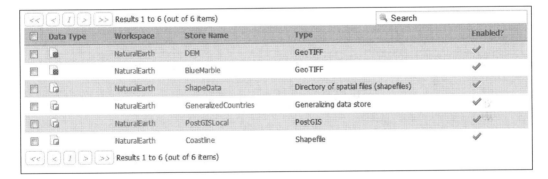

Of course, a new layer is listed.

Data stores that work with multiple files, such as the shapefile store, must be sent as a ZIP archive. When uploading a standalone file, set `Content-type` appropriately based on the file type. If you are loading a ZIP archive, set `Content-type` to `application/zip`.

Managing layers with REST

In the previous recipe, you loaded a shapefile with REST. A data store and a layer were created and your data is now published on WMS. If you go to the layer preview page and select the **ne_110m_coastline layer** layer, you should see a map like this:

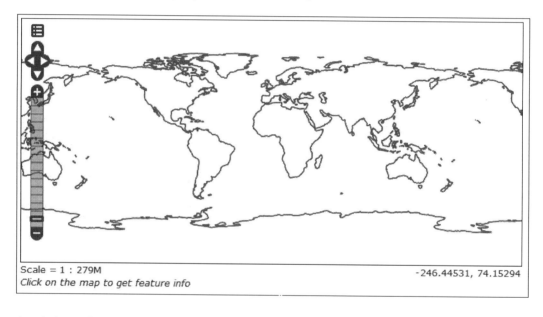

A style is applied to the data and all mandatory layer parameters were compiled by GeoServer when you issued the data store creation request.

While this is enough to get data properly configured on your server, in a real-world case your automation workflow should provide more control over data publication. The GeoServer REST interface gives you control over the layer item. In this recipe, you will see how to create a new layer and edit an existing one.

How to do it...

1. Let's retrieve information from the **ne_110m_coastline** layer:

```
$ curl -u admin:geoserver -XGET -H 'Accept: text/xml'
  http://localhost:8080/geoserver/rest/
  layers/ne_110m_coastline -o ne_110m_coastline.xml
```

2. Now let's perform the same operation using Python:

```
>>> myUrl = 'http://localhost:8080/geoserver
  /rest/layers/ne_110m_coastline'
>>> headers = {'Accept': 'text/xml'}
>>> resp = requests.get(myUrl, auth=('admin','geoserver'),
  headers=headers)
```

3. Open the XML file containing details about the layer:

```xml
<layer>
  <name>ne_110m_coastline</name>
  <type>VECTOR</type>
  <defaultStyle>
    <name>line</name>
    <atom:link xmlns:atom="http://www.w3.org/2005/Atom"
      rel="alternate" href="http://localhost:8080/
      geoserver/rest/styles/line.xml"
      type="application/xml"/>
  </defaultStyle>
  <resource class="featureType">
    <name>ne_110m_coastline</name>
    <atom:link xmlns:atom="http://www.w3.org/2005/Atom"
      rel="alternate" href="http://localhost:8080/
      geoserver/rest/workspaces/NaturalEarth/
      datastores/Coastline/featuretypes/
      ne_110m_coastline.xml" type="application/xml"/>
  </resource>
  <attribution>
    <logoWidth>0</logoWidth>
    <logoHeight>0</logoHeight>
  </attribution>
</layer>
```

4. There is a link to the feature type used by this layer; retrieve information about it using cURL:

```
$ curl -u admin:geoserver -XGET -H 'Accept: text/xml'
  http://localhost:8080/geoserver/rest/workspaces
  /NaturalEarth/datastores/Coastline/featuretypes/
  ne_110m_coastline.xml -o ne_110m_coastline_ft.xml
```

5. As usual, you can do the same operation using the Python code:

```
>>> myUrl =  'http://localhost:8080/geoserver/rest
  /workspaces/NaturalEarth/datastores/
  Coastline/featuretypes/ne_110m_coastline.xml'
>>> headers = {'Accept': 'text/xml'}
>>> resp = requests.get(myUrl, auth=('admin','geoserver'),
  headers=headers)
```

6. The XML file contains a lot more information than that of the corresponding layer. Here, we have an extract; look at the file you extracted for a full view:

```
<featureType>
  <name>ne_110m_coastline</name>
  <nativeName>ne_110m_coastline</nativeName>
  <namespace>
    <name>NaturalEarth</name>
    <atom:link xmlns:atom="http://www.w3.org/2005/Atom"
      rel="alternate" href="http://localhost:8080/geoserver
      /rest/namespaces/NaturalEarth.xml"
      type="application/xml"/>
  </namespace>
  <title>ne_110m_coastline</title>
  <keywords>
    <string>ne_110m_coastline</string>
    <string>features</string>
  </keywords>
  <nativeCRS>
...
</nativeCRS>
  <srs>EPSG:4326</srs>
  <nativeBoundingBox>
    <minx>-180.0</minx>
    <maxx>180.00000044181039</maxx>
    <miny>-85.60903777459774</miny>
    <maxy>83.64513</maxy>
    <crs>
...
    </crs>
  </nativeBoundingBox>
```

```
    <latLonBoundingBox>
...
    </latLonBoundingBox>
    <projectionPolicy>NONE</projectionPolicy>
    <enabled>true</enabled>
    <store class="dataStore">
      <name>Coastline</name>
      <atom:link xmlns:atom="http://www.w3.org/2005/Atom"
        rel="alternate" href="http://localhost:8080/geoserver
        /rest/workspaces/NaturalEarth/datastores
        /Coastline.xml" type="application/xml"/>
    </store>
    <maxFeatures>0</maxFeatures>
    <numDecimals>0</numDecimals>
    <attributes>
      <attribute>
        <name>the_geom</name>
        <minOccurs>0</minOccurs>
        <maxOccurs>1</maxOccurs>
        <nillable>true</nillable>
        <binding>com.vividsolutions.jts.geom.
          MultiLineString</binding>
      </attribute>
...
    </attributes>
</featureType>
```

7. Now you should change the layer, using different styles to render coastline features. Prepare an XML file containing the following code and name it `changeStyle.xml`:

```
<layer>
  <defaultStyle>
    <name>simple_roads</name>
  </defaultStyle>
  <enabled>true</enabled>
</layer>
```

8. Then, make a PUT request to change configuration for the layer:

```
$ curl -u admin:geoserver -XPUT -H 'Content-type: text/xml' -d
  @changeStyle.xml http://localhost:8080/geoserver
  /rest/layers/ne_110m_coastline
```

9. To perform the same action with Python, use the following code snippet:

```
>>> myUrl =  'http://localhost:8080/geoserver/
    rest/layers/ne_110m_coastline'
>>> file = open('changeStyle.zip','r')
>>> payload = file.read()
>>> headers = {'Content-type': 'application/zip'}
>>> resp = requests.put(myUrl, auth=('admin','geoserver'),
    data=payload, headers=headers)
>>> resp.status_code
200
```

10. Now, go to the web interface and check the publishing properties for the coastline layer.

How it works...

Layers and feature types are strictly linked and some users get confused about them. If you check the **Layer** properties in the GeoServer web interface, you'll find a lot of information. However, when you retrieved the information for the coastline layer, the response contained only a few of the properties. Most of the missing information was in the response to your request for feature type:

```
$ curl -u admin:geoserver -XGET -H 'Accept: text/xml' http://
localhost:8080/geoserver/rest/workspaces/NaturalEarth/datastores/
Coastline/featuretypes/ne_110m_coastline.xml -o ne_110m_coastline_ft.xml
```

A feature type is a vector dataset configured on GeoServer, while a layer is its representation. The former contains most of the details about the data.

You may have more layers pointing to the same feature type if you want to represent them in different ways, for instance using different styles.

There's more...

As most of the vector datasets are contained in the feature type, you need to send a request to it if you want to update layer properties.

You can change the keyword and layer name and description by issuing a `PUT` request.

First of all, you need to prepare an XML file with the desired changes. You will again use the coastline layer, giving it a more concise name and a proper description:

```
<featureType>
  <name>Coastline</name>
  <nativeName>ne_110m_coastline</nativeName>
  <title>Coastline</title>
  <keywords>
    <string>Coastline</string>
    <string>Natural Earth Data</string>
  </keywords>
  <abstract>Ocean coastline, including major islands. Coastline is
  matched to land and water polygons. Courtesy of Natural Earth
  project</abstract>
  <enabled>true</enabled>
</featureType>
```

Then, you will send it to GeoServer:

```
$ curl -u admin:geoserver -XPUT -H 'Content-type: text/xml' -d
  @coastline.xml http://localhost:8080/geoserver/rest/
  workspaces/NaturalEarth/datastores/Coastline
  /featuretypes/ne_110m_coastline
```

Alternatively, the same using Python:

```
>>> myUrl = 'http://localhost:8080/geoserver/rest/
  workspaces/NaturalEarth/datastores/
  Coastline/featuretypes/ne_110m_coastline'
>>> file = open('coastline.xml','r')
>>> payload = file.read()
>>> headers = {'Content-type': 'application/zip'}
>>> resp = requests.put(myUrl, auth=('admin','geoserver'),
  data=payload, headers=headers)
>>> resp.status_code
200
```

If your data is not static, the bounding boxes should be recalculated. If you add new features that are put of the bounding box that was calculated when you first added the layer on GeoServer, you can't see them in the map until you inform GeoServer of the extent.

Again you need a `PUT` request, a very simple one, as in this case you don't need to send any XML code:

```
$ curl -u admin:geoserver -XPUT -H 'Content-type: text/xml' -d
  @coastline.xml http://localhost:8080/geoserver/rest/
  workspaces/NaturalEarth/datastores/Coastline/
  featuretypes/ne_110m_coastline&recalculate=nativebbox,latlonbbox
```

Uploading and updating styles with REST

In *Chapter 3, Advanced Styling*, you learned a lot about styles and SLD. You used a very powerful extension, the CSS module, to create styles avoiding the complexity of SLD syntax. There are many options to create SLD, and some users prefer using external tools to manage them.

Whatever you prefer to use to create and edit your styles in order to configure a proper visualization, you should upload them on GeoServer and publish them.

REST offers you two resources to manage styles:

- `/styles`
- `/workspaces/<ws>/styles`

The former points to styles not associated to a workspace while the latter contains the workspaces with associated styles.

Adding a new style is a routine task if you are going to publish data with REST. We will retrieve an existing style from GeoServer, update it, and then upload it to GeoServer as a new one.

How to do it...

1. We will use the `Capitals` style as the template for our new style. Send a request to GeoServer to retrieve it and save to the `CapitalsBlue.xml` file:

   ```
   $ curl -u admin:geoserver -XGET -H 'Accept:
     application/vnd.ogc.sld+xml' http://localhost:8080/
     geoserver/rest/styles/Capitals -o CapitalsBlue.xml
   ```

2. You can also use the following commands in Python:

   ```
   >>> myUrl = 'http://localhost:8080/geoserver
     /rest/styles/Capitals'
   >>> headers = {'Accept':'application/vnd.ogc.sld+xml'}
   ```

```
>>> resp = requests.get(myUrl, auth=('admin','geoserver'),
  headers=headers)
>>> file = open('CapitalsBlue.xml','w')
>>> file.write(resp.text)
>>> file.close()
```

3. Now open the `CapitalsBlue.xml` file. Unless you use an editor that can format XML in a more readable way, you will see just one line containing all the code. Locate this code fragment:

```
</sld:LabelPlacement>
<sld:Fill>
  <sld:CssParameter name="fill">#ffffff</sld:CssParameter>
</sld:Fill>
</sld:TextSymbolizer>
```

4. Then, edit the `font` and `fill` parameters to change the font color from black to blue:

```
<sld:Fill>
  <sld:CssParameter name="fill">#0000ff</sld:CssParameter>
</sld:Fill>
```

5. Go to the beginning of the code and replace the old name with this new one:

```
<sld:Name>CapitalsBlue</sld:Name>
```

6. Save the file and close it. Now, we will create a new style with this file. Send a POST request to create `CapitalsBlue style`:

```
$ curl -u admin:geoserver -XPOST -H 'Content-type:
  application/vnd.ogc.sld+xml' -d @CapitalsBlue.xml
  http://localhost:8080/geoserver/rest/styles
```

7. Alternatively, do the same operation in Python:

```
>>> myUrl = 'http://localhost:8080/geoserver/rest/styles'
>>> file = open('CapitalsBlue.xml','r')
>>> payload = file.read()
>>> headers = {'Content-type':
  'application/vnd.ogc.sld+xml','Accept': 'text/xml'}
>>> resp = requests.post(myUrl, auth=('admin','geoserver'),
  data=payload, headers=headers)
>>> resp.status_code
201
```

How it works...

You are now quite used to the REST syntax, so nothing seems too strange in the execution steps. You are probably wondering why we used a different header:

```
$ curl -u admin:geoserver -XGET -H 'Accept:
  application/vnd.ogc.sld+xml'
```

This format is to tell GeoServer we actually want the SLD format. If you specify `text/xml`, as in the previous recipes, you will get only a description of what the SLD is and not the rendering rules. Send the request modified as shown here:

```
$ curl -u admin:geoserver -XGET -H 'Accept:
  text/xml'http://localhost:8080/geoserver/rest/styles/Capitals -o
  CapitalsBlue.xml
```

Then, open the `CapitalsBlue.xml` file:

```
<style>
  <name>Capitals</name>
  <sldVersion>
    <version>1.0.0</version>
  </sldVersion>
  <filename>Capitals.sld</filename>
</style>
```

This is not really what you need to inspect drawing rules and then edit them!

Managing layers with the GWC REST API

You were already in contact with cached layers in *Chapter 5, Advanced Configurations*. You had a quick tour of GeoWebCache (`http://geowebcache.org/`), which is a Java open source project. Like any caching system, it acts as a proxy between the clients and the map server. There is a standalone version that works with any map server being compliant with the WMS standard.

Indeed, GeoWebCache uses the WMS syntax to retrieve tiles from the map server. It exposes the tiles in several ways, with the GeoServer integrated version you can use:

- **Web Map Service (WMS)**
- **WMS Tiling Client Recommendation (WMS-C)**
- **Web Map Tiling Service (WMTS)**
- **Tile Map Service (TMS)**

You used the integrated version of GeoWebCache and it is a good choice as there are many advantages in using the internal one. You can use a single interface to administer both GeoServer and GeoWebCache, and you don't have to use a custom URL or a special endpoint. Also, all the layers you publish on GeoServer are automatically configured as cached. You just have to set the caching properties on layers and layer groups.

Of course, you can use REST operations to control GeoWebCache settings and behavior.

How to do it ...

1. First of all, have a look at what layers are cached in your GeoServer. As usual, we start with cURL:

   ```
   $ curl -u admin:geoserver -XGET -H 'Accept: text/xml'
   http://localhost:8080/geoserver/gwc/rest/layers -o
   gwc_layers.xml
   ```

2. Then perform the same operation with Python:

   ```
   >>> myUrl = 'http://localhost:8080/geoserver/gwc/rest/layers'
   >>> headers = {'Accept':'text/xml'}
   >>> resp = requests.get(myUrl, auth=('admin','geoserver'),
       headers=headers)
   >>> file = open('gwc_layers_py.xml','w')
   >>> file.write(resp.text)
   >>> file.close()
   ```

3. Now examine the result:

   ```
   <layers>
     <layer>
       <name>NaturalEarth:Coastline</name>
       <atom:link xmlns:atom="http://www.w3.org/2005/Atom"
         rel="alternate" href="http://localhost:8080/
           geoserver/gwc/rest/layers/Natur
           alEarth%3ACoastline.xml" type="text/xml"/>
     </layer>
     ...
   </layers>
   ```

4. Now, retrieve the information of a single layer:

   ```
   $ curl -u admin:geoserver -XGET -H 'Accept: text/xml'
   http://localhost:8080/geoserver/gwc/
   rest/layers/NaturalEarth:Coastline.xml -o gwc_coastline.xml
   ```

5. Again, do the same with Python:

```
>>> myUrl = 'http://localhost:8080/geoserver/gwc/
    rest/layers/NaturalEarth:Coastline.xml'
>>> headers = {'Accept':'text/xml'}
>>> resp = requests.get(myUrl, auth=('admin','geoserver'),
    headers=headers)
>>> file = open('gwc_coastline_py.xml','w')
>>> file.write(resp.text)
>>> file.close()
```

6. Open the XML file retrieved. There is a lot of information:

```xml
<?xml version="1.0" encoding="UTF-8"?>
<GeoServerLayer>
  <id>LayerInfoImpl--5b67a624:145e68c7cdc:-7ffc</id>
  <enabled>true</enabled>
  <name>NaturalEarth:Coastline</name>
  <mimeFormats>
    <string>image/jpeg</string>
    <string>image/png</string>
  </mimeFormats>
  <gridSubsets>
    <gridSubset>
      <gridSetName>EPSG:900913</gridSetName>
      <extent>
        <coords>
          <double>-2.003750834E7</double>
          <double>-2.003750834E7</double>
          <double>2.003750834E7</double>
          <double>1.8440002895114224E7</double>
        </coords>
      </extent>
    </gridSubset>
    <gridSubset>
      <gridSetName>EPSG:4326</gridSetName>
      <extent>
        <coords>
          <double>-180.0</double>
          <double>-85.60903777459774</double>
          <double>180.0</double>
          <double>83.64513</double>
        </coords>
      </extent>
    </gridSubset>
```

```
      </gridSubsets>
      <metaWidthHeight>
         <int>4</int>
         <int>4</int>
      </metaWidthHeight>
      <expireCache>0</expireCache>
      <expireClients>0</expireClients>
      <parameterFilters>
         <styleParameterFilter>
            <key>STYLES</key>
            <defaultValue></defaultValue>
         </styleParameterFilter>
      </parameterFilters>
      <gutter>0</gutter>
   </GeoServerLayer>
```

7. Now you will modify the layer, removing the grid set in CRS EPSG:900913. From the XML file saved, remove the following lines:

```
      <gridSubset>
         <gridSetName>EPSG:900913</gridSetName>
         <extent>
            <coords>
               <double>-2.003750834E7</double>
               <double>-2.003750834E7</double>
               <double>2.003750834E7</double>
               <double>1.8440002895114224E7</double>
            </coords>
         </extent>
      </gridSubset>
```

8. Save the file and send this request to update the layer configuration:

```
$ curl -u admin:geoserver -XPOST -H 'Content-type: text/xml' -
d @gwc_coastline.xml http://localhost:8080/geoserver/
gwc/rest/layers/NaturalEarth:Coastline.xml
```

9. Again, do the same with the following Python code:

```
>>> myUrl = 'http://localhost:8080/geoserver/
gwc/rest/layers/NaturalEarth:Coastline.xml'
>>> file = open('gwc_coastline.xml','r')
>>> payload = file.read()
>>> headers = {'Content-type': 'text/xml','Accept':
'text/xml'}
```

```
>>> resp = requests.post(myUrl, auth=('admin','geoserver'),
    data=payload, headers=headers)
>>> resp.status_code
200
```

10. Check the configuration on the web interface.

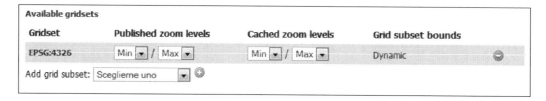

How it works ...

Configuring cached layers is really similar to performing operations on GeoServer layers. In the web interface, the configuration is indeed perfectly integrated and only on the REST interface you have a different entry point for your operations.

Please note that, by default, when you add a new layer on GeoServer, it is also automatically added to the GeoWebCache configuration.

In the first request of this recipe, you retrieved the layers' list and it should contain all layers unless you changed the GeoServer's default behavior.

However, any action you perform on a layer from the GWC REST interface does work on the uncached layer. Let's see, for instance, what happens when we delete the coastline layer using the GWC REST interface.

As usual, we firstly used cURL to do it:

```
$ curl -u admin:geoserver -XDELETE -H 'Content-type: text/xml'
  http://localhost:8080/geoserver/gwc/rest/
  layers/NaturalEarth:Coastline.xml
```

Then switched to Python code:

```
>>> myUrl = 'http://localhost:8080/geoserver/gwc/
  rest/layers/NaturalEarth:Coastline.xml'
>>> headers = {'Content-type': 'text/xml'}
>>> resp = requests.delete(myUrl, auth=('admin','geoserver'),
  headers=headers)
>>> resp.status_code
200
```

If you now open the layer configuration and go to the **Tile Caching** tab, you can see it's empty.

Managing cache tiles with the GWC REST API

Managing the cache is a more complex task than just managing the layer configuration. Cache is composed of map tiles that you may create at once by seeding the layer or waiting for the users to issue GetMap requests that have gone through the GeoWebCache and are stored as maps tile in the GeoWebCache repository.

The GWC REST interface supports the seeding, truncating, and managing tiles of cached layers.

How to do it...

1. Create a new XML file, insert the following code, and save it as `seedCoastline.xml`:

```xml
<seedRequest>
  <name>NaturalEarth.Coastline</name>
  <srs>
    <number>4326</number>
  </srs>
  <zoomStart>1</zoomStart>
  <zoomStop>8</zoomStop>
  <format>image/png</format>
  <type>seed</type>
  <threadCount>4</threadCount>
</seedRequest>
```

2. Send a cURL request to start seeding for the **NaturalEarth:Coastline** layer:

```
$ curl -u admin:geoserver -XPOST -H 'Content-type: text/xml' -
d @seedCoastline.xml http://localhost:8080/geoserver/
gwc/rest/seed/NaturalEarth:Coastline.xml
```

3. Alternatively, do the same operation in Python:

```
>>> myUrl = 'http://localhost:8080/geoserver/
gwc/rest/seed/NaturalEarth:Coastline.xml'

>>> file = open('seedCoastline.xml','r')

>>> payload = file.read()

>>> headers = {'Content-type': 'text/xml','Accept':
'text/xml'}

>>> resp = requests.post(myUrl, auth=('admin','geoserver'),
data=payload, headers=headers)

>>> resp.status_code

200
```

4. Now, go to the tile layers list and press the **Seed/Truncate** link for the **NaturalEarth:Coastline** layer. You should see four listed processes that are calculating tiles for you, as shown in the following screenshot:

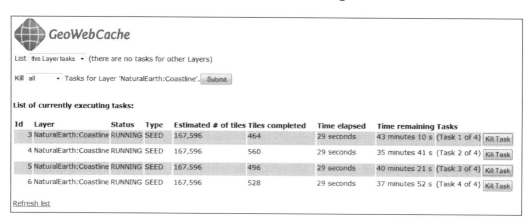

How it works...

Map tiles need to be created and then saved on filesystems, and sometimes may require a lot of disk space and a lot of time.

To check the status of the seed operation, you can use the web interface as in the previous screenshot, but we prefer to leverage on REST. The code is as follows:

```
$ curl -u admin:geoserver -XGET
  http://localhost:8080/geoserver/gwc/rest
  /seed/NaturalEarth:Coastline.json -o seedingProcesses.json
```

This returns a list of running process for a specific layer:

```
{"long-array-array":[[3072,167596,581,7,1],
  [4592,167596,374,8,1],[5840,167596,290,9,1],
  [2640,167596,684,10,1]]}
```

The JSON file contains an array of arrays. Each array corresponds to a single seeding/truncating task. The meaning of each long value in each thread array is shown as follows:

```
[tiles processed, total number of tiles to process, estimated
    number of second to end, Task ID, Task status]
```

The task status value returned will be one of the following:

- -1 = ABORTED
- 0 = PENDING
- 1 = RUNNING
- 2 = DONE

So, in our case, we have something like this:

Tiles processed	Total tiles to process	Seconds to the end	Task ID	Task status
3072	167596	581	7	RUNNING
4592	167596	374	8	RUNNING
5840	167596	290	9	RUNNING
2640	167596	684	10	RUNNING

Of course, it is always possible to totally halt the seeding process with a simple GET request. It can be issued to a single layer, as shown in the following code snippet. This halts all processes running for the **NaturalEarth.Coastline** layer:

```
$ curl -u admin:geoserver -XGET -d 'kill_all=all'
  http://localhost:8080/geoserver/gwc/rest/
  seed/NaturalEarth:Coastline
```

You have several processes that are creating tiles for many layers. If you need to stop them all, the REST interface gives you an operation to stop them all. Regardless of the layer, you shall use /gwc/rest/seed as the entry point. The following line of code halts all seeding and truncating processes on the server:

```
$ curl -u admin:geoserver -XGET -d 'kill_all=all'
  http://localhost:8080/geoserver/gwc/rest/seed
```

You can also erase all tiles for a layer; this may be useful when your data needs to be updated and the cache is no more useful. Just prepare an XML file similar to that previously prepared for the seeding and insert truncate as the operation type, as shown in the following example:

```
<seedRequest>
  <name>NaturalEarth.Coastline</name>
  <srs>
    <number>4326</number>
  </srs>
  <zoomStart>1</zoomStart>
  <zoomStop>8</zoomStop>
  <format>image/png</format>
  <type>truncate</type>
  <threadCount>4</threadCount>
</seedRequest>
```

Then, send it to GeoServer and all processes will be halted:

```
$ curl -u admin:geoserver -XPOST -H 'Content-type: text/xml' -d
  @seedStopCoastline.xml http://localhost:8080/geoserver/gwc
  /rest/seed/NaturalEarth:Coastline.xml
```

7
Advanced Visualizations

In this chapter, we'll cover the following recipes:

- Adding time to WMS maps
- Using the WMS animator
- Keyhole Markup Language styling
- Using z-order creatively
- Using transparency creatively
- Using symbology encoding

Introduction

Advanced Visualization is a key factor in producing beautiful maps. Here, beautiful maps are intended not just as the art of producing something that other people consider nice to look at. Maps are your way to communicate your interpretation of data to others.

Spatial data are not objective by nature; all data behaves the same with regards to this aspect. Maps are not a specular representation of the real world. They're propositions, models of the world, and the clearer and readable you design your model, the more understandable it'll appear to other people.

We already had a tour of how to style data in *Chapter 3, Advanced Styling*. This chapter follows the work you started there and shows you other topics relevant to representing your spatial data, as usual using GeoServer.

Adding time to WMS maps

Most users are comfortable with static 2D data, where a shape is represented on a surface and is invariant throughout time.

While most maps are built with this type of data, GeoServer offers you the possibility to explore even the third spatial dimension, which is elevation.

Besides, GeoServer can also publish data that changes over time. In this recipe, we'll see how to use data that changes over time using a set of points mimicking the path of a vehicle on a highway.

Getting ready

For this recipe, we need some new data. We will create a new dataset on PostGIS with data simulating a vehicle tracking path. It contains a set of points using `timestamp`.

First, we need to create a repository for the data. Execute the following SQL code to create a table:

```
CREATE TABLE vehicletrack (
    gid integer NOT NULL,
    "time" timestamp without time zone,
    geom geometry(Point,32633)
);

CREATE SEQUENCE vehicletrack_gid_seq
    START WITH 1
    INCREMENT BY 1
    NO MINVALUE
    NO MAXVALUE
    CACHE 1;

ALTER SEQUENCE vehicletrack_gid_seq OWNED BY vehicletrack.gid;

ALTER TABLE ONLY vehicletrack ALTER COLUMN gid SET DEFAULT
    nextval('vehicletrack_gid_seq'::regclass);

ALTER TABLE ONLY vehicletrack
    ADD CONSTRAINT vehicletrack_pkey PRIMARY KEY (gid);

CREATE INDEX vehicletrack_geom_gist ON vehicletrack USING gist
    (geom);
```

You can find the preceding code in the `ch07_vehicleTable.sql` file in the code bundle.

Now, we can insert the data. Use the `ch07_vehiclePoints.sql` file, which you can download from this book's site and execute it, as shown in the following statement:

```
$ psql -U gissuser -d gisdata
psql (9.3.1)
Type "help" for help.


gisdata=> \i ch07_vehiclePoints.sql
```

Now, we need to publish the layer on GeoServer. The publication workflow follows the ordinary flow. Please note the **Dimensions** tab. The **Time** flag is enabled, as shown in the following screenshot:

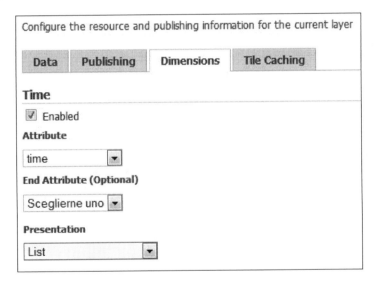

GeoServer has a proper attribute, so it gives you an option to use it to enable the time for the layer. After you flag it, three more controls appear. From the **Attribute** list, select **time**. We have no **End Attribute** value; this is the case when you have a period, that is, a range of validity time for each feature. In the **Presentation** list, select the **List** value.

How to do it...

1. Take the three files with the `.html` extension and place them in the `ROOT` folder under `<CATALINA_HOME>/webapps` on your Tomcat.

2. Open your browser and point it to the following URL to send GeoServer a request for a map containing an OpenStreetMap basemap and your new layer:

   ```
   http://localhost:8080/ch07_timeWMS.html
   ```

3. You should see a map that looks like the following screenshot:

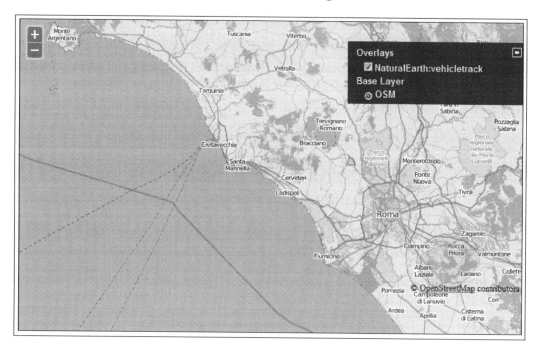

4. The `vehicletrack` layer is shown in the layers list but no features are represented on the map. Now try the following URL:

   ```
   http://localhost:8080/ch07_timeWMSALL.html
   ```

5. This time you can see the sample points tracking the position of the vehicle on the trip, as shown in the following screenshot:

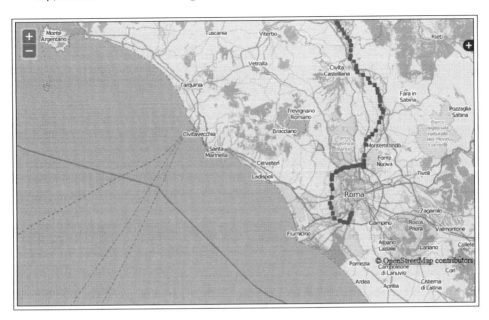

6. Load the following URL in your browser: `http://localhost:8080/ch07_timeWMSRange.htm`. Now you can see that just a subset of positions are shown on the map:

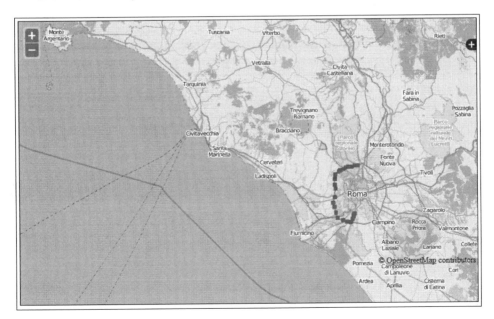

How it works...

After you enabled the time dimension for the layer, you can use an additional parameter in your request to GeoServer: `time`. In fact, the simple OpenLayers app you used in this recipe uses it. Let's see how the code works in detail.

First of all, you need to get the OpenLayers package. In the script, an absolute reference to the OpenLayers official site is used. When building a real application, you may want to incorporate the package in your app and so you will be using a relative path:

```
<script type="text/javascript"
    src="http://openlayers.org/api/2.13.1/OpenLayers.js"></script>
```

Just after it, there is the JavaScript snippet that creates the map and loads two layers. We create a map object, which will be the canvas that shows the result of the `GetMap` request to GeoServer. Note that you need to explicitly set the projection to `EPSG:3857`, the standard code for the Web Mercator CRS. In fact, we'll use OpenStreetMap tiles as the basemap and these are only available in this CRS:

```
<script type="text/javascript">
    var map, layer;
    function init(){
        map = new OpenLayers.Map(
            {div: 'myMap',
            projection: 'EPSG:3857'}
        );
```

We now have the `vehicletrack` layer, which you created in this recipe. We set it as transparent, to avoid it hiding the underlying basemap. We also set the `isBaseLayer` property to `False` to avoid OpenLayers from loading it as an alternative basemap:

```
        var demolayer = new OpenLayers.Layer.WMS(
            'NaturalEarth:vehicletrack','../geoserver/
            NaturalEarth/wms',
            {layers: 'NaturalEarth:vehicletrack',
             format: 'image/png',
             transparent: true
             },
            {singleTile: 'True',
             isBaseLayer: false}
        );
        map.addLayer(demolayer);
```

Then, we add the OpenStreetMap layer. This is really straightforward. Using the OSM class, we just need to provide a name for it, which will be used in the layerSwitcher control. The OSM class points, by default, to the following:

```
var layer = new OpenLayers.Layer.OSM("OSM");
map.addLayer(layer);
```

The final step is to center the map on an area containing the vehicle data, and add the control to switch the layer visibility on or off:

```
map.setCenter(
    new OpenLayers.LonLat(12.0,42.0).transform(
        new OpenLayers.Projection("EPSG:4326"),
        map.getProjectionObject()
    ), 9
);
map.addControl(new OpenLayers.Control.LayerSwitcher({
    ascending: false
}));
}
</script>
```

Although you add the layer, the vehicletrack layer in this case, it doesn't show on the map. The layer name is listed in the LayerSwitcher control, so there is no error in the script. It is just that you did not specify the time parameter, so no point is returned by GeoServer.

If you inspect the code contained in the ch07_timeWMSALL.html file, you will see that the only difference is in the creation of the vehicletrack layer:

```
var demolayer = new OpenLayers.Layer.WMS(
    'NaturalEarth:vehicletrack','../geoserver/
    NaturalEarth/wms',
    {layers: 'NaturalEarth:vehicletrack',
     format: 'image/png',
     transparent: true,
     time: '2014-05-26'
    },
    {singleTile: 'True',
     isBaseLayer: false}
);
```

Now you have the value 2014-05-26 for the time parameter and all the points have a timestamp in that day, so all points are shown.

You can define the time value using the `yyyy-MM-ddThh:mm:ss.SSSZ` format and you can also specify a range; in this case, you set the start and end date using the same format and separate them with the `/` character.

In the `ch07_timeWMSRange.html` file, a two-hour range is specified and just a subset of points is displayed on the map:

```
time: '2014-05-26T11:00:00.0Z/2014-05-26T12:00:00.0Z'
```

Using the WMS animator

You've been using WMS since the start of this book. You are an expert with `GetMap` requests, so it's perfectly clear to you that such a request can only produce a static map, that is, a representation of your data according to the styles and other parameters you submitted with the query.

Sometimes it may be useful to produce a dynamic map, something more similar to an animation. In fact, an animation is composed of an ordered sequence of pictures, so a map animation only requires you to produce an ordered sequence of maps.

A common use case is a map changing its extent to simulate a move over the data. In this recipe, you will learn how to produce a small animation, which shows a map moving toward the east.

How to do it...

1. Start your GeoServer instance and go to the web interface.

2. On the left panel, select the **Layer** option and then check that the following layers are listed among the available layers:

   - **NaturalEarth:populatedplaces**

   - **NaturalEarth:GeneralizedCountries**

3. We created them in the *Improving performance with pregeneralized features* recipe, *Chapter 1*, *Working with Vectors*. In case you skipped it, you should at least load the data and publish them in GeoServer.

4. Now open your browser and point it to the following URL:

```
http://localhost:8080/geoserver/wms/animate?layers=NaturalEa
rth:populatedplaces,NaturalEarth:GeneralizedCountries&width=6
00&aparam=bbox&avalues=-7\,40\,0\,47,-6.5\,40\,0.5\,47,-6\,4-
0\,1\,47,-5.5\,40\,1.5\,47,-5\,40\,2\,47,-4.5\,40\,2.5\,47,-
4\,40\,3\,47,-3.5\,40\,3.5\,47,-3\,40\,4\,47,-
2.5\,40\,4.5\,47,-2\,40\,5\,47,-1.5\,40\,5.5\,47,-1\,40\,6\,47
```

5. Wait for GeoServer to elaborate on your request. A map will then appear in the browser showing a short animation, which will display a map shifting from Spain to France. The map should look like the following screenshot:

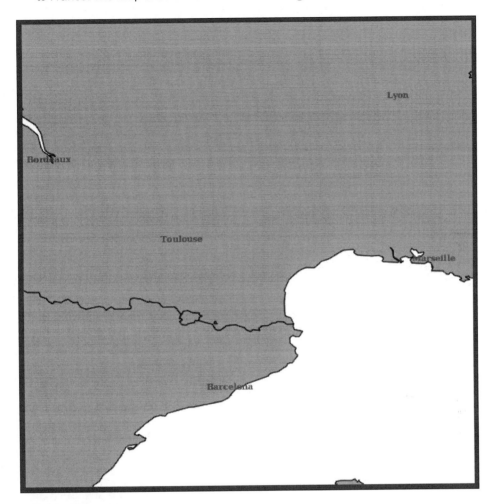

How it works...

The small animation you requested GeoServer to create for you is stored inside an animated GIF. You can check it if you right-click on the picture and use the **Save** image function. If you check the GIF properties, you will see that it contains 13 pictures or frames.

Each frame is a static map with a different extent. You can produce it with 13 `GetMap` requests, and then use an external tool to merge all 13 pictures in an animation. GeoServer does it all for you. The small, but fundamental, difference in the request of an ordinary `GetMap` is in the path.

For a simple `GetMap` request, you could use the `http://localhost:8080/geoserver/wms` path. In this case, you shall use the `http://localhost:8080/geoserver/wms/animate` path. So your request is recognized as an animation request and extra parameters, such as the `animator` parameter, are allowed.

You need to forward some more information to instruct GeoServer on how to produce the animation. Basically, you have to set the `aparam` and `avalue` parameters:

- `aparam`: This parameter specifies the name of the parameter that will change in the frames. In this recipe, we used the `bbox` parameter, so GeoServer will expect different bounding boxes for each frame.

- `avalue`: This parameter specifies the actual value that should be used for each frame. In this recipe, we listed a set of bounding boxes, each containing four numbers, for the top, bottom, left, and right.

 Please note that we used the escape character \ for some commas. In fact, commas are recognized by GeoServer as the separator for different values, but in this case, each value is composed of numbers separated by commas.

The other parameters are the same you would use in a standard `GetMap` request. Please note that the animator parameter has default values for almost all `GetMap` parameters; the only one you need to explicitly set is `layers` to indicate what data should be represented in the map.

The previous requests, in fact, do not contain the format, as they defaults to `image/gif;subtype=animated`. In fact, with GeoServer 2.5.x release, the animated GIF is the only supported format for animation.

There's more...

The GeoServer animator gives you options of speed and looping for your animation. To set them, you can use the following two custom parameters:

- `gif_loop_continuosly`: This parameter controls whether the animation will run just once or loop continuously. The default value is false and, in fact, in this recipe, the animation just plays once. Try to run it again adding `&gif_loop_continuosly=true` at the end of the URL.

- `gif_frames_delay`: This parameter specifies the frame delay in milliseconds. The default is 1,000 milliseconds, which is the value used in the previous request. Add `&gif_frame_delay=500` at the end of the URL and run it again.

We'll explore the preceding two parameters using data from the previous recipe. We'll create an animation showing the path of the vehicle. In fact, you just have to specify time as the animation parameter, as shown in the following request:

```
http://localhost:8080/geoserver/wms/animate?layers=NaturalEarth:vehi
cletrack&width=200&aparam=time&avalues=2014-05-26T11:00:00.0Z/2014-
05-26T11:05:00.0Z,2014-05-26T11:05:00.0Z/2014-05-26T11:10:00.0Z,2014-
05-26T11:10:00.0Z/2014-05-26T11:15:00.0Z,2014-05-26T11:15:00.0Z/2014-
05-26T11:20:00.0Z,2014-05-26T11:20:00.0Z/2014-05-26T11:25:-
00.0Z,2014-05-26T11:25:00.0Z/2014-05-26T11:30:00.0Z,2014-05-
26T11:30:00.0Z/2014-05-26T11:35:00.0Z,2014-05-26T11:35:00.0Z/2014-05-
26T11:40:00.0Z,2014-05-26T11:40:00.0Z/2014-05-26T11:45:00.0Z,2014-05-
26T11:45:00.0Z/2014-05-26T11:50:00.0Z,2014-05-26T11:50:00.0Z/2014-05-
26T11:55:00.0Z,2014-05-26T11:55:00.0Z/2014-05-26T12:00:00.0Z,2014-
05-26T12:00:00.0Z/2014-05-26T12:05:00.0Z,2014-05-26T12:05:00.0Z/2014-
05-26T12:10:00.0Z,2014-05-26T12:10:00.0Z/2014-05-26T12:15:00.0Z,2014-
05-26T12:15:00.0Z/2014-05-26T12:20:00.0Z,2014-05-26T12:20:00.0Z/2014-
05-26T12:25:00.0Z,2014-05-26T12:25:00.0Z/2014-05-26T12:30:00.0Z&gif_
loop_continuosly=true&gif_frame_delay=500
```

The `avalues` parameter contains a set of ranges, and each one spans over a five-minute interval; the resulting screenshot shows you the path of the vehicle in that period. You can also control some `animator` parameters globally.

In the GeoServer web interface, locate the **WMS** setting in the left pane, as shown:

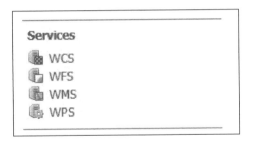

Scroll down until you reach the **WMS-Animator Options** section, as shown in the following screenshot:

```
WMS-Animator Options

Max allowed frames
2147483647

Max rendering time (ms)


Max rendering size (bytes)


Frames Delay (ms, default 1s)
1000

[ ] Loop Continuously
```

You'll find the two previous custom parameters, and from here, you can change the default behavior. For instance, you may want GeoServer to loop the animation continuously by default. The first option lets you set the maximum number of frames allowed in a single animation, which as you can see is a very high value by default. You may want to reduce it to avoid a huge load on your server triggered by some user. The other two values let you set the maximum time GeoServer should work on an animation before discarding it and also, the maximum animation size. Again, these values let you protect your server from dangerous requests.

Keyhole Markup Language styling

Keyhole Markup Language (**KML**) is an XML-based language built by Google™ and is mainly used in its desktop mapping product, Google Earth™. It allows the user to virtually view, pan, and fly around the imagery of the Earth.

Playing with imagery can be really nice; if you haven't yet, you should try just wandering on remote areas of the planet and explore areas where once the **Here be Dragons** label were the most common among labels: (http://en.wikipedia.org/wiki/Here_be_dragons).

However, the program is way more than a videogame and if you add it to your data, it becomes a very powerful and accessible tool for 3D visualization.

How do you make GeoServer and Google Earth™ interoperate? It is here that KML comes to your rescue. Google Earth™ can read and visualize data formatted in KML; on the other hand, GeoServer is capable of responding to your requests on formatting data in KML. Then, every layer published on GeoServer can easily be used in Google Earth.

Getting ready

To complete this recipe, you need to have a working installation of Google Earth™ on your workstation. Installing it is really simple; just point your browser to the following download page:

```
http://www.google.co.uk/intl/en_uk/earth/download/ge/agree.html
```

Please read the license agreement carefully. The software can be used freely for noncommercial use. If you plan to use it in your company, you should check whether the intended use violates the license agreement.

There are binaries for Windows, Mac OS X, and Linux, both 32-bit and 64-bit editions. Just after you click on the **Agree and Download** button, the proper installer for your OS is downloaded and the browser will prompt you to save it in a local folder; now run it, after which installation will be executed in minutes.

Apart from the size of the download, you should be aware that using Google Earth™ requires you to have access to a good Internet connection. All the imagery shown in the software is downloaded as you move around the globe.

How to do it...

1. Start your GeoServer instance and go to the web interface.

2. On the left panel, select the **Layer** option and then check that the **NaturalEarth:EuropeCountries** layer is listed among the available layers. We created it in the *Creating a SQL view* recipe, *Chapter 1, Working with Vectors*; in case you skipped it, you should at least load the data and publish it in GeoServer.

3. You can see that in the **Common Formats** column, a link named **KML** is shown. Click on it.

4. The browser will prompt you to select an action for the file. Select the radio button, **Open with**, click on the button to its right, and select Google Earth™ as the program to process the downloaded data.

5. Click on the **OK** button and Google Earth ™ will open. It could take a while for it to show you the exact location of your data; eventually, you should look at a map similar to the following screenshot:

6. Quite an ordinary map but you got your data inside Google Earth. Now you will try something more complex.

7. Download the ch07_KMLEurope.sld file from http://www.packtpub.com/geoserver-cookbook/book in the **Support** section and save it on your filesystem.

8. From the left panel of the GeoServer interface, select the **Styles** item.

9. Click on the **Add a new Style** button, as shown in the following screenshot:

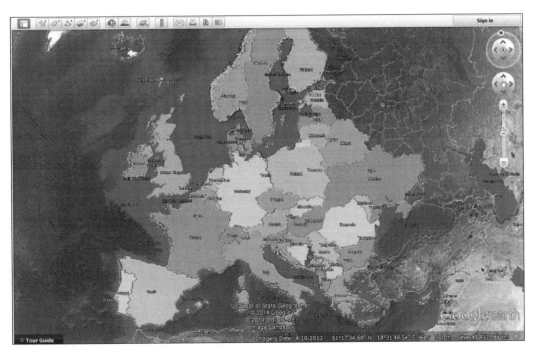

10. Insert KMLEurope as the name for the new style, and then click on the **Browse** button and locate the file you previously saved on the filesystem. Click on the **Submit** button to save the style in the GeoServer configuration.

11. Now, on your browser, insert the following URL:

    ```
    http://localhost:8080/geoserver/NaturalEarth/wms/kml?layers=Nat
    uralEarth:EuropeCountries&styles=KMLEurope
    ```

12. When you are prompted for an action on the file, select Google Earth ™ as you did before. Once the program completes loading your data, you should have a map that looks like the following screenshot:

How it works...

When you clicked on the KML link in the **Layers** preview page, you probably noticed the following URL:

```
http://localhost:8080/geoserver/NaturalEarth/wms/kml?layers=NaturalEa
rth:EuropeCountries
```

As you can see, this link is really shorter and simpler than a standard `GetMap` WMS request. In fact, you can have GeoServer outputting KML in response to your request by changing the format of the response to `format=application/vnd.google-earth.kml+XML`. Using the short form is possible because of the KML reflector.

It is a facility that uses default values for almost all the parameters; you just have to explicitly set the `layers` parameter. The default values are shown as follows:

Key	Value
request	GetMap
service	Wms
version	1.1.1
srs	EPSG:4326
format	applcation/vnd.google-earth.kmz+xml
width	2048
height	2048
bbox	<layer bounds>
kmattr	True
kmplacemark	false
kmscore	40
styles	Uses the default style for the layer

Of course, you can override the default style, as you did in the second request. The first map used the default style for the **EuropeCountries** layer, and then you inserted the `&styles=KMLEurope` value.

You can override almost all parameters; for instance, you may want to change the size of the image by setting different values for `width` and `height`. The parameter that has the greatest impact on the map and what we will focus on is `styles`. Using it, you can control how the features will be rendered.

You can also add vendor parameters, such as `cql_filter`, provided by GeoServer to easily filter features in the `GetMap` request. The following URL sends a request for features, which is contained in four countries of the `populatedplaces` layer:

```
http://localhost:8080/geoserver/NaturalEarth/wms/kml?layers=NaturalEa
rth:populatedplaces&styles=Capitals&cql_filter=adm0name%20in%20('Spai
n','Greece','France','Italy')
```

The resulting map is as shown in the following screenshot:

There's more...

When adding GeoServer data to Google Earth, you don't need to start from the **Layers** preview page. We did it just for the sake of understanding, but now that you've learned how it works, it is simpler to add a reference to the data in the Google Earth ™ configuration.

You can add a reference to GeoServer by opening the **Add** menu in Google Earth and selecting the **Network Link** item. In the dialog box, you have to specify a name for the resource and a URL pointing to your GeoServer, as shown in the following screenshot:

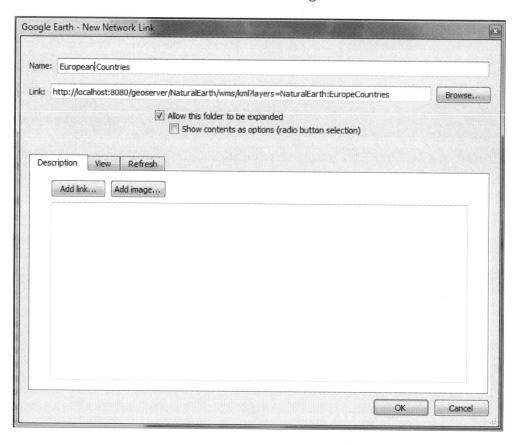

This way, your link will be saved in the **Places** library under the **Temporary Places** category, as shown in the following screenshot. Using the checkbox, you can turn it on or off and make it visible on the globe.

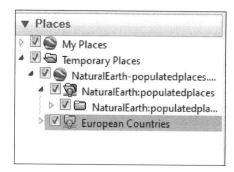

Using z-order creatively

In the *Creating scale-dependent rules* recipe, *Chapter 3, Advanced Styling*, we already used a complex symbol produced by merging simple symbols. In this recipe, we will now focus on the concept of z-order, that is, the order that GeoServer uses to draw symbols on the map.

Understanding this lets you use features and symbols in the proper way, along with producing some advanced symbology.

How to do it...

1. In this recipe, we will use the **NaturalEarth:populatedplaces** layer, which you configured in *Chapter 3, Advanced Styling*. If you missed that chapter, please read through the instructions on how to download and configure the dataset and install the CSS module.

2. Download the code for the chapter from the Packt site and extract the `ch07_Places.css` file.

3. Open the GeoServer web interface and from the left panel, select **CSS Styles**.

4. Choose **Create a new Style** and insert `places` as the name.

5. Choose **NaturalEarth:populatedplaces** as layers to preview the style.

6. Now copy the content of the `ch07_Places.css` file and paste it in the editor window.

7. Click on the **submit** button and open the map preview; your map should look like the following screenshot:

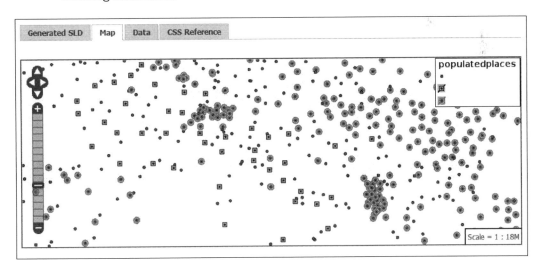

How it works...

Let's inspect the CSS file to understand the z-order logic. In the beginning, you define a category to classify features that hold two values, which is `Admin-1 capital` and `Admin-0 capital`, in their fields. For this category, you select three mark symbols, all of the `circle` type, as follows:

```
[featurecla = 'Admin-1 capital'] ,[featurecla = 'Admin-0 capital']
  {
  mark: symbol('circle'), symbol('circle'), symbol('circle');
}
```

Then, you define `size`, `fill`, and the `stroke` color for the first of these symbols, that is, placed on bottom of the drawing order. In fact GeoServer first draws a red circle with with an orange fill:

```
[featurecla = 'Admin-1 capital'] ,[featurecla = 'Admin-0 capital']
  :nth-mark(1) {
  size: 10px;
  fill: orange;
  stroke: red;
}
```

Repeat the same step to define the size and color for the other two symbols as follows:

```
[featurecla = 'Admin-1 capital'] ,[featurecla = 'Admin-0 capital']
  :nth-mark(2) {
  size: 6px;
  fill: brown;
}
[featurecla = 'Admin-1 capital'], [featurecla = 'Admin-0 capital']
  :nth-mark(3) {
  size: 2px;
  fill: black;
}
```

According to your instructions, GeoServer draws a smaller brown circle, then a tiny black circle.

The resulting symbol is a complex one produced from the overlay of the three. Of course, you have to carefully select sizes, with the symbol getting smaller as you scale up the z-order.

Using transparency creatively

A common task in producing maps is to mix different layers in a single output. This causes some masking of the overlapping objects, as we explored in the previous recipe. When you work with the raster data, of course, masking is an issue as the top raster layer could totally hide the bottom layers.

In this recipe, we'll explore how to use transparency to avoid masking and merge several raster layers in a single map.

Getting ready

In the *Rendering transformations for raster data* recipe of *Chapter 3, Advanced Styling*, we downloaded a dataset from USGS to explore how rendering works for raster data. We will now use the same dataset, producing a complementary dataset.

> If you didn't read *Chapter 3, Advanced Styling*, you should at least download and publish the DEM following the instructions given in the *Rendering transformations for raster data* recipe in *Chapter 3*.

We will use the `gdaldem` tool, available among the GDAL command utilities, to create a shaded relief representation from the digital elevation model.

> We already introduced GDAL/OGR in the *Using different WFS versions in OpenLayers* recipe in *Chapter 1, Working with Vectors*, to process the blueMarble dataset. GDAL/OGR is a powerful open library to process raster and vector dataset.
>
> You can find a lot of detailed information from the main site at `http://www.gdal.org/`.
>
> Many different formats are supported; look at the following link for raster's formats:
>
> `http://www.gdal.org/formats_list.html`
>
> Also, look at the following link for vector data formats:
>
> `http://www.gdal.org/ogr_formats.html`

Open a command shell and insert the following code:

```
$ gdaldem hillshade dem.tiff shadedRelief.tiff -z 5 -s 111120 -az 90
  -of GTiff -co COMPRESS=DEFLATE -co TILED=YES
```

We will now produce another derived dataset; it is a colored representation of the DEM and we'll again use the `gdaldem` utility to produce it.

First of all, we need to create a set of colors to transform `dem.tiff` from a grey scale picture to a full RGB one. Using a text editor, create a new file called `colours.txt` and insert the following text lines inside it; be careful not to add extra lines or other characters:

```
65535 255 255 255
1400 254 254 254
1000 121 117 10
700 151 106 47
350 127 166 122
175 213 213 149
1 218 179 122
```

For your interest, the color palette used in this recipe is publicly available at `http://www.colourlovers.com/palette/1374547/ Landcarpet_Europe`.

COLOURLovers is a nice place where you can find many more hints on how to create a beautiful output from your data.

After saving the file in the same folder that contains the `dem.tiff` file, open the command shell and execute the following command:

```
$ gdaldem color-relief dem.tiff colours.txt colourRelief.tiff -of
  GTiff -co COMPRESS=DEFLATE -co TILED=YES
```

Now that two new datasets are created, go to the GeoServer interface and publish them as layers. You can call them **NaturalEarth:shadedRelief** and **NaturalEarth:colourRelief** to use the same names contained in the following steps, or modify the steps according to your choice.

How to do it...

1. Log on to the GeoServer web interface. From the left panel, select the **Stores** option and click on the **Add new store** button.

2. Select **GeoTIFF** as the datastore type, insert a name, and then point it to the `shadedRelief.tiff` file you created previously.

3. Click on **Save** and publish the file.

4. Repeat the previous steps for the `colourReflief.tiff` file.

5. Take the `ch07_transparencyWMS.html` file and place it in the ROOT folder under `<CATALINA_HOME>/webapps` on your Tomcat.

6. Open your browser and point it to the following URL:

   `http://localhost:8080/ch07_transparencyWMS.html`

7. Your map should look like the following screenshot:

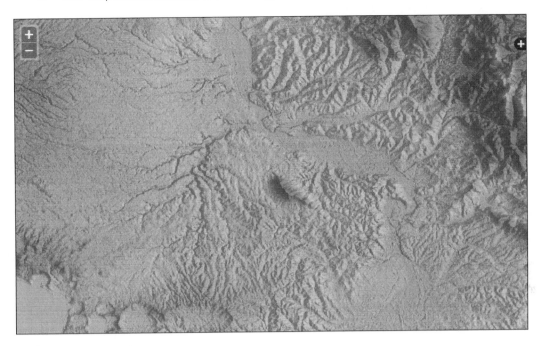

How it works...

If you look at the datasets you produced, in the layers preview section of GeoServer, you will find that they are quite different from the original DEM. The **shadedRelief** dataset uses a well-known technique among cartographers to produce a map that uses shadows to give the user a realistic representation of relief.

Hill-shading is a well known technique among cartographers. It was widely used before digital cartography was invented. At that time, cartography was quite related to the art of painting. If you are curious about it, you can take a look at http://en.wikipedia.org/wiki/Shaded_relief#Shaded_relief.

A brief and nice summary about how the technique developed can also be found in an article by Karen A. Mulcahy at http://www.geo.hunter.cuny.edu/terrain/ter_hist.html.

The following screenshot shows the shaded relief output:

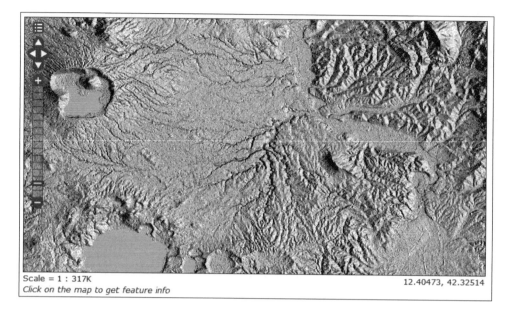

Scale = 1 : 317K

Click on the map to get feature info

12.40473, 42.32514

To produce a map with better representation, we then created a color representation of the DEM. When you define the color palette, each row contains an elevation value in the first column, and the red, green, and blue values that define the color to be used for that elevation.

The `gdaldem` utility then produces a smoothing transition among the classes you define and the final output is a map like the following screenshot:

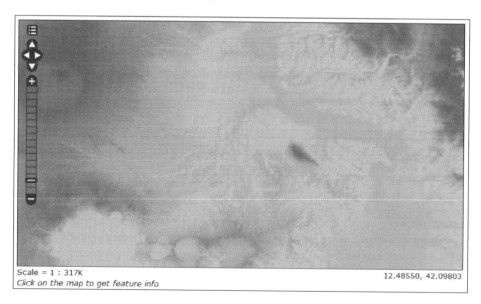

Scale = 1 : 317K

Click on the map to get feature info

12.48550, 42.09803

To produce the final output, the OpenLayers application makes two WMS `GetMap` requests and GeoServer produces two pictures that are then overlaid in the browser. The magic is in the following setting:

```
var colourRelief = new OpenLayers.Layer.WMS(
    'NaturalEarth:colourRelief','../geoserver/NaturalEarth/wms',
    {layers: 'NaturalEarth:colourRelief',
     format: 'image/png',
     transparent: true
     },
    {singleTile: 'True',
     opacity: 0.65,
     isBaseLayer: false}
);
```

If you set the opacity of the second layer to a value lower than one, it is visually merged with the underlying picture and the resulting visual effect is that of a single layer.

Using symbology encoding

Thematic mapping is one of the more common uses of spatial data, and the most used thematic maps are the choropleth maps that we already used in several recipes in this book.

 Take a look at the following Wikipedia page for more information about choropleth maps:

http://en.wikipedia.org/wiki/Choropleth_map

Until now, the examples showed you how to produce a thematic map with fixed values in the attributes. SLD specifications define some functions that let you classify your data using related attributes in a dynamic way.

In this recipe, we will explore how to apply symbology encoding to GeoServer layers.

 Symbology encoding is a standard defined by OGC; you can read the official paper at the following URL:

http://www.opengeospatial.org/standards/symbol

How to do it...

1. Log on to the GeoServer web interface. From the left panel, select the **Styles** option and click on the **Add a new Style** button.

2. In the **Styles** editor, insert `InterpolatePop` as the new name, and then select **polygon** as the default style to copy from, as shown in the following screenshot:

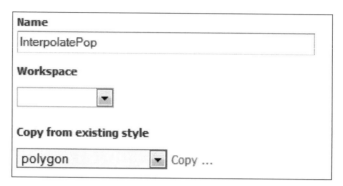

3. The XML code is loaded in the editor window. Search for the rule to draw the grey polygon and select it using the following code snippet:

```
<PolygonSymbolizer>
    <Fill>
        <CssParameter name="fill">
            <ogc:Function name="Interpolate">
                <ogc:PropertyName>pop_est</ogc:PropertyName>

                <ogc:Literal>0</ogc:Literal>
                <ogc:Literal>#A1A690</ogc:Literal>

                <ogc:Literal>1000000</ogc:Literal>
                <ogc:Literal>#299BCD</ogc:Literal>

                <ogc:Literal>50000000</ogc:Literal>
                <ogc:Literal>#0AAA50</ogc:Literal>

                <ogc:Literal>500000000</ogc:Literal>
                <ogc:Literal>#EE1C25</ogc:Literal>

                <ogc:Literal>1500000000</ogc:Literal>
```

```
        <ogc:Literal>#EB0C8B</ogc:Literal>

        <ogc:Literal>color</ogc:Literal>

    </ogc:Function>
  </CssParameter>
  </Fill>
</PolygonSymbolizer>
```

4. Click on the **Validate** button, check that no errors are reported, and then click on the **Submit** button.

5. Now open the **Layers** section from the left panel of the GeoServer interface and click on the **NaturalEarth:countries** layer.

6. Switch to the **Publishing** panel and add the **InterpolatePop** style to the layer configuration, as shown in the following screenshot:

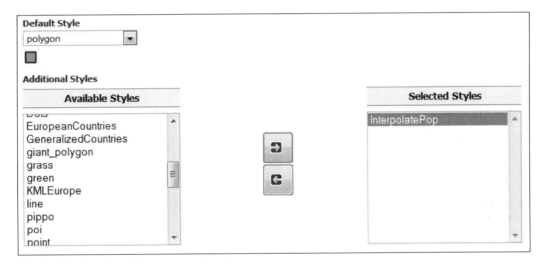

7. Now open the **Layer** preview for the **NaturalEarth:countries** layer and the options toolbar, and select **InterpolatePop** as the style; your map should look like the following screenshot:

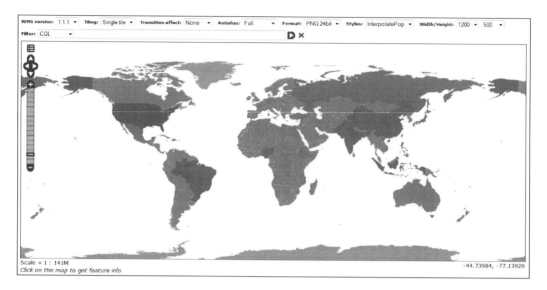

How it works...

You have now created a thematic map where the color applied to features is determined by an interpolation curve. In a simpler thematic map, you create a set of rules, where you set a specific color in each class that applies to all the matching features.

Using the `interpolate` function, you just need to create a single rule that defines the interpolation curve that will transform a continuous-valued attribute into another continuous range of values.

In this case, the valued attribute is `pop_est`, which contains the population value for each country, and the range of these values is the RGB colors. The transformation is defined by a set of (input/output) control points chosen along a desired mapping curve. Piecewise interpolation along the curve is used to compute an output value for any input value.

You set the following five control points to define your curve:

```
<ogc:Literal>0</ogc:Literal>
<ogc:Literal>#A1A690</ogc:Literal>

<ogc:Literal>1000000</ogc:Literal>
<ogc:Literal>#299BCD</ogc:Literal>

<ogc:Literal>50000000</ogc:Literal>
```

```
<ogc:Literal>#0AAA50</ogc:Literal>

<ogc:Literal>500000000</ogc:Literal>
<ogc:Literal>#EE1C25</ogc:Literal>

<ogc:Literal>1500000000</ogc:Literal>
<ogc:Literal>#EB0C8B</ogc:Literal>
```

The last line defines the interpolation method, `color` in this case, as we want to output RGB values:

```
<ogc:Literal>color</ogc:Literal>
```

8
Monitoring and Tuning

In this chapter, we'll cover the following recipes:

- ▶ Installing the control flow module
- ▶ Setting a per-user limit
- ▶ Setting a per-request limit
- ▶ Installing the monitoring extension
- ▶ Configuring the monitoring extension
- ▶ Creating reports from the monitoring database
- ▶ Limiting the GeoWebCache disk use

Introduction

Among the main features that can make your web service a successful one, there is reliability and speed. Almost every user hates slow applications and broken sessions. One of the most frustrating experiences is to stare at your browser waiting for the page to load completely, and unless you are a network engineer, checking whether the services are broken is not all that fun.

So, monitoring your services is a crucial point to assure your users that they will have a fast and reliable response. There are many specialized tools to monitor a task; as an example, a general purpose tool such as Nagios (http://www.nagios.org/) is a valid open source option.

GeoServer offers a specialized extension to collect data about incoming requests. This data can quickly be visualized in a few ready-to-use reports. We'll also explore how to use them for service analysis to create custom reports. Also, to avoid your instance from collapsing under too much load, the control flow module extension is a very nice option. It allows you to properly limit the requests' flow, creating a queue when in peak time.

Installing the control flow module

The control flow module is an official GeoServer extension. Installation, as usual, is quite easy. You may find the package listed among the other extension downloads on the GeoServer download page (`http://geoserver.org/download/`). In order to avoid compatibility issues, please ensure that you download a version of the extension exactly matching the GeoServer version you are using.

How to do it...

1. Download the ZIP archive. Please verify that the version number in the filename is the same as the GeoServer WAR file you installed. For the 2.5.2 release, the link is as follows:

   ```
   http://sourceforge.net/projects/geoserver/files/
   GeoServer/2.5.2/extensions/geoserver-2.5.2-control-flow-plugin.
   zip
   ```

   > If you don't remember your GeoServer's release, you may look for it in the web admin interface at `http://localhost/geoserver/web/?wicket:bookmarkablePage=:org.geoserver.web.AboutGeoServerPage`.

2. Stop your GeoServer instance and then extract the contents of the ZIP archive into the `/WEB-INF/lib/` directory in the GeoServer webapp. For example, if you have deployed the GeoServer WAR file, you should place the control flow module's JAR file in `CATALINA_HOME/webapps/geoserver/WEB-INF/lib/`.

3. After extracting the extension, restart GeoServer in order for the changes to take effect. In this case, the installation does not cause any change on the web interface that you can look for to check whether the installation was successful.

4. Open your favorite text editor, create a new file, and insert following line:

   ```
   ip.blacklist=127.0.0.1
   ```

5. Now save the file with the name `controlflow.properties` inside the `<GEOSERVER_DATA_DIR>` folder.

6. Restart GeoServer to have your configuration reloaded.

7. Point your browser to the following URL:

   ```
   http://localhost:8080/geoserver/web
   ```

8. You should see an error page similar to the one shown in the following screenshot:

HTTP Status 403 - This IP has been blocked. Please contact the server administrator

type Status report

message This IP has been blocked. Please contact the server administrator

description Access to the specified resource has been forbidden.

Apache Tomcat/7.0.41

How it works...

The control flow module, as its name clearly explains, controls the flow of requests to your GeoServer. That is, every request coming to GeoServer is filtered by the module and then submitted, queued, or rejected.

In this recipe, you inserted the loopback address of your machine in the blacklist, so you can no longer use GeoServer. Of course, this is a very unlikely situation; just useful to demonstrate that the module is working properly.

A more common use of the extension is to limit the concurrent requests from the same user or a service to avoid an overwhelming amount of load that can block your GeoServer.

Setting a per-user limit

GeoServer usually serves data to several users. According to the size of your organization, the actual number may range from a few to several hundred concurrent requests.

As with any other shared resource, we will ensure that none can exceed a certain amount of processing power, leaving others waiting for what remains.

This is handled by the control flow module, which uses a per user limit setting. We will implement it in this recipe.

How to do it...

1. Using your favorite text editor, open the previously created `controlflow.properties` file and modify its contents as follows:

```
#ip.blacklist=127.0.0.10
# Maximum number of concurrent requests per user
user=2
```

2. Now save the file and close it.

3. Open your browser and point it to the GeoServer **Layer preview** page.

4. Click on the OpenLayers preview for the **NaturalEarth:blueMarble** layer. A new tab will open with the usual simple app to browse the data.

5. Now, open the Firebug console and switch to the **Net** panel. Click on the **Activate firebug for the current website** button. An empty list of requests will be shown in the window, as shown in the following screenshot:

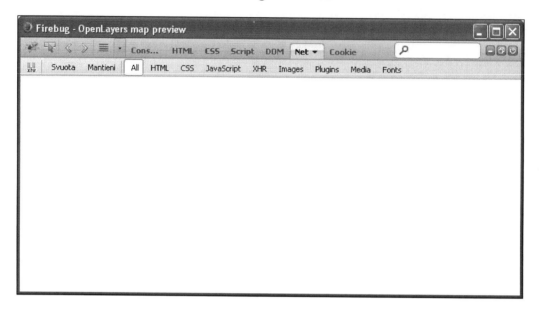

 In the preceding steps, we use Firefox and its debug extension Firebug. Firebug is not available by default in the browser but you can easily add it from the add-in page.

If you are more comfortable with Chrome, you may follow the instructions using the Developers tools' console; it opens when you press *Ctrl + Shift + I*.

6. In the OpenLayers preview page for **NaturalEarth:blueMarble**, open the options toolbar, and from the **Tiling** combo, select the **Tiled** option, as shown in the following screenshot:

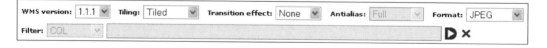

7. Now, when you switch to the Firebug console window, you should see a few concurrent requests sent to GeoServer, as shown in the following screenshot:

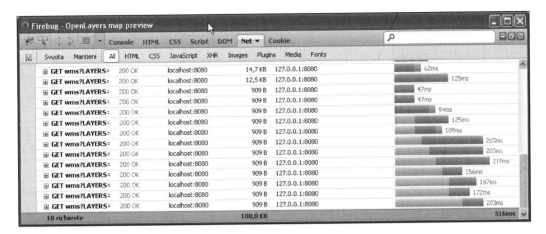

How it works...

In the previous steps, you set a limit of two concurrent requests per user. This is a very small number and you may want to increase it during a production installation.

When calculating the proper number to insert, you have to consider not only the GeoServer capacity to stand against user requests, but also if your users use a web application, consider that browser's limit by default as the concurrent requests you may send to the same host.

 With Firefox, you may check its limit and also change it by opening the about:config URL and searching for the network.http.max-persistent-connections-per-server parameter (defaulting to six limits for the current release).

To check how this works, you open the layer preview page. The simple OpenLayers application contained sends a GetMap request to GeoServer, but a single request will not trigger the limit. So how can you test whether it is really working?

Using the **Tiled** mode does the magic! Of course, when selecting it, the application, instead of sending a single request upon your map actions, sends requests for tiles that compose your map. It uses a regular tessellation and you can check it by having a look at the parameters for each GetMap request.

Using Firebug, inspect the details for the requests sent; you can control all `GetMap` requests to have a 256 x 256 size as follows:

Using tiles lets you produce many concurrent requests, as shown in one of the earlier screenshots.

To check how GeoServer handles them and to be sure that the control flow module is properly working, open the log file. You should see something similar to the following:

```
2014-06-16 17:28:01,902 DEBUG [org.geoserver.ows] - Getting layers
    and styles from LAYERS and STYLES
2014-06-16 17:28:01,902 DEBUG [org.geoserver.ows] - establishing
    raster style for NaturalEarth:blueMarble
2014-06-16 17:28:01,902 DEBUG [org.geoserver.ows] - Getting layers
    and styles from LAYERS and STYLES
2014-06-16 17:28:01,902 DEBUG [org.geoserver.ows] - establishing
    raster style for NaturalEarth:blueMarble
2014-06-16 17:28:01,902 DEBUG [org.geoserver.flow] -
    UserFlowController(4,GS_CFLOW_-2cd39e64:146a546eaa8:-8000) queue
    size 2
2014-06-16 17:28:01,902 DEBUG [org.geoserver.flow] -
    UserFlowController(4,GS_CFLOW_-2cd39e64:146a546eaa8:-8000) queue
    size 2
2014-06-16 17:28:01,902 DEBUG [org.geoserver.flow] -
    UserFlowController(4,GS_CFLOW_-2cd39e64:146a546eaa8:-8000) total
    queues 1
2014-06-16 17:28:01,902 DEBUG [org.geoserver.flow] -
    UserFlowController(4,GS_CFLOW_-2cd39e64:146a546eaa8:-8000) total
    queues 1
2014-06-16 17:28:01,902 DEBUG [org.geoserver.flow] -
    UserFlowController(4) purged 0 stale queues
```

As you can see, the module properly handles your requests, queuing them, and avoiding your GeoServer instance from getting overwhelmed by too many concurrent requests.

GeoServer logging has several profiles. To find information about the control flow module processing requests, select the `GEOSERVER_DEVELOPER_LOGGING` profile.

Setting a per-request limit

Setting the per user limit is nice, but you may want to have a more fine-grained control on how requests are processed by GeoServer. For instance, you may want to have some service, for example, WMS, be given priority over WFS or WCS.

The control flow module lets you set specific limits for each service and you can also configure limits at the request-type level, as we will do in this recipe.

Getting ready

In this recipe, we need to test the control flow module against a higher number of concurrent requests. Unless you're running this recipe on a GeoServer production site, where several real users run ten or more requests each second, you may find it difficult to send many requests by your browser just interactively.

Hence, I want to introduce you to an open-source tool that can help you in creating a stress test. Although there are many similar tools available, JMeter is the most famous and probably the simplest one to use.

JMeter is an open source project from the Apache foundation (`http://jmeter.apache.org/`). The installation is really easy; it being a Java ™ application, you just need to have a JDK or JRE installed on the same machine. If you're going to use the same machine that hosts GeoServer, that is a nice idea; you of course have already installed a Java ™ environment.

So download a recently released archive, at the time of writing Version 2.11 is the latest, from `http://jmeter.apache.org/download_jmeter.cgi`. Then, extract the files to a folder and you are done.

 JMeter is a desktop application with a clean and powerful interface. In this recipe, you will be only asked to use a test suite we created for you, but you may be interested in exploring its features. If this is the case, we want to point you to two extremely useful sources of information:

First of all, the official project documentation that you may find online at `http://jmeter.apache.org/usermanual/index.html`.

Secondly, if you are more comfortable with books, you can refer to *Performance Testing with JMeter 2.9, Packt Publishing*.

How to do it...

1. Using your favorite text editor, open the previously created `controlflow.properties` file and modify its content according to the following snippet:

```
# Maximum number of concurrent requests to all services
ows.global=30
# Maximum number of concurrent WMS GetMap requests
ows.wms=20
# Maximum number of concurrent WCS GetCoverage requests
ows.wcs=4
# Maximum number of concurrent WFS GetFeature requests
ows.wfs=6
# Maximum number of concurrent requests per user
user=6
```

2. Now save the file, close it, and then restart GeoServer.

3. From the Packt site for this book (`https://www.packtpub.com/hardware-and-creative/geoserver-cookbook`), download the `ch08_workflowTest.jmx` file and save it to a folder on the same machine where you installed JMeter.

4. Launch JMeter using the `jmeter.bat` or `jmeter.sh` script according to your operating system.

5. From the **File** menu, select **Open**, and browse for the folder where you saved the JMX file. You should see a test suite loaded in JMeter, as shown in the following screenshot:

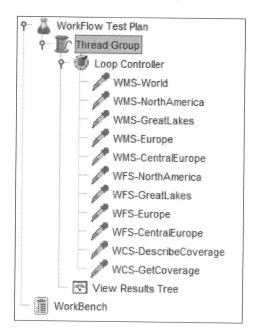

6. Start the test suite by selecting the item **Run**, and then click on **Start** from the JMeter menu.

7. Open the `geoserver.log` file. If the control flow is running properly, you should see many rows similar to the following:

```
2014-06-18 23:11:11,577 INFO [geoserver.flow] - Running
   requests: 9, processing through flow controllers: 0
2014-06-18 23:11:11,862 INFO [geoserver.flow] - Running
   requests: 7, processing through flow controllers: 0
2014-06-18 23:11:11,683 INFO [geoserver.flow] - Running
   requests: 8, processing through flow controllers: 0
2014-06-18 23:11:12,216 INFO [geoserver.flow] - Running
   requests: 6, processing through flow controllers: 0
2014-06-18 23:11:12,268 INFO [geoserver.flow] - Running
   requests: 5, processing through flow controllers: 0
2014-06-18 23:11:12,439 INFO [geoserver.wms] -
   Request: getServiceInfo
```

How it works...

When you run the test suite, especially if JMeter is on the same machine where GeoServer is installed, you would have surely seen a lot of CPU activity. In fact, this test runs many requests on GeoServer.

In the test suite, there is an element called **Thread Group**; if you click on it in the tree view, the right panel shows its content, as shown in the following screenshot:

The **Number of Threads (users)** field is where you set the number of concurrent users you want to run in the test suite, 10 in this case. The **Ramp-Up Period (in seconds)** field is the time JMeter takes to reach the full number of concurrent users. You may set a longer time duration if you experience problems with your machine, as starting many concurrent threads is very challenging for your system.

The **Loop count** field is the number of times the test suite has to be repeated; this may prove useful when you want to test the reliability of a system in the long run.

In our test, we simulate 10 users sending all the requests 10 times. In fact, as the test starts, you may control how many users are running from the JMeter toolbar; to its right end, there is a control that shows you the running / total number of users, as shown in the following screenshot:

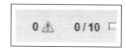

Just under the **Thread Group** item, there is another element, the **User Defined Variables** item. It is a place where you can set values common to all the requests inside your test; it is a convenient way to change them easily according to your needs, as shown in the following screenshot:

User Defined Variables

Name: User Defined Variables

Comments:

User Defined Variables

Name:	Value
hostname	localhost
port	8080

We use two variables: one for the hostname of the server where GeoServer is installed and one for the TCP port. You may want to change them if, for instance, you're running JMeter from a different machine.

Then, there are a set of HTTP Request items, each named with a string referring to what the request is designed for.

The first one is WMS-World, which unsurprisingly send a WMS `GetMap` request asking for a full extent view of the **NaturalEarth:blueMarble** layer.

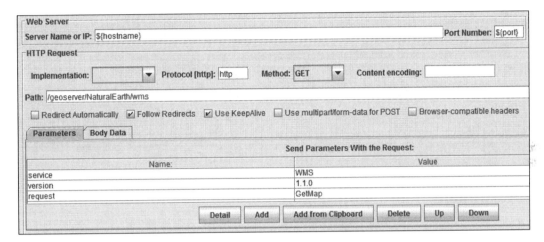

In the preceding screenshot, we can see the two variables defined before, for hostname and port, and a path for the request. Then, a set of parameters define exactly what we want GeoServer to represent in this map.

You may browse the other requests to check the differences.

The bottom element, called **View Results Tree**, is a fundamental one to control if all is okay with your test. As requests are fulfilled by GeoServer, the results are listed in this control, with a green icon for the successful entries and a red one for the errors.

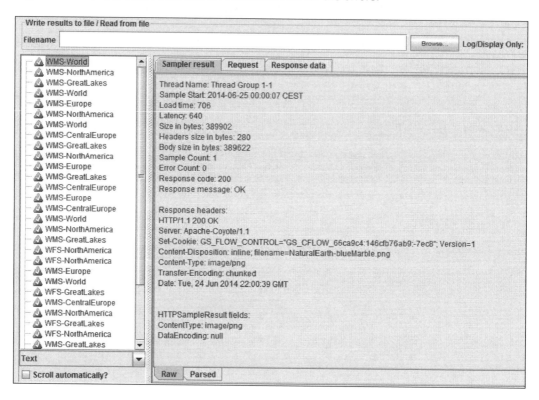

When you click on an item in the right panel, you can see all the details about the request performed, the response from GeoServer, and also the data itself, for example, a map for a WMS request or GML code for a WFS request.

I hope this brief tour raised your curiosity about this wonderful tool. When you're in need of performing a functional or performance test on a web service, JMeter is your friend!

> In fact, JMeter is not useful just for web services. Although an illustration is out of the scope of this book, you'd probably be interested to know that it can also run tests against databases, filesystems, and LDAP.

Installing the monitoring extension

In the previous recipe, you learned how to control the requests flow your users send to GeoServer. You may also become interested in monitoring them, for instance, in order to check what the most used services and datasets are.

A low-level approach, and it is the only possible one, is to analyze the GeoServer logs and the web server logs. All requests are in some way tracked there, so it's just a matter of how to find a convenient way to extract and organize them in a structured data model.

Getting ready

Analyzing the logs may be quite challenging. Besides, according to the detail level, you may find too much information or totally miss the piece you are looking for.

Luckily, GeoServer developers have been working on a clever extension that helps you to analyze what requests GeoServer has been receiving. Unsurprisingly, it is called **Monitor Extension**.

You can find the package listed among the other extension downloads on the GeoServer download page (http://geoserver.org/download/).

Note that in this case, the extension is packaged in two downloads; you need to download both the core and hibernate archive.

Miscellaneous

- Chart Symbolizer
- Control Flow
- Cross Layer Filtering
- CSS Styling
- GeoSearch
- CAS
- Monitor (Core, Hibernate)
- Importer (Core, BDB Backend)
- INSPIRE

How to do it...

1. Download the two ZIP archives. Please verify that the version number in the filenames is the same as the GeoServer WAR file you installed.

> If you don't remember your GeoServer's release, you can look for it in the web admin interface at `http://localhost/geoserver/web/?wicket:bookmarkablePage=:org.geoserver.web.AboutGeoServerPage`.

2. Stop your GeoServer instance, and then extract the contents of the ZIP archives into the `/WEB-INF/lib/` directory in the GeoServer webapp. For example, if you have deployed the GeoServer WAR file, you should place the control flow module's JAR file in `CATALINA_HOME/webapps/geoserver/WEB-INF/lib/`.

3. After extracting the extension, restart GeoServer in order for the changes to take effect. Open the GeoServer web interface and log in as the administrator. On the left panel, you will see a new section, as shown in the following screenshot:

4. The installation also modified your GeoServer data directory. It now contains a folder called `monitoring`:

```
$ ls -ag /opt/geoserver_data_dir/monitoring
-rw-r--r-- 1 root    521 Jun 20 10:59 db.properties
-rw-r--r-- 1 root    396 Jun 20 10:59 filter.properties
-rw-r--r-- 1 root    370 Jun 20 10:59 hibernate.properties
-rw-r--r-- 1 root 131072 Jun 20 10:59 monitoring.1.log.db
-rw-r--r-- 1 root 131120 Jun 20 10:59 monitoring.data.db
-rw-r--r-- 1 root 131120 Jun 20 10:59 monitoring.index.db
-rw-r--r-- 1 root    100 Jun 20 10:59 monitoring.lock.db
-rw-r--r-- 1 root   9352 Jun 20 10:59 monitoring.trace.db
-rw-r--r-- 1 root   1232 Jun 20 10:59 monitor.properties
```

5. Open the GeoServer web interface and go to the **Layer** preview section. Open the OpenLayers preview for some of the configured layers and browse the maps by panning and zooming.

6. After a while, turn back to the GeoServer web interface and go to the **Monitor** section. Open the **Activity** link, click on the **Daily** tab, and you should see a graph of requests, as shown in the following screenshot:

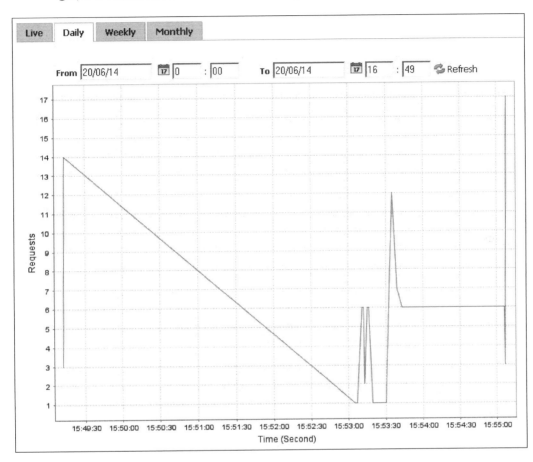

How it works...

The monitoring extension adds a few controllers to your GeoServer.

These objects check each incoming request and save some details for further reference. In fact, you might have noted that the timestamp of the request is saved, and you can produce a graph plotting the number of requests over time.

Besides the timestamp, other details persist and you can, for instance, see a quick view of which service is the most requested.

From the GeoServer web interface, go to the **Monitor** section on the left panel and click on the **Reports** link.

This is a simple tool to create quick pie charts with statistics about the GeoServer activity:

Reports

Monitoring Reports

OWS Request Summary

Click on the **OWS Request Summary** link to open the preconfigured charts and go to the **WMS** tab. Here, you will find a chart that represents a proportion of each WMS operation, as shown in the following screenshot:

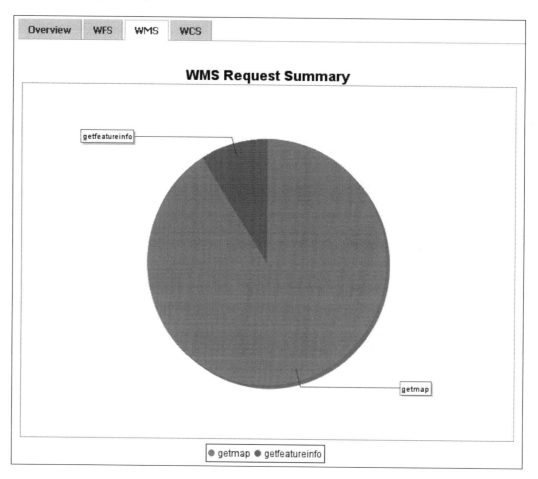

These simple reports are built using the information persisted; indeed, the service and operation are among the saved details.

A full reference of the captured information is available in the GeoServer official documentation (`http://docs.geoserver.org/stable/en/user/extensions/monitoring/reference.html`).

This is a good starting point if you plan to analyze the monitoring data using external tools and build your own stats and charts.

However, before considering how to integrate external tools, we need to explore where the information is actually persisted.

Configuring the monitoring extension

In the previous recipe, we started to explore the monitoring extension. You managed to store information for some requests and created a chart showing the proportion of each operation for WMS.

We haven't discussed yet where the information is stored. After viewing the chart, try to restart GeoServer and then open the reports section again. You'll be surprised that this time no data is shown; all the information previously collected is gone.

This happens because, by default, the monitoring extension uses the memory as a data repository, so information vanishes each time you restart GeoServer.

In this recipe, we'll configure a more robust approach for information storage, which is especially helpful if you need to save information over a wide range of time.

Getting ready

In this recipe, we're going to store information in an RDBMS. The monitoring extension supports different software, such as H2, PostgreSQL, or Oracle ™.

We'll use PostgreSQL, a powerful and open source software, which, with its extension PostGIS, is the most famous open spatial database. The installation is very easy; for Linux distro, the easiest way is to use binary packages from the official repository. On Debian-like distributions, you can use the `apt` package manager:

```
$ sudo apt-get install postgresql-9.1
```

This way you'll have the recent release up and running in a few seconds.

For Windows, a good choice is to download the binary package by Enterprise DB:

`http://www.enterprisedb.com/products-services-training/pgdownload#windows`

How to do it...

1. Stop GeoServer.

2. Open the `db.properties` file with a text editor and change its content. Comment the section for H2 and uncomment the PostgreSQL configuration. Please verify your settings and change the properties accordingly:

   ```
   driver=org.postgresql.Driver
   url=jdbc:postgresql://localhost:5432/gisdata
   username=gisuser
   password=gisuser
   defaultAutoCommit=false
   ```

3. Save the file and open the `hibernate.properties` file located in the same folder. You need to change only the following two properties:

   ```
   # PostgreSQL dialect
   databasePlatform=org.hibernate.dialect.PostgreSQLDialect
   database=POSTGRESQL
   ```

4. Open the `monitor.properties` file and change the storage settings to include the extension using the DB:

   ```
   storage=hibernate
   ```

5. Restart GeoServer to have your configuration reloaded. After it starts, you can check that inside the PostgreSQL database, there are two new tables:

   ```
   $ psql -U gisuser -d gisdata
   gisdata=> \dt req*
                   List of relations
      Schema |         Name        |  Type  |  Owner
     --------+---------------------+--------+---------
      public | request             | table  | gisuser
      public | request_resources   | table  | gisuser
   ```

6. Open the GeoServer web interface and go to the **Layer** preview section. Open the OpenLayers preview for some of the configured layers and browse the maps by panning and zooming.

7. After a while, turn back to the GeoServer web interface and go to the **Monitor** section. Open the **Activity** link, click on the **Daily** tab and you should see a graph showing the request number over time, as shown in the *How to do it...* section of the previous recipe.

8. Connect to the database and check for records stored in the two new tables:

```
gisdata=> select count(*) from request;

 count
-------
    45

gisdata=> select status, http_method, service, operation from
   request limit 5;

  status   | http_method | service | operation
-----------+-------------+---------+-----------
 FINISHED  | GET         | WMS     | GetMap
 FINISHED  | GET         | WMS     | GetMap
 FINISHED  | GET         | WMS     | GetMap
 FINISHED  | GET         | WMS     | GetMap
 FINISHED  | GET         | WMS     | GetMap
```

How it works...

Using an RDBMS is a robust way to persist information safely. An RDBMS is also a very flexible tool to retrieve information and elaborate it in order to prepare usage reports.

The monitoring extension configuration is based on four properties files. The one called `monitor.properties` holds the general settings.

The `mode` parameter sets how the information is collected and updated. By default, it is in the `history` mode, that is, information is stored after the request completion. The `live` mode makes GeoServer collect information in real time. In this mode, you can also use a real-time monitor from the GeoServer web interface.

The `storage` property controls where the monitoring information is stored. It can assume two values: `memory`, which is the default value, and `hibernate`.

We selected the `hibernate` mode, and hence GeoServer will search for a database acting as a repository. To connect to the database, more parameters are required. They are contained in the `hibernate.properties` and `db.properties` files. GeoServer reads them and uses the contained information to connect to the RDBMS and store information inside it.

> Hibernate is a Java ™ library to map objects contained in a relational database, such as PostgreSQL or Oracle, to an object-oriented model such as the one used by GeoServer internally.
>
> It is widely used and you may find a lot of detailed information about it.
>
> A good starting point is `http://hibernate.org/`.

In the first file, we instruct hibernate on what kind of database we're using, shown as follows:

```
# hibernate dialect
databasePlatform=org.hibernate.dialect.PostgreSQLDialect
database=POSTGRESQL
```

In the latter, we insert the connection parameters as follows:

```
# sample configuration for postgres
driver=org.postgresql.Driver
url=jdbc:postgresql://localhost:5432/gisdata
username=gisuser
password=gisuser
defaultAutoCommit=false
```

We changed the default H2 database to PostgreSQL; you're already using it as a spatial repository for your data and it is a very powerful piece of software. It is also very interoperable with many reporting tools.

If your organization uses Oracle, you may as well be use it to monitor information storage. In `hibernate.properties`, insert the following code snippet:

```
# hibernate dialect
databasePlatform=org.hibernate.dialect.OracleDialect
database=ORACLE
```

Then, insert the following code snippet in the `db.properties` file:

```
driver=oracle.jdbc.driver.OracleDriver
url=jdbc:oracle:thin:@localhost:1521\:ORCL
username=gisuser
password=gisuser
```

Obviously, whatever RDBMS flavor you're using, the information stored is the same. You probably noted the `crs` field in the request table. Along with the `minx`, `miny`, `maxx`, and `maxy` fields, it records the envelope for each request:

```
gisdata=> select crs, round(minx::numeric,2) as minx,
  round(miny::numeric,2) as miny, round(maxx::numeric,2) as maxx,
  round(maxy::numeric,2) as maxy from request where crs is not null;
```

crs	minx	miny	maxx	maxy
EPSG:4326	-180.00	-90.00	180.00	90.00
EPSG:4326	-17.84	28.48	40.17	57.48
EPSG:4326	-4.09	36.12	24.92	50.63
EPSG:4326	2.79	39.95	17.29	47.20

In the `monitor.properties` file, you can set the CRS used to log the envelopes, by default, WGS84 Lat Long, which is EPSG:4326. You may change it to another one, of course, being careful to select one that makes sense to all your data extent.

This is the output of requests to the **NaturalEarth:blueMarble** layer after changing the setting to EPSG:3857 in the `monitor.properties` file:

```
gisdata=> select crs, round(minx::numeric,2) as minx,
  round(miny::numeric,2) as miny, round(maxx::numeric,2) as maxx,
  round(maxy::numeric,2) as maxy from request where crs is not null;
```

crs	minx	miny	maxx	maxy
EPSG:3857	-5126784.36	1967710.95	7788015.94	13111054.46
EPSG:3857	-1966571.86	3704742.20	4490828.29	8524724.33
EPSG:3857	-381573.65	4668514.96	2847126.43	7007058.96
EPSG:3857	-381573.65	4668514.96	2847126.43	7007058.96

The last configuration file, `filter.properties`, controls what requests are monitored. By default, it contains some filters to avoid monitoring some requests:

```
/rest/monitor/**
/web
/web/**
```

All requests forwarded to the GeoServer web interface and the Monitor REST API are not collected. According to your needs, you can add more filters.

The syntax is quite simple to manage; you have to specify the complete URL after `/geoserver` and before the key pair values.

For instance, if you want to filter out all requests to a namespace, you can use a filter such as the following one:

```
NaturalEarth/ows
```

Now, WMS, WCS, and WFS requests such as the following will be ignored by the monitoring module, but obviously they will be processed by GeoServer:

```
http://localhost/geoserver/NaturalEarth/ows?service=WCS&version=1.
  0.0&request=DescribeCoverage&coverage=NaturalEarth:dem
http://localhost/geoserver/NaturalEarth/ows?service=WCS&version=1.
  0.0&request=GetCoverage&coverage=NaturalEarth:dem&crs=
  EPSG:4326&bbox=12.06,42.03,12.88,42.50&bands=1
http://localhost/geoserver/NaturalEarth/ows?service=WFS&version=1.
  0.0&request=GetFeature&typeName=
  NaturalEarth:populatedplaces&bbox=-157.1484375,13.88671875,-
  41.1328125,71.89453125
```

Creating reports from the monitoring database

The collected monitoring data can be very useful, but you probably want to use it in a more flexible way than just staring at the custom report included in the GeoServer interface.

Reports can be designed to show usage stats or check the safety state of your server. You can group them in several ways, as with any other source of alphanumerical data. There are several different tools you can use for this, most of them coming from the business intelligence, data warehousing, and analytics branches of Information Technology.

In this recipe, we want to focus again on the spatial component of the data. You may wonder what the most queried area of your datasets is, for example, and want analyze whether there are some preferential areas where your user browses for data. This may prove useful in order to tune your GeoServer for better performance, and it'll be more useful if a wider extent is covered by your data.

We'll create a point layer from the request by taking the centroid of envelopes, and then render it as **Heatmap**.

How to do it...

1. Open a shell console and connect to the database where GeoServer stores the monitoring information, as follows:

   ```
   $ psql -U gisuser -d gisdata
   ```

2. Execute the following script to create a new table from the existing information:

   ```
   create table heatmap as
   select
       name,
       crs,
       service,
       operation,
       ST_Centroid(ST_GeomFromText('POLYGON
           ((' || minx || ' ' || maxy || ',' || maxx || ' ' || maxy ||
           ',' || maxx || ' ' || miny || ',' || minx || ' ' || miny ||
           ',' || minx || ' ' || maxy || '))', 4326))   as geom
   from
       request join request_resources on (request_id = id)
   where
       crs is not null;
   ```

3. Execute the following SQL statement to create a spatial index on the new table:

```
CREATE INDEX heatmap_geom_gist  ON public.heatmap USING
gist(geom);
```

4. Now open the GeoServer interface and publish the table as a new layer. Then, go to the **Layer** preview and check what your map shows. It shows many points, each corresponding to a request, as shown in the following screenshot:

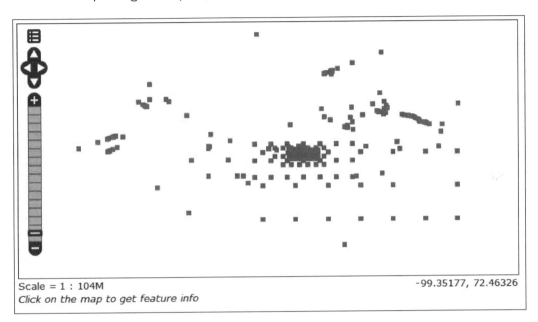

Scale = 1 : 104M   -99.35177, 72.46326
Click on the map to get feature info

5. Now take the `ch08_heatmap.sld` file from the code accompanying this chapter and create a new GeoServer style with it. Then, change the configuration for the **Heatmap** layer, assigning the new style as its default.

6. Take the `ch08_heatmapWMS.html` file and save it in the `<CATALINA_HOME>/webapps/ROOT` folder, and then point your browser to the following URL:

```
http://localhost:8080/ch08_heatmapWMS.html
```

7. Now the map shows you the area where concentrated requests are in blue and turn to light green as the density of the requests decreases, as shown in the following screenshot:

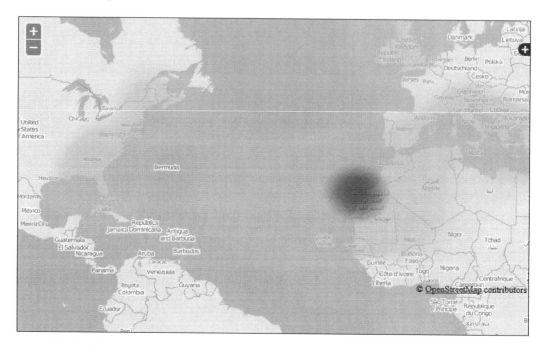

How it works...

In this recipe, we simulated a very minimalistic data warehouse. We selected a set of information, transformed it, and created a new dataset. This is usually done with an ETL procedure, and our SQL query may be considered a very simple **Extract, Transform, and Load** (**ETL**) procedure.

ETL is used to process data from a data source to another. If this is totally new to you, a good starting point might be here:

`http://en.wikipedia.org/wiki/Extract,_transform,_load`

General purpose ETL tools are not usually spatially aware, but in the last few years, a few robust solutions have been developed. Among proprietary solutions, the champion is **Feature Manipulation Engine** (**FME**) by Safe, which is available at `http://www.safe.com/fme/`.

An open source solution is GeoKettle, which is available at `http://www.spatialytics.org/projects/geokettle/`.

The key transformation we did to the data is to create its geometry from the numeric description of bounding boxes:

```
ST_Centroid(ST_GeomFromText('POLYGON
  ((' || minx || ' ' || maxy || ',' || maxx || ' ' || maxy ||
  ',' || maxx || ' ' || miny || ',' || minx || ' ' || miny ||
  ',' || minx || ' ' || maxy || '))', 4326))  as geom
```

Concatenating the `minx`, `miny`, `maxx`, and `maxy` values properly, we build a polygon, actually a rectangular shape, and then we ask PostGIS to calculate its barycenter and set this as the geometric property of the request. For instance, have a look at the following request:

minx	miny	maxx	maxy	crs
-181.80000	-90.868171	181.800013	84.5022735	EPSG:4326

The preceding request produces the following polygon:

```
POLYGON((-181.800003051758 84.5022735595703,181.800018310547 84.5
022735595703,181.800018310547 -90.8681716918945,-181.800003051758
-90.8681716918945,-181.800003051758 84.5022735595703))
```

Polygon's barycenter is shown as follows:

```
POINT(7.6293944864863e-06 -3.1829490661621)
```

The other transformation on the data is on the rendering side.

In fact, we used the rendering transformation capability of GeoServer to transform a vector data, the point layer, in a raster map. The transformation is inside the style:

```
...
        <Abstract>A heatmap for monitoring data</Abstract>
        <FeatureTypeStyle>
          <Transformation>
           <ogc:Function name="gs:Heatmap">
             <ogc:Function name="parameter">
               <ogc:Literal>data</ogc:Literal>
             </ogc:Function>
...
```

Here, we refer to the `gs:Heatmap` process, which is a function delivered by the WPS extension, which creates the raster data according to the point density. We used the WPS extension in *Chapter 4, Geoprocessing*; consult it for instructions about its installation and configuration.

The other core information delivered by the style is the color ramp used to represent the point density. We use a `RasterSymbolizer` element where you can customize a set of classes with color and the associated quantity, as follows:

```
...
        <RasterSymbolizer>
          <Geometry>
            <ogc:PropertyName>geom</ogc:PropertyName>
          </Geometry>
          <Opacity>0.6</Opacity>
          <ColorMap type="ramp" >
            <ColorMapEntry color="#FFFFFF" quantity="0"
              label="nodata" opacity="0" />
            <ColorMapEntry color="#44FF44" quantity=".05"
              label="nodata" />
            <ColorMapEntry color="#00FFAA" quantity=".45"
              label="values" />
            <ColorMapEntry color="#0000FF" quantity="1.0"
              label="values" />
          </ColorMap>
        </RasterSymbolizer>
...
```

 You can read about the details of rendering transformations available in GeoServer from the official documentation available at `http://docs.geoserver.org/stable/en/user/styling/sld-extensions/rendering-transform.html`.

There's more...

You learned how to use the default reports to display the monitoring information, and how to create a custom report by directly accessing the database.

GeoServer also offers you a simple HTTP API to retrieve the monitoring information. This will prove very useful if you have to integrate reports in an external application that may not be comfortable accessing the database, for instance, a web application running on a remote system.

The basic form of the request is shown as follows:

```
http://<host>:<port>/geoserver/rest/monitor/requests.<format>
```

The basic request lets you get all the information formatted according to your choice. The options available for the format parameters are:

- ▶ HTML
- ▶ ZIP
- ▶ CSV
- ▶ XLS

For instance, if you send an HTTP GET request to obtain all the requests formatted in HTML, the right syntax is as follows:

```
$ curl -XGET http://localhost:8080/geoserver/
  rest/monitor/requests.html -O requests.html
```

The `requests.html` file will contain all the requests collected since GeoServer started. When you open the file in a browser, you'll have a list of data sources, as shown in the following screenshot:

Id	Status	Server	Method	Path	Query
1	FINISHED	localhost	GET	/NaturalEarth/wms	service=WMS&version=1.1.0&request=GetMap&layers=Na
2	FINISHED	localhost	GET	/openlayers/theme/default/style.css	null
3	FINISHED	localhost	GET	/openlayers/OpenLayers.js	null
4	FINISHED	localhost	GET	/openlayers/img/east-mini.png	null
5	FINISHED	localhost	GET	/openlayers/img/cancel.png	null
6	FINISHED	localhost	GET	/options.png	null
9	FINISHED	localhost	GET	/openlayers/img/west-mini.png	null
10	FINISHED	localhost	GET	/openlayers/img/zoom-minus-mini.png	null
7	FINISHED	localhost	GET	/openlayers/img/north-mini.png	null
13	FINISHED	localhost	GET	/openlayers/img/zoom-plus-mini.png	null
11	FINISHED	localhost	GET	/openlayers/img/zoombar.png	null
12	FINISHED	localhost	GET	/openlayers/img/slider.png	null
8	FINISHED	localhost	GET	/openlayers/img/south-mini.png	null
14	FINISHED	localhost	GET	/NaturalEarth/wms	LAYERS=NaturalEarth:GeneralizedCountries&STYLES=&F
15	FINISHED	localhost	GET	/NaturalEarth/wms	REQUEST=GetFeatureInfo&EXCEPTIONS=application/vnd.
16	FINISHED	localhost	GET	/NaturalEarth/wms	LAYERS=NaturalEarth:GeneralizedCountries&STYLES=&F
17	FINISHED	localhost	GET	/NaturalEarth/wms	LAYERS=NaturalEarth:GeneralizedCountries&STYLES=&F

As you can see, not all fields are returned. Be aware that the previous request will return all the records in the monitoring repository, so the resulting output can be very huge.

A few options help to filter and sort the output according to your needs. You can display the output by using the `count` and `offset` parameters, if you send the following request:

```
$ curl -XGET http://localhost:8080/
  geoserver/rest/monitor/requests.html?count=10&offset=13 -O
  requests.html
```

Now, you'll obtain a short list of 10 items starting from the 14th ID, as shown in the following screenshot:

Id	Status	Server	Method	Path	Query
14	FINISHED	localhost	GET	/NaturalEarth/wms	LAYERS=NaturalEarth:GeneralizedCountries&STYLES=&F
15	FINISHED	localhost	GET	/NaturalEarth/wms	REQUEST=GetFeatureInfo&EXCEPTIONS=application/vnd.
16	FINISHED	localhost	GET	/NaturalEarth/wms	LAYERS=NaturalEarth:GeneralizedCountries&STYLES=&F
17	FINISHED	localhost	GET	/NaturalEarth/wms	LAYERS=NaturalEarth:GeneralizedCountries&STYLES=&F
18	FINISHED	localhost	GET	/NaturalEarth/wms	LAYERS=NaturalEarth:GeneralizedCountries&STYLES=&F
19	FINISHED	localhost	GET	/NaturalEarth/wms	LAYERS=NaturalEarth:GeneralizedCountries&STYLES=&F
20	FINISHED	localhost	GET	/NaturalEarth/wms	LAYERS=NaturalEarth:GeneralizedCountries&STYLES=&F
21	FINISHED	localhost	GET	/NaturalEarth/wms	LAYERS=NaturalEarth:GeneralizedCountries&STYLES=&F
22	FINISHED	localhost	GET	/NaturalEarth/wms	LAYERS=NaturalEarth:GeneralizedCountries&STYLES=&F
23	FINISHED	localhost	GET	/NaturalEarth/wms	REQUEST=GetFeatureInfo&EXCEPTIONS=application/vnd.

Another option to filter the resulting set is to send a time range. There are two available parameters, from and to, and both require a timestamp, as shown in the following example, where all requests for the 24th of June are requested:

```
$ curl -XGET http://localhost:8080/geoserver/
rest/monitor/requests.html?from=2014-06-26T00:00:00&to=2014-06-
26T24:00:00 -O requests.html
```

If you need more information about a single request, you can send a specific request using the internal identifier, that is, use the ID as a filter:

```
$ curl -XGET http://localhost:8080/
geoserver/rest/monitor/requests/13.html -O requests.html
```

Limiting the GeoWebCache disk use

We already explored GeoWebcache in the earlier chapters. In the *Setting up GeoWebCache* recipe of *Chapter 5, Advanced Configurations*, you configured it properly to store your tiles. In fact, you changed the default folder, that is, Temp under the Tomcat installation path, to a custom location.

The cache size may grow very large and fill your filesystem. Luckily, among its features, there is one feature that enables you to fine-tune the amount of space occupied by cache tiles on the disks.

How to do it...

1. From the GeoServer administration interface, go to the **Tile Caching** section on the left panel, as shown in the following screenshot:

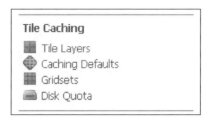

2. Click on the **Disk Quota** link to open the panel to customize settings:

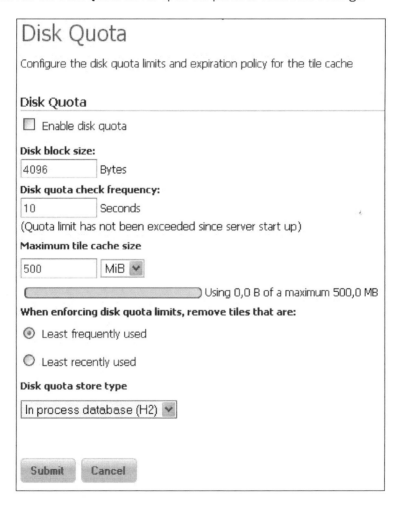

3. By default, there is an upper limit for the cache size, that is, 500 MB; however, the **Enable disk quota** flag is unchecked. Check it and click on the **Submit** button.

4. Now select **Tile Layers** link from the **Tile Caching** section on the left panel.

5. A list of layers is shown. Locate the **NaturalEarth:GeneralizedCountries** layer and open the preview for it by selecting the **EPSG:4326/jpeg** gridset, as shown in the following screenshot:

 Gridsets are caching schemas. When you decide to store tiles for a layer, you have to define the common properties for the tiles set. The logical entities where you store these properties are the gridsets.

The properties you can configure in a gridset are the CRS, the tile sizes (in pixels), the number and scale of zoom levels, and the bounds of the gridset. Once you define a gridset and bind it to a layer, your client requests must conform to the caching schema, that is, the gridset, or GeoWebCache will be unable to fulfill your request.

6. An OpenLayers-based app will be opened. Browse the map by panning and zooming for a little.

7. Get back to the **Tile Layers** list and check what it shows now.

8. Open again, go to the **Disk Quota** panel and change the **Maximum tile cache size** value to 5 **MiB**, and then click on the **Submit** button.

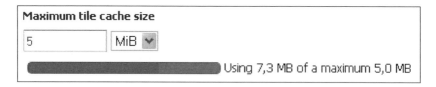

9. Wait for 10 seconds and then open the the **Disk Quota** panel again. You can now see that GeoWebCache has enforced the limit, reducing the cache size.

> **Maximum tile cache size**
>
> 5   MiB ⌄
>
> [████████████░░░░░░░░░░░░░░░] Using 2,86 MB of a maximum 5,0 MB
>
> **When enforcing disk quota limits, remove tiles that are:**

How it works...

The GeoWebCache disk quota feature is quite simple to use but very effective in controlling your storage occupation.

Apart from the basic settings explained in the previous steps, an important setting is the block size used by the filesystem where you store tiles. The provided default, that is, 4096 bytes, is quite common. If you feel unsure, you can check it; for example, on Linux, you may use the `dumpe2fs` utility:

```
$ dumpe2fs -h /dev/mapper/ubuntu1204x64vm-root | grep 'Block size'
dumpe2fs 1.42 (29-Nov-2011)
Block size:               4096
```

In this case, we can safely go with the default value; in case your result is different, insert a proper value in the **Disk block size** textbox as follows:

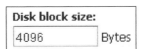

Another important setting is the time interval for GeoWebCache to perform the check on the cache size. The default time of 10 seconds is a good trade off, but you may insert a higher value. A very low value will degrade the performance.

The most important setting is the upper limit for your cache size. There is no magic rule here. It depends on how many layers you have to cache and of course how much space is available.

If you're using a non-dedicated filesystem for your tiles, consider that there may be other processes creating temporary objects on the filesystem and select a conservative value that leaves at least 20 percent of the filesystem always free. On the other hand, if you have a dedicated filesystem for your cache, you can insert a value near to 99 percent of the total size. Avoid setting it to a value equal to your filesystem size; filling it completely can produce weird errors and corruption.

You may wonder what happens to tiles when the upper limit is hit. You have two options for the criteria used to select the tiles to be deleted. The default option selects lesser used tiles, which is usually a good choice as long as your site contains a static set of layers. If you frequently add new layers, there are chances that older ones are used less, so select the **Least frequently used** option as shown in the following screenshot:

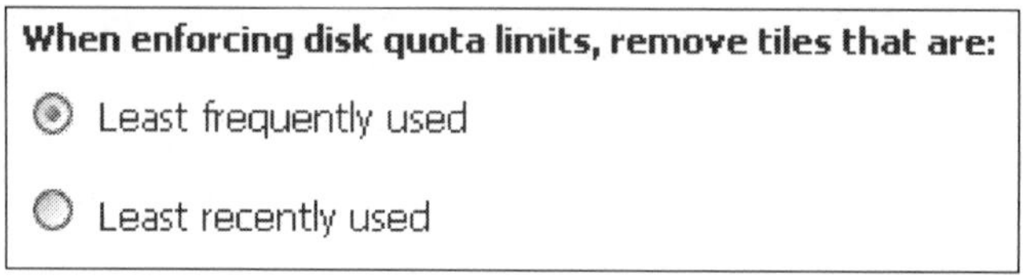

OGC for ESRI Professionals

In this appendix, we will cover the following topics:

- ArcGIS versus GeoServer
- Understanding standards
- WMS versus the mapping service
- WFS versus feature access
- Publishing raster data with WCS

Introduction

This is the final part of this book; if you're still reading, you weren't scared by the term *Appendix*. Appendices are often seen as something with minor importance or somehow collateral to the main topics of the book. Also, its location at the end of the book doesn't help much to attract readers.

Anyway, because you are the kind of reader that starts from page number one and goes on through each chapter or just because you read the introduction and recognized yourself as a member of the ESRI community, we're going to have explore in the borderline land that crosses the proprietary and open source software.

 ArcGIS for Server is not available without a proper license. You need to request your local distributor for an evaluation code if you want to try out the examples described in this appendix.

ArcGIS versus GeoServer

As an ESRI professional, you obviously know the server product from this vendor that can be compared to GeoServer well. It is called ArcGIS for Server and in many ways it can play the same role as that of GeoServer, and the opposite is true as well, of course.

Undoubtedly, the big question for you is: why should I use GeoServer and not stand safely on the vendor side, leveraging on integration with the other software members of the big ArcGIS family?

Listening to colleagues, asking to experts, and browsing on the Internet, you'll find a lot of different answers to this question, often supported by strong arguments and somehow by a religious and fanatic approach.

There are a few benchmarks available on the Internet that compare performances of GeoServer and other open source map servers versus ArcGIS for Server. Although they're not definitely authoritative, a reasonably objective advantage of GeoServer and its OS cousins on ArcGIS for Server is recognizable.

Anyway, I don't think that your choice should overestimate the importance of its performance. I'm sorry but my answer to your original question is another question: why should you choose a particular piece of software?

This may sound puzzling, so let me elaborate a bit on the topic. Let's say you are an IT architect and a customer asked you to design a solution for a GIS portal. Of course, in that specific case, you have to give him or her a detailed response, containing specific software that'll be used for data publication. Also, as a professional, you'll arrive to the solution by accurately considering all requirements and constraints that can be inferred from the talks and surveying what is already up and running at the customer site.

Then, a specific answer to what the software best suited for the task is should exist in any specific case. However, if you consider the question from a more general point of view, you should be aware that a map server, which is the best choice for any specific case, does not exist.

You may find that the licensing costs a limit in some case or the performances in some other cases will lead you to a different choice. Also, as in any other job, the best tool is often the one you know better, and this is quite true when you are in a hurry and your customer can't wait to have the site up and running.

So the right approach, although a little bit generic, is to keep your mind open and try to pick the right tool for any scenario.

However, a general answer does exist. It's not about the vendor or the name of the piece of software you're going to use; it's about the way the components or your system communicate among them and with external systems. It's about standard protocol.

This is a crucial consideration for any GIS architect or developer; nevertheless, if you're going to use an ESRI suite of products or open source tools, you should create your system with special care to expose data with open standards.

Understanding standards

Let's take a closer look at what standards are and why they're so important when you are designing your GIS solution.

The term *standard* as mentioned in Wikipedia (`http://en.wikipedia.org/wiki/Technical_standard`) may be explained as follows:

> *"An established norm or requirement in regard to technical systems. It is usually a formal document that establishes uniform engineering or technical criteria, methods, processes and practices. In contrast, a custom, convention, company product, corporate standard, etc. that becomes generally accepted and dominant is often called a de facto standard."*

Obviously, a lot of standards exist if you consider the Information Technology domain. Standards are usually formalized by standards organization, which usually involves several members from different areas, such as government agencies, private companies, education, and so on.

In the GIS world, an authoritative organization is the **Open Geospatial Consortium** (**OGC**), which you may find often cited in this book in many links to the reference information.

In recent years, OGC has been publishing several standards that cover the interaction of the GIS system and details on how data is transferred from one software to another. We'll focus on three of them that are widely used and particularly important for GeoServer and ArcGIS for Server:

- ▶ **WMS**: This is the acronym for Web Mapping Service. This standard describes how a server should publish data for mapping purposes, which is a static representation of data.
- ▶ **WFS**: This is the acronym for Web Feature Service. This standard describes the details of publishing data for feature streaming to a client.
- ▶ **WCS**: This is the acronym for Web Coverage Service. This standard describes the details of publishing data for raster data streaming to a client. It's the equivalent of WFS applied to raster data.

Now let's dive into these three standards. We'll explore the similarities and differences among GeoServer and ArcGIS for Server.

WMS versus the mapping service

As an ESRI user, you surely know how to publish some data in a map service. This lets you create a web service that can be used by a client who wants to show the map and data. This is the proprietary equivalent of exposing data through a WMS service.

With WMS, you can inquire the server for its capabilities with an HTTP request:

```
$ curl -XGET -H 'Accept: text/xml'
  'http://localhost:8080/geoserver/wms?service=WMS
  &version=1.1.1&request=GetCapabilities' -o capabilitiesWMS.xml
```

Browsing through the XML document, you'll know which data is published and how this can be represented.

If you're using the proprietary way of exposing map services with ESRI, you can perform a similar query that starts from the root:

```
$ curl -XGET 'http://localhost/arcgis/rest/services?f=pjson' -o
  capabilitiesArcGIS.json
```

The output, in this case formatted as a JSON file, is a text file containing the first of the services and folders available to an anonymous user. It looks like the following code snippet:

```
{
  "currentVersion": 10.22,
  "folders": [
   "Geology",
   "Cultural data",
...
   "Hydrography"
  ],
  "services": [
   {
    "name": "SampleWorldCities",
    "type": "MapServer"
   }
  ]
}
```

At a glance, you can recognize two big differences here. Firstly, there are logical items, which are the folders that work only as a container for services. Secondly, there is no complete definition of items, just a list of elements contained at a certain level of a publishing tree.

To obtain specific information about an element, you can perform another request pointing to the item:

```
$ curl -XGET 'http://localhost/arcgis/rest/
  services/SampleWorldCities/MapServer?f=pjson' -o
  SampleWorldCities.json
```

 Setting up an ArcGIS site is out of the scope of this book; besides, this appendix assumes that you are familiar with the software and its terminology. Anyway, all the examples use the SampleWorldCities service, which is a default service created by the standard installation.

In the new JSON file, you'll find a lot of information about the specific service:

```
{
  "currentVersion": 10.22,
  "serviceDescription": "A sample service just for demonstation.",
  "mapName": "World Cities Population",
  "description": "",
  "copyrightText": "",
  "supportsDynamicLayers": false,
  "layers": [
   {
    "id": 0,
    "name": "Cities",
    "parentLayerId": -1,
    "defaultVisibility": true,
    "subLayerIds": null,
    "minScale": 0,
    "maxScale": 0
   },
  ...
  "supportedImageFormatTypes":
    "PNG32,PNG24,PNG,JPG,DIB,TIFF,EMF,PS,PDF,GIF,SVG,SVGZ,BMP",
  ...
  "capabilities": "Map,Query,Data",
  "supportedQueryFormats": "JSON, AMF",
  "exportTilesAllowed": false,
  "maxRecordCount": 1000,
  "maxImageHeight": 4096,
  "maxImageWidth": 4096,
  "supportedExtensions": "KmlServer"
}
```

Please note the information about the image format supported. We're, in fact, dealing with a map service. As for the operation supported, this one shows three different operations: Map, Query, and Data. For the first two, you can probably recognize the equivalent of the GetMap and GetFeatureinfo operations of WMS, while the third one is little bit more mysterious. In fact, it is not relevant to map services and we'll explore it in the next paragraph.

If you're familiar with the GeoServer REST interface, you can see the similarities in the way you can retrieve information.

We don't want to explore the ArcGIS for Server interface in detail and how to handle it. What is important to understand is the huge difference with the standard WMS capabilities document. If you're going to create a client to interact with maps produced by a mix of ArcGIS for Server and GeoServer, you should create different interfaces for both. In one case, you can interact with the proprietary REST interface and use the standard WMS for GeoServer.

However, there is good news for you. ESRI also supports standards. If you go to the map service parameters page, you can change the way the data is published.

The situation shown in the previous screenshot is the default capabilities configuration. As you can see, there are options for **WMS**, **WFS**, and **WCS**, so you can expose your data with ArcGIS for Server according to the OGC standards.

If you enable the **WMS** option, you can now perform this query:

```
$ curl -XGET 'http://localhost/arcgis/
  services/SampleWorldCities/MapServer/
  WMSServer?SERVICE=WMS&VERSION=1.3.0&REQUEST=GetCapabilities'
  -o capabilitiesArcGISWMS.xml
```

The information contained is very similar to that of the GeoServer capabilities. A point of attention is about fundamental differences in data publishing with the two software. In ArcGIS for Server, you always start from a map project. A map project is a collection of datasets, containing vector or raster data, with a drawing order, a coordinate reference system, and rules to draw.

It is, in fact, very similar to a map project you can prepare with a GIS desktop application. Actually, in the ESRI world, you should use ArcGIS for desktop to prepare the map project and then publish it on the server.

In GeoServer, the map concept doesn't exist. You publish data, setting several parameters, and the map composition is totally demanded to the client. You can only mimic a map, server side, using the group layer for a logical merge of several layers in a single entity.

In ArcGIS for Server, the map is central to the publication process; also, if you just want to publish a single dataset, you have to create a map project, containing just that dataset, and publish it.

Always remember this different approach; when using WMS, you can use the same operation on both servers. A `GetMap` request on the previous map service will look like this:

```
$ curl -XGET 'http://localhost/arcgis/services/
  SampleWorldCities/MapServer/WMSServer?service=
  WMS&version=1.1.0&request=GetMap&layers=fields&styles
  =&bbox=47.130647,8.931116,48.604188,29.54223&srs=
  EPSG:4326&height=445&width=1073&format=img/png' -o map.png
```

Please note that you can filter what layers will be drawn in the map. By default, all the layers contained in the map service definition will be drawn.

WFS versus feature access

If you open the capabilities panel for the ArcGIS service again, you will note that there is an option called feature access. This lets you enable the feature streaming to a client.

With this option enabled, your clients can acquire features and symbology information to ArcGIS and render them directly on the client side. In fact, feature access can also be used to edit features, that is, you can modify the features on the client and then post the changes on the server.

Select and configure capabilities

☑ Mapping (always enabled)   ☐ WCS

☐ WMS   ☑ Feature Access

☐ Schematics   ☐ Mobile Data Access

☐ Network Analysis   ☑ KML

☐ WFS

Feature Access Configuration

URLs

REST URL: http://localhost/arcgis/rest/services/SampleWorldCities/FeatureServer

SOAP URL: http://localhost/arcgis/services/SampleWorldCities/MapServer/FeatureServer

Operations Allowed

☑ Create   ☑ Query   ☑ Update
☐ Sync   ☑ Delete

Properties

☐ Allow Geometry Updates

   ☐ Allow update of true curves

☐ Apply default to features with z-values

   Default z-value when inserting or updating features: | 0 |

☐ Enable ownership-based access control on features

   Operations allowed on features created by other users

   ☑ Query   ☐ Update   ☐ Delete

When you check the **Feature Access** option, many specific settings appear. In particular, you'll note that by default, the **Update** operation is enabled, but the **Geometry Updates** is disabled, so you can't edit the shape of each feature.

If you want to stream features using a standard approach, you should instead turn on the **WFS** option. ArcGIS for Server supports versions 1.1 and 1.0 of WFS. Moreover, the transactional option, also known as WFS-T, is fully supported.

As you can see in the previous screenshot, when you check the WFS option, several more options appear. In the lower part of the panel, you'll find the option to enable the transaction, which is the editing feature. In this case, there is no separate option for geometry and attributes; you can only decide to enable editing on any part of your features.

After you enable the WFS, you can access the capabilities from this address:

```
$ curl -XGET 'http://localhost/arcgis/services/
SampleWorldCities/MapServer/WFSServer?SERVICE=WFS&VERSION=1.1.
0&REQUEST=GetCapabilities' -o capabilitiesArcGISWFS.xml
```

Also, a request for features is shown as follows:

```
$ curl -XGET "http://localhost/arcgis/services/SampleWorldCities
/MapServer/WFSServer?service=wfs&version=1.1.0
&request=GetFeature&TypeName=SampleWorldCities:
cities&maxFeatures=1" -o getFeatureArcGIS.xml
```

This will output a GML code as a result of your request. As with WMS, the syntax is the same. You only need to pay attention to the difference between the service and the contained layers:

```
<wfs:FeatureCollection xsi:schemaLocation
 ="http://localhost/arcgis/services/SampleWorldCities/
 MapServer/WFSServer http://localhost/arcgis/services/
 SampleWorldCities/MapServer/WFSServer?request
 =DescribeFeatureType%26version=1.1.0%26typename=cities
 http://www.opengis.net/wfs http://schemas.opengis.net
 /wfs/1.1.0/wfs.xsd">
  <gml:boundedBy>
```

```
        <gml:Envelope srsName="urn:ogc:def:crs:EPSG:6.9:4326">
            <gml:lowerCorner>-54.7919921875 -
                176.1514892578125</gml:lowerCorner>
            <gml:upperCorner>78.2000732421875
                179.221923828125</gml:upperCorner>
        </gml:Envelope>
    </gml:boundedBy>
    <gml:featureMember>
        <SampleWorldCities:cities gml:id="F4__1">
            <SampleWorldCities:OBJECTID>1</SampleWorldCities:OBJECTID>
            <SampleWorldCities:Shape>
                <gml:Point>
                    <gml:pos>-15.614990234375 -
                        56.093017578125</gml:pos>
                </gml:Point>
            </SampleWorldCities:Shape>
            <SampleWorldCities:CITY_NAME>Cuiaba</
SampleWorldCities:CITY_NAME>
            <SampleWorldCities:POP>521934</SampleWorldCities:POP>
            <SampleWorldCities:POP_RANK>3</SampleWorldCities:POP_RANK>
            <SampleWorldCities:POP_CLASS>500,000 to
                999,999</SampleWorldCities:POP_CLASS>
            <SampleWorldCities:LABEL_FLAG>0</SampleWorldCities:LABEL_
FLAG>
        </SampleWorldCities:cities>
    </gml:featureMember>
</wfs:FeatureCollection>
```

Publishing raster data with WCS

The **WCS** option is always present in the panel to configure services. As we already noted, WCS is used to publish raster data, so this may sound odd to you. Indeed, ArcGIS for Server lets you enable the **WCS** option, only if the map project for the service contains one of the following:

> ▸ A map containing raster or mosaic layers

> ▸ A raster or mosaic dataset

> ▸ A layer file referencing a raster or mosaic dataset

> ▸ A geodatabase that contains raster data

If you try to enable the WCS option on SampleWorldCities, you won't get an error. Then, try to ask for the capabilities:

```
$ curl -XGET "http://localhost/arcgis/services
  /SampleWorldCities/MapServer/
  WCSServer?SERVICE=WCS&VERSION=1.1.1&REQUEST=GetCapabilities" -o
  capabilitiesArcGISWCS.xml
```

You'll get a proper document, compliant to the standard and well formatted, but containing no reference to any dataset. Indeed, the sample service does not contain any raster data:

```
<Capabilities xsi:schemaLocation="http://www.opengis.net/wcs/1.1
  http://schemas.opengis.net/wcs/1.1/wcsGetCapabilities.xsd
  http://www.opengis.net/ows/1.1/
  http://schemas.opengis.net/ows/1.1.0/owsAll.xsd"
  version="1.1.1">
    <ows:ServiceIdentification>
        <ows:Title>WCS</ows:Title>
        <ows:ServiceType>WCS</ows:ServiceType>
        <ows:ServiceTypeVersion>1.0.0</ows:ServiceTypeVersion>
        <ows:ServiceTypeVersion>1.1.0</ows:ServiceTypeVersion>
        <ows:ServiceTypeVersion>1.1.1</ows:ServiceTypeVersion>
        <ows:ServiceTypeVersion>1.1.2</ows:ServiceTypeVersion>
        <ows:Fees>NONE</ows:Fees>
        <ows:AccessConstraints>None</ows:AccessConstraints>
    </ows:ServiceIdentification>

  ...

    <Contents>
        <SupportedCRS>urn:ogc:def:crs:EPSG::4326</SupportedCRS>
        <SupportedFormat>image/GeoTIFF</SupportedFormat>
        <SupportedFormat>image/NITF</SupportedFormat>
        <SupportedFormat>image/JPEG</SupportedFormat>
        <SupportedFormat>image/PNG</SupportedFormat>
        <SupportedFormat>image/JPEG2000</SupportedFormat>
        <SupportedFormat>image/HDF</SupportedFormat>
    </Contents>
</Capabilities>
```

If you want to try out **WCS**, other than the `GetCapabilities` operation, you need to publish a service with raster data; or, you may take a look at the sample service from ESRI arcgisonline™.

Try the following request:

```
$ curl -XGET "http://sampleserver3.arcgisonline.com/
  ArcGIS/services/World/Temperature/ImageServer/
  WCSServer?SERVICE=WCS&VERSION=1.1.0&REQUEST=GETCAPABILITIES" -o
  capabilitiesArcGISWCS.xml
```

Parsing the XML file, you'll find that the contents section now contains coverage, raster data that you can retrieve from that server:

```
  ...
  <Contents>
    <CoverageSummary>
      <ows:Title>Temperature1950To2100_1</ows:Title>
      <ows:Abstract>Temperature1950To2100</ows:Abstract>
      <ows:WGS84BoundingBox>
        <ows:LowerCorner>-179.99999999999994 -55.5</ows:LowerCorner>
        <ows:UpperCorner>180.00000000000006 83.5</ows:UpperCorner>
      </ows:WGS84BoundingBox>
      <Identifier>1</Identifier>
    </CoverageSummary>
    <SupportedCRS>urn:ogc:def:crs:EPSG::4326</SupportedCRS>
    <SupportedFormat>image/GeoTIFF</SupportedFormat>
    <SupportedFormat>image/NITF</SupportedFormat>
    <SupportedFormat>image/JPEG</SupportedFormat>
    <SupportedFormat>image/PNG</SupportedFormat>
    <SupportedFormat>image/JPEG2000</SupportedFormat>
    <SupportedFormat>image/HDF</SupportedFormat>
  </Contents>
```

You can, of course, use all the operations supported by standard. The following request will return a full description of one or more coverages within the service in the GML format.

An example of the URL is shown as follows:

```
$ curl -XGET "http://sampleserver3.arcgisonline.com/
  ArcGIS/services/World/Temperature/ImageServer/
  WCSServer?SERVICE=WCS&VERSION=1.1.0&REQUEST=DescribeCoverage&
  COVERAGE=1" -o describeCoverageArcGISWCS.xml
```

Also, you can obviously request for data, and use requests that will return coverage in one of the supported formats, namely GeoTIFF, NITF, HDF, JPEG, JPEG2000, and PNG:

Another URL example is shown as follows:

```
$ curl -XGET "http://sampleserver3.arcgisonline.com/
  ArcGIS/services/World/Temperature/ImageServer/
  WCSServer?SERVICE=WCS&VERSION=1.0.0
  &REQUEST=GetCoverage&COVERAGE=1&CRS=EPSG:4326
  &RESPONSE_CRS=EPSG:4326&BBOX=-158.203125,-
  105.46875,158.203125,105.46875&WIDTH=500&HEIGHT=500&FORMAT=jpeg" -o
  coverage.jpeg
```

Index

polygon style, creating with 81-85
URL 78

CSS module
about 78
installing 79-81

cURL
about 116, 152
URL 116, 153

D

data
filtering, with CQL 25-28
filtering, with CQL spatial operators 28-32

data stores
about 160
creating, with REST 160-166
editing, with REST 160-166

DEBUG parameter 129
Digital Elevation Model (DEM) 96
dot density chart
creating 99-102
URL 99

DUMP parameter 129

E

EarthExplorer
URL 54

ECQL
about 25, 113
references 25

Enterprise DB
URL 8

European Petroleum Survey Group (EPSG)
about 135
URL 135

ExpandToRGB property 62
Extended Common Query Language. *See* ECQL

Extract, Transform, and Load (ETL)
about 236
reference link 236

F

feature access
versus WFS 251-253

Feature Manipulation Engine (FME)
about 236
URL 236

file
metadata, checking of 15

fill property 83
filters
adding, to style 85-88

Firebug 13

G

GARBAGE COLLECTOR parameter 128
gdaldem tool
using 203

GDAL formats
adding 66-69

GDAL/OGR
about 203
URL 203

gedit 127
GeoKettle
URL 236

geometrical center of contiguous USA
about 137
URL 137

geoprocessing
about 103
WPS process builder, using 106-111

GeoServer
about 103
installing 104
upgrading 122-124
URL 39
versus ArcGIS for Server 246, 247

GeoServer extension
URL, for downloading 214

GeoServer views 35
GeoWebCache
about 174

N

Nagios
  URL 213
Name property 62
NASA Earth Observatory
  URL 8
Natural Earth
  URL 8
NaturalEarth workspace 92
NEWSIZE parameter 128
nonspatial filters, WFS
  using 16-19

O

official EPSG code
  overriding 140-142
Open Geospatial Consortium (OGC) 247
OpenGIS® Web Processing Service. *See* **WPS**
OpenLayers
  dealing, with WFS version 8-14
out of memory case (OOM) 129

P

parametric view
  creating 36-38
PERM parameter 129
per request limit
  setting 219-224
per user limit
  setting 215-218
pgAdmin
  about 148
  URL 148
PGC parameter 128
polygon style
  creating, with CSS 81-85
PostGIS installation, on Linux
  URL 8
PostGIS raster data source
  adding 70-75
pregeneralized features
  performances, improving with 39-43

pyramids
  using 62-65
Python
  about 116, 152
  URL 116, 153

Q

QGIS
  URL 46

R

raster data
  publishing, with WCS 254-257
  transformations, rendering for 96-98
raster data source, PostGIS
  adding 70-75
RDBMS
  GeoServer configuration, storing 145-149
rendering transformations, GeoServer
  URL, for documentation 238
reports
  creating, from monitoring database 234-240
Representational State Transfer. *See* **REST**
Reprojection console
  using 135-139
Requests library
  about 116, 153
  URL 116, 153
REST
  about 151, 152
  data stores, creating 160-166
  data stores, editing 160-166
  reference link 152
  used, for managing layers 166-172
  used, for updating styles 172-174
  used, for uploading styles 172-174
  workspaces, managing with 153-159

S

scale
  creating 91-95

Thank you for buying
GeoServer Cookbook

About Packt Publishing

Packt, pronounced 'packed', published its first book "*Mastering phpMyAdmin for Effective MySQL Management*" in April 2004 and subsequently continued to specialize in publishing highly focused books on specific technologies and solutions.

Our books and publications share the experiences of your fellow IT professionals in adapting and customizing today's systems, applications, and frameworks. Our solution based books give you the knowledge and power to customize the software and technologies you're using to get the job done. Packt books are more specific and less general than the IT books you have seen in the past. Our unique business model allows us to bring you more focused information, giving you more of what you need to know, and less of what you don't.

Packt is a modern, yet unique publishing company, which focuses on producing quality, cutting-edge books for communities of developers, administrators, and newbies alike. For more information, please visit our website: www.packtpub.com.

About Packt Open Source

In 2010, Packt launched two new brands, Packt Open Source and Packt Enterprise, in order to continue its focus on specialization. This book is part of the Packt Open Source brand, home to books published on software built around Open Source licenses, and offering information to anybody from advanced developers to budding web designers. The Open Source brand also runs Packt's Open Source Royalty Scheme, by which Packt gives a royalty to each Open Source project about whose software a book is sold.

Writing for Packt

We welcome all inquiries from people who are interested in authoring. Book proposals should be sent to author@packtpub.com. If your book idea is still at an early stage and you would like to discuss it first before writing a formal book proposal, contact us; one of our commissioning editors will get in touch with you.

We're not just looking for published authors; if you have strong technical skills but no writing experience, our experienced editors can help you develop a writing career, or simply get some additional reward for your expertise.

Python Geospatial Development
Second Edition

ISBN: 978-1-78216-152-3   Paperback: 508 pages

Learn to build sophisticated mapping applications from scratch using Python tools for geospatial development

1. Build your own complete and sophisticated mapping applications in Python.

2. Walks you through the process of building your own online system for viewing and editing geospatial data.

3. Practical, hands-on tutorial that teaches you all about geospatial development in Python.

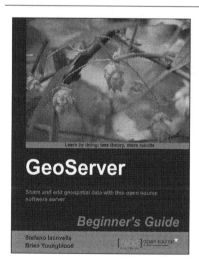

GeoServer Beginner's Guide

ISBN: 978-1-84951-668-6   Paperback: 350 pages

Share and edit geospatial data with this open source software server

1. Learn free and open source geospatial mapping without prior GIS experience.

2. Share real-time maps quickly.

3. Learn step-by-step with ample amounts of illustrations and usable code/list.

Please check **www.PacktPub.com** for information on our titles

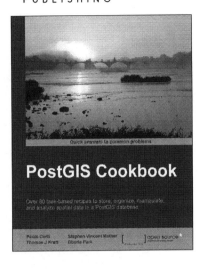

PostGIS Cookbook

ISBN: 978-1-84951-866-6   Paperback: 484 pages

Over 80 task-based recipes to store, organize, manipulate, and analyze spatial data in a PostGIS database

1. Integrate PostGIS with web frameworks and implement OGC standards such as WMS and WFS using MapServer and GeoServer.

2. Convert 2D and 3D vector data, raster data, and routing data into usable forms.

3. Visualize data from the PostGIS database using a desktop GIS program such as QGIS and OpenJUMP.

4. Easy-to-use recipes with advanced analyses of spatial data and practical applications.

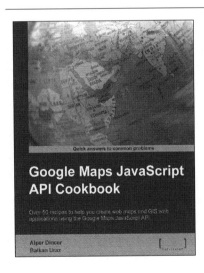

Google Maps JavaScript API Cookbook

ISBN: 978-1-84969-882-5   Paperback: 316 pages

Over 50 recipes to help you create web maps and GIS web applications using the Google Maps JavaScript API

1. Add to your website's functionality by utilizing Google Maps' power.

2. Full of code examples and screenshots for practical and efficient learning.

3. Empowers you to build your own mapping application from the ground up.

Made in the USA
Middletown, DE
03 March 2017